WHAT'S BOTHERING RASHI?

A GUIDE TO
IN-DEPTH ANALYSIS OF
HIS TORAH COMMENTARY

AVIGDOR BONCHEK

DEVARIM

FOCUS ON RASHI AND THE BA'ALEI HATOSAFOS

JERUSALEM FELDHEIM PUBLISHERS NEW YORK

Published in collaboration with
THE INSTITUTE FOR THE STUDY OF RASHI

First Published 2002
ISBN 1-58330-564-5

FELDHEIM PUBLISHERS
POB 35002 / Jerusalem, Israel

202 Airport Executive Park
Nanuet, NY 10954

www.feldheim.com

10 9 8 7 6 5 4 3 2 1

Printed in Israel

Designed & Produced by
LASER PAGES PUBLISHING LTD.
Jerusalem
972-2-652-2226

בס"ד

שמואל קמנצקי
Rabbi S. Kamenetsky

Study: 215-473-1212
Home: 215-473-2798

2018 Upland Way
Philadelphia, Pa 19131

פעיה"ק פילאדלפיא יצ"ו

לכבוד ידידי יקירי הרב הגאון
ר' אליעזר הכהן דונר שליט"א

אשר הראני מכתב דבריו אשר לובן וגם ותחלתו
ודרך של התורה. אמת שמתי לבי לספר המובן של ספר
שלם ציה ומתבערת ... מילין דרי תפתה ...
ואין אומר מקום ודרב"מ שם הלכה ... ואם כן ...
כל הפועל ... הקהל, ... ביאולטם שמים ...
ואמונה.

ויהי רצון ... לרבים ונהרות וגלוי הלכות
אין ... כבולם לדרכה, להפיץ
דבריו ... של ... בכל פנים
ויהי ... כמה ... וכרוב ...
... וכו'.

דו"ש ביקרא ... שאול
שמואל קמנצקי

Rabbi Nachman Bulman
Yeshivat Ohr Somayach
Ohr Lagolah

הרב נחמן בולמן
ישיבת אור שמח
אור לגולה

בס"ד

כד' בניסן תשנ"ז
May 1, 1997

The writer of these lines has seen a notable new work on Rashi — "What's Bothering Rashi? A Guide to In-Depth Analysis of Rashi's Torah Commentary" by Avigdor Bonchek.

Students of Rashi are uniquely affected by his elemental simplicity of style. Children are indelibly stirred by his words, masters of Torah see in his words the heights of Torah genius. Over the centuries C'lal Yisroel sees Rashi as our companion in the eternal climb to Sinai. Commentary on Rashi has been as limitless as our people's preoccupation with Torah.

Central to the Torah revival of our time has therefore also been Rashi-commentary in English — except for one characteristic of classical Rashi learning; namely that Rashi learning "put us" as it were into his laboratory. We asked with him, we probed with him, we lived his solution. He took us to Sinai again with him.

R. Bonchek's work again takes us, as it were, into Rashi's cheder and Beis HaMedrash. He puts "us into Rashi" and not just "Rashi into us." Many will be grateful to him for his guide to learning Rashi.

Rabbi Nachman Bulman

137/21 Ma'alot Daphna, Jerusalem 97762 Israel • Tel: 02-824321 :טל • 97762 ירושלים 137\21 מעלות דפנה

INSTITUTE FOR
THE STUDY OF
R🄰S H I
AND EARLY TORAH COMMENTARIES

For the appreciation and the glorification of Torah

The Institute for the Study of Rashi and Early Commentaries is proud to present this, the fifth and final volume of the *"What's Bothering Rashi?"* series. This volume continues the tradition of analyzing, in easily understandable language and in a clearly reasoned fashion, the methods of learning *Rashi* and other Torah commentaries, in depth.

With the completion of this series, one of the goals of the Institute has been achieved, praise to the Creator of all. We plan on producing, G-d willing, a series of books which highlight the rules of *P'shat* interpretation of the Torah. At the same time, we are preparing school-level workbooks with a detailed teacher's manual that will make the teaching of the Torah and its classic commentaries an exciting and intellectually challenging classroom experience in Torah study. We also plan on producing audiocassettes for individual adult study. These works are to be translated into Hebrew for the non-English reading public.

The purpose of the Institute is to make available to the Torah community, both student and adult, both neophyte and scholar, the wonders of in-depth study of the Written Torah. *Chumash-and-Rashi* has been the foundation of Torah study for generations of Jews. Quite commonly, however, the special techniques necessary to engage the student to think on his own, have not been emphasized. The ability to apply one's innate analytical powers to grasp the inner logic of the commentator's message has not received sufficient consideration. In such cases, the student has been deprived of the exhilarating experience of viewing the Torah through the eyes of our classic Torah commentators. The question-and-answer method of learning, so essential to a deep understanding of *Rashi,* is likewise crucial to a better appreciation of all the classical Torah commentaries. The emphasis of all the works of the Institute, present and planned, is to guide the student in a method of self-discovery which will enable him to proceed in his learning to achieve a constantly expanding appreciation of the wisdom and beauty of our Written Torah.

Sincerely,

Avigdor Bonchek, Ph.D.
Director

2 Wisconsin Circle, Suite 700, Chevy Chase, Maryland 20815   Tel: (301) 656 5540

In Loving Memory
of our parents

Chaim and Miriam Kasper ע״ה
רי חיים יצחק בן שמריהו ז״ל
מרים בת ר׳ חיים יעקב ע״ה

They survived the holocaust while courageously
preserving their *Yiddiskeit*.
In America they built a home based on
Ahavas Chesed and *Mitzvos*.

Their children

Shulamis and Avigdor Bonchek
and grandchildren

—Contents—

המכין מצעדי גבר

Every morning the believing Jew recites this blessing. "Blessed are You, *Hashem* King of the universe, who prepares man's steps." A person wakes up in the morning and begins his activities by putting one foot down before the other. The path he takes that day, while planned by him, is in truth guided by a higher force. He can never know how his day will end and what may transpire between sunrise and sunset. Do we need any more riveting reminder of this than the horrifying events of September 11th?

As I bring this fifth and final volume of *What's Bothering Rashi?* to the printers, that *bracha* and its message ring in my ears. Though it was only about six years ago that I began this endeavor, I cannot remember what thoughts and what brazen conceit prompted me to undertake this mission. Of course, I am certainly glad that I did. It has enabled me to come to places - spiritual, personal and geographical - that I never could have dreamt of when I first began my finger-pecking at the computer keyboard. I originally got involved in this work because of my life-long fascination with Torah and Rashi's commentary. I began with a small *Bereishis* volume, never thinking that it might lead to more. But He Who guided my steps led me along this path to its completion. My gratefulness to. *Hashem* is deeply felt and cannot adequately be expressed in words. I am immeasurably grateful that He has shown me more of the Torah's wonders than I could ever have imagined. These books have given me the privilege of being involved with Torah education to an extent that I never thought possible; to pique the curiosity of Torah students whom I would never have met otherwise. This endeavor has brought me in contact with many people for whom Torah is an inspiration and a never-ending intellectual challenge. From many of these people I have heard many interesting *p'shatim* on Rashi and learned an amazing amount. One delicious example of what I learned is the following Torah thought.

When Joseph tells his father and brothers his dream of the sun, moon and stars bowing to him, his father becomes upset and says (Genesis 37:10):

"Shall we come, I, your mother and your brothers, to prostrate before you..?"

Rashi comments: **Shall we come?:** *Rashi:* "Has not your mother already died?"

Rashi is saying that Jacob realized the dream could not be true because the "sun and the moon" referred to father and mother, but Rachel, the mother, had already died during Benjamin's birth.

If we look at the Hebrew verse we see an unusual thing.

"וַיְסַפֵּר אֶל אָבִיו וְאֶל אֶחָיו וַיֹּאמֶר לוֹ מַה הַחֲלוֹם הַזֶּה אֲשֶׁר חָלָמְתָּ
הֲבוֹא נָבוֹא אֲנִי וְאִמְּךָ וְאַחֶיךָ לְהִשְׁתַּחֲוֹת לְךָ אָרְצָה?"

And if we examine closely these words אֲשֶׁר **חָלָמְתָּ הֲבוֹא** we see the successive letters **רָחֵל מֵתָה** which mean "Rachel has died."!

Astounding, no? This was told to me by a fourth grade teacher as a discovery of one of his 9 year old pupils! What better evidence that the Torah's wonders are accessible to all. The accessibility of Torah insights to all, is the motif of these books. It is my belief that once certain basic principles of interpretation are grasped by the student he too can see new insights in the Torah and in the commentaries. He too can join that illustrious tradition of Torah scholars who have provided the people of Israel with its ongoing tradition of intellectual excitement and spiritual enhancement.

During the years of working on these books, I have always been cognizant of the fact that the final product could not be achieved by me alone. The support, intellectual, emotional and financial, that I have had all the way through, from family, friends and sponsors, has been indispensable.

A guiding light to me throughout these volumes has been the teachings of Nechama Leibowitz ע"ה. Her thorough familiarity with the Torah and its commentaries and her life-long mission of propagating the depth and beauty of the Written Torah all have been an important inspiration for the special educational approach which I have tried to convey in these works. In addition her deep faith in *Hashem* and her authentic modesty conveyed a profound *musar* message far better than any lecture could.

So, too, I again thank all those who have continued to help me. And beyond their letters of approbation, I am greatly indebted to Rav Nachman Bulman, שליט"א, and Rav Shmuel Kamenetsky, שליט"א for their warm encouragement to me in my work.

May G-d grant them both good health so they may be able to continue their immense contribution to the propagation of Torah in our generation.

I am most appreciative to Dr. Jerry Hochstein and the Memorial Foundation for Jewish Culture for their grant which helped in the publication of this volume.

I am happy to mention Elcya Weiss and her dedicated staff, especially to Nitza, at Laser Pages who provided the important technical know how for publication. I remain indebted to my long time friend, Harvey Klineman; his artistic talents made possible the beautiful graphics of the book's cover. Much thanks and gratitude to my friend Ya'akov Feldheim and to the efficient staff at Feldheim Publishers who did so much to make these volumes as attractive and reader friendly as they are.

I am most of all indebted to my wife, Shulamis for the unfailing encouragement and help she has given me in this project, as she has always done in all of my endeavors. Our children, Chanoch, Elisheva, Yehoshua, Michal, Shira and Avi, have also been a source of pride and encouragement to us. Each has helped me in this work in so many ways – technical assistance, intellectual stimulation, the give and take of Torah discussion, encouragement and love. May *Hashem* grant them His blessings always — in all ways.

Appreciating the *Ba'alei haTosafos*

The term *Ba'alei haTosafos* refers to those Talmudic scholars of the 12th-14th centuries who lived in Northern France and Germany. This is a group of several hundred scholars, many of whom are identified with what is known as the "School of Rashi" or in Hebrew as בית מדרשו של רש"י. They wrote commentaries on the Talmud, frequently in relation to Rashi's Talmudic commentary. Some of the most famous, like the Rashbam and Rabbeinu Ya'akov Tam, were offspring of Rashi himself. The name *Tosafos* means "additions" and is derived from the idea that these commentaries were essentially additions to the Master's, Rashi's, seminal Talmudic commentary. In fact they are much more than mere additions. They developed an in-depth analytical approach to Rashi's commentary and to the Talmud itself. A major difference between their Talmudic commentary and Rashi's is that the *Tosafos* took as their task reconciling differences that became apparent when different parts of the Talmud were compared to each other. Rashi's approach is more focused on the text in front of him and rarely involves itself in comparative analysis.

Few of the *Ba'alei haTosafos* authored an organized and systematic commentary on the Torah, as Rashi did. There are throughout the Talmud occasional forays into Torah commentary, but these are incidental to the *Tosafos's* primary task. But there do exist several printed compilations of *Tosafos'* commentaries on the Chumash, the most famous being *Das Zekeinim Ba'alei haTosafos*, which is printed in many *Mikraos Gedolos* editions. Other compilations are the *Moshav Zekeinim, Hadar Zekeinim, Imrei Noam,* and *Panei'ach Raza.* Two of the most famous *Ba'alei haTosafos* who have compiled systematic Torah commentaries are Rabbi Samuel son of Meir (the Rashbam) (1080-1160), Rashi's grandson, and Rabbi Joseph Bechor Shor (1140-?), one of the Talmudic *Tosafos*, who lived a generation after the Rashbam. Their commentaries were unknown for centuries until the past century when rare manuscripts of each of their Torah commentaries were found. Another commentary, whose complete manuscript has yet to be found is that of Rabbi Joseph Kara (1065-?). He was a contemporary of Rashi and the Rashbam and had a very original approach to *p'shat*(not to be confused with Joseph Kairo (1488-1575), the author of the *Shulchan Aruch)*. His commentary on the Prophets exists and can be found in *Mikraos Gedolos*. In fact his name "Kara" probably derives from his interest and expertise in Scriptures (Mikra). It is almost certain that he also wrote a commentary on the Torah, but no manuscript of his has been found. The Rashbam, Bechor Shor and the *Das Zekeinim* all refer to his commentary in their commentaries. There is some reasonable speculation that a manuscript of his Torah commentary exists today in a church library in Italy, but it has not yet been made available for inspection.

TORAH COMMENTARY AND *P'SHAT*

I have chosen the *Ba'alei Tosafos* as the focus of this volume because of the importance some of them place on *p'shat* interpretation. Rashi declared early on (Genesis 3:8) that his commentary would focus on *p'shat*. This does not mean that he did not make abundant use of *drash*; he certainly drew on other modes of interpretation in addition to *p'shat*. (I have discussed the whole question of Rashi's commentary being exclusively or significantly *p'shat* in the *Bereishis* volume of *What's Bothering Rashi?*) Regarding the *Ba'alei Tosafos,* only some of them emphasized *p'shat* in their comments on Torah, but those who did, did so with more single-mindedness than even Rashi. But many of the other *Ba'alei Tosafos* encompass the full gamut of interpretive methods used by Torah commentaries. These include straightforward *p'shat, aggadic drash*, and *gematrios*. The compilations noted above (*Das Zekeinim, Hadar Zekeinim* and *Moshav Zekeinim*) all contain comments based on a variety of interpretative approaches.

The reader will find in this volume (in addition to the analyses of Rashi) a focus on the commentaries that emphasized *p'shat,* in particular the Rashbam and the Bechor Shor. The interest in *p'shat* interpretation gained ascendancy in the 11th and 12th centuries in the Ashkenazi Yeshivos in Northern France and Germany. Further south in Spain and Southern France, the Sephardim had already developed an approach to *p'shat* earlier. The Ibn Ezra (1089-1164) is the outstanding example of Spanish Torah scholarship. He was the quintessential *p'shat* commentator. Two generations after Rashi, the Ramban (1194-1270) also in Spain, made his profound contribution to *p'shat* interpretation. The Spanish influence may explain to some extent the flourishing of *p'shat* interpretation among the Ashkenazim. It is known that the Ibn Ezra traveled a lot and lived for a while in Northern France and knew of the commentaries of the Ashkenazi scholars, Rashi, Rashbam and Bechor Shor.

Two Characteristics of *P'shat*

There are two characteristics of *p'shat*, which differentiate it from *drash*, which should be mentioned.

One is that *p'shat* is based exclusively on text and on context, while *drash* is not bound by this limitation. In *drash* meanings are ascribed which may take the interpretation completely out of its time or place context. The second difference is that *p'shat* can be derived by any student as long as he can support his interpretation by reasonable evidence from text and context. *Drash* on the other hand, was handed down by the Talmudic Sages, it is part and parcel of the Oral Tradition, and is based on the rules of *drash* interpretation, given to Moses at Sinai. This second point, the element of originality in *p'shat*, is quite significant for it allows much room for creative and original interpretations. We will see examples of this from the Rashbam and the Bechor Shor. The Ramban, in his seminal Torah commentary, also offers many original and enlightening interpretations. His commentary was the focus of the *Shemos* volume of *"What's Bothering Rashi?"*; it won't be central in this volume.

Rabbi Joseph Kara on *P'shat*

To illustrate how these *Reshonim* saw the centrality of *p'shat,* I offer the following quote from the commentary of Rabbi Joseph Kara. Joseph Kara was not really one of the *Ba'alei Tosafos*; he was a younger contemporary and personal friend of Rashi, and was certainly influenced by him. The following is from his commentary to I Samuel 3:

> "You should be aware that when the Prophecy was written, it was written complete, with all its solutions, so that future generations should not stumble in it. It lacks nothing in its place [to be fully understood.] There is thus no need to offer proofs from other sources nor from the *midrash*. For the Torah is complete and complete it was given to us …but the purpose of the *midrash* of the Sages is to enhance Torah and glorify it. But he who does not know the Simple Meaning, פשוטו של מקרא , and turns to the *midrash* is similar to one who is swept along by the torrents as the depths of the sea overwhelm him and he grasps on to anything that comes to his hand to save himself. But were he to have paid close attention to the word of G-d he would have investigated and searched for the *p'shat* and he would have found [the solution to his problem]. So it says 'If you seek it like silver and like hidden treasure you search for it, then you will understand the fear of G-d and you shall find G-dly knowledge (Proverbs 2:4)."

What Joseph Kara advocates is what is today termed a "close reading" of the text. Modern academic scholars pride themselves as having discovered a new approach to Torah interpretation. But, in fact, this is the approach that was developed by Rashi and his students, among them Kara, nearly a thousand years ago.

P'SHAT AND DRASH IN THE BA'ALEI TOSAFOS

In both the Rashbam and Bechor Shor we find two central and seemingly contradictory aspects of their approach to Torah interpretation.

1) Their unswerving search and preference for *p'shat* as opposed to Talmudic *drash,* on the one hand, and

2) Their great & unqualified respect for the centrality of Talmudic *drash,* on the other.

Let us see a representative quote from the Rashbam:

Rashbam (Genesis 37:2):

Let those who love reason know and understand that which our Rabbis taught us (*Shabbos* 63a) that "A verse never departs from its *p'shat* (Plain Meaning)." It is still true that in essence the Torah's purpose is to teach us and relate to us teachings, rules of conduct and laws which we derive from hints within the Plain Meaning of the Scriptures, through superfluous wording, through the thirty two principles of Rabbi Eliezer, the son of Rabbi Yosi the Galilean, or the thirteen principles of Rabbi Ishmael. Due to their piety the earliest scholars devoted their time to *midrashic* explanations which are the essence of Torah. As a result they never became attuned to the profundities of the Plain Meaning of the Scriptures....As it says "I was eighteen years old and I had studied the entire Talmud yet I had never realized that "a verse never departs from its *p'shat* (Plain Meaning) — פשוטו של מקרא".

Similarly Rabbi Shlomo, (Rashi) my mother's father, who illumined the eyes of all the Diaspora, who wrote commentaries on the Torah, Prophets and the Writings, set out to explain the *p'shat* of the Scriptures. However, I, Samuel, the son of his son-in-law, Meir, may the memory of the righteous be a blessing, argued with him in front of him. He admitted to me that had he had the time he would have written new commentaries based on the interpretations of the *p'shat* of Scripture that are newly thought of each day."

This quote is both informative and touching. Through it we are afforded a rare glimpse into Rashi's thinking. Rashi, says the Rashbam, his grandson, would have made changes in his classic Torah commentary "had he the time." This gives us pause to think what kinds of changes he would have made. But more significant than this tantalizing personal tidbit, is the Rashbam's own statement about his attitude towards *p'shat* and *drash*. Although in his Torah commentary he is an unswerving advocate of *p'shat*, nevertheless he forcefully defends the centrality of *drash* interpretations as the essence of Torah. He says of both the Talmudic Sages and the earlier Torah scholars, that "Due to their piety they devoted their time to *midrashic* explanations which are the essence of Torah." That is to say that while the Rashbam's own contribution would be to a *p'shat* interpretation of the Torah — which he would at times defend in an uncompromising, vigorous manner — he realized that this was not "the essence of Torah." That is because Torah is to be lived — not just studied — and the *drash* interpretations teach us the rules by which the Jew is to live, rule which are to shape our daily lives.

Another quote from his commentary reinforces our impression of the Rashbam's stand *vis-a-vis p'shat* and *drash* (Exodus 21:2):

> Let those who love wisdom know and understand that my purpose, as I explained in Genesis, is not to offer halachic interpretations wherein aggados and halachos are derived from superfluities in Scriptural language. Even though these interpretations are the most essential ones. Some of those explanations can be found in the work of our teacher, Sholomo, my mother's father. But my purpose is to explain the *p'shat* of the Scripture. I will explain the laws and rules [of the Torah] in a manner that conforms to the way of the world (meaning, simple *p'shat*). Nevertheless it is the halachic interpretations that is the most essential one, as the Rabbis said (*Sota* 16a) '*Halacha* uproots the Biblical text."

SOME CHARACTERISTICS OF RASHBAM'S TORAH COMMENTARY

There are certain aspects of Torah interpretation which are central to the Rashbam's commentary. We will look at three of them. 1) Originality in interpretation; 2) His principle of 'Introductions'; and 3) His approach to redundancies.

ORIGINALITY IN INTERPRETATION

As an outstanding illustration of how the Rashbam can offer an original *p'shat* interpretation to verses which are interpreted quite differently by the Talmudic Sages, we cite the following (long) example from Exodus of the laws of *shomrim,* custodians.

> *Exodus 22:6-12:*
> 6. "If a man shall give money or vessels to his fellow to safeguard and it is stolen from the house of the man, if the thief is found, he shall pay double. 7. If the thief is not found, the householder shall approach the judges that he had not laid his hand upon his fellow's property. 8. For every item of liability, whether an ox, a donkey, a sheep or a garment, regarding any lost item about which he says 'This is it.' To the judges shall come both their claims. Whomever the judges find guilty shall pay double to his fellow.
> 9. If a man shall give his fellow a donkey or an ox or a sheep or any animal to safeguard and it died or was broken or was looted without a witness. 10. An oath of *Hashem* shall be between both of them that he did not lay his hand on the property of his fellow, the owner shall accept it and he shall not pay. 11. If it was stolen from him, he shall pay the owners. 12. If it shall be torn to death, he shall bring a witness; for a torn animal he does not pay."

The verses above are interpreted by the Talmud (*Baba Metzia* 94b) in the following way. The first paragraph (verses 6-8) refers to a case of an unpaid custodian, *shomer chinum.* The second paragraph (verses 9-12) refers to a case of a paid custodian, a *shomer sachar.* That is why, according to the Talmud, in the first case — the man who watched his friend's property for nothing — if it was stolen or lost he need only take an oath and he is cleared. But in the second case (verses 9-12) the man bears more responsibility since he was paid for the safekeeping. Thus if the article was stolen or lost he must pay for it.

Rashi quotes these laws in his commentary. All Talmudists know these laws, the Rashbam knew them as well.

Nevertheless, the Rashbam offers a very original *p'shat* interpretation of these verses, which differs significantly from the Talmudic interpretation. Following is a synopsis of his interpretation of these verses. The Rashbam first notes the Talmudic interpretation of theses verses, then he comments:

The first section frees the *shomer* of obligation to pay, in cases of stolen or lost articles because these are moveable objects ('silver or vessels') which he guards in his home as he does own possessions. Therefore, if these are stolen, he is free because he has guarded them as well as he did own possessions. But the second section speaks of animals and these are ordinarily kept out in the field. So if he was given them to watch, he certainly had to take responsibility for whatever might happen while they are out in the field. Therefore he would be responsible if they are stolen or lost, because their owner gave them to him with that intention.

This is a very neat and reasonable interpretation of these verses. While the Rashbam makes note of the Talmudic interpretation which is based on the different kinds of *shomrim*, he says this is not *p'shat*. He offers his interpretation as *p'shat* which deals only with what is written in the Torah without any additional assumptions. Here is an example where the Rashbam offers an interpretation which disagrees with the Sages' *drash* in an important halachic matter. If one reads this interpretation of the Rashbam without knowing of his respect and even his preference for the Sages' *drash*, he would misunderstand the Rashbam. This illustrates the complexity of the Rashbam's approach — respecting *drash* as the essence of Torah while pursuing *p'shat* for the sake of understanding the Torah on that level. This dual approach to Torah interpretation is true for all Torah scholars. But it is most evident in the commentaries of the *Ba'alei haTosafos*. This is because their *p'shat* interpretations were so original while at the same time they were outstanding Talmudic scholars intimately familiar with *drash*.

RASHBAM'S RULE OF 'INTRODUCTIONS'

The Rashbam developed an approach to commentary based on the idea of "introductions." Best is to let the Rashbam speak himself. Here is part of his commentary to the first verse in Genesis:

This too is of the main aspects of *p'shat* according to the Scriptures. It is customary to mention something which is not presently necessary (to the story) but which is necessary for something that is mentioned later (in the Torah). As it says, "Shem, Ham and Yeffes." (Genesis 9:18) And it says "Ham is the father of Canaan." (This is only mentioned) because later (9:25) it says "cursed is Canaan." Had it not previously explained who Canaan is, we wouldn't know why he was cursed. ....Likewise in the story of the

Creation in six days, Moses introduced this in order to appreciate what G-d said at the Giving of the Torah "Remember the Sabbath day to sanctify it …. because in six days *Hashem* made the heavens and the earth, the sea and all that is in it and He rested on the seventh day." That is why it is written (in Genesis) "And it was evening and it was morning *the* sixth day." That very same sixth day which is identified with what *Hashem* said at Sinai. Therefore Moses told Israel to let them know that the word of G-d is truth.

WHAT IS THE RASHBAM SAYING?

The Rashbam's comment is based on the fact that the Torah says 'And it was evening and it was morning *the* sixth day.' The use of the definite article, the הי' הידיעה, before "sixth day" means that the Torah is referring to an already known 'sixth day'— that day is the Sabbath. But we only know of the Sabbath later when we are told of the Ten Commandments in the book of Exodus. This comment is quite startling. His idea is that the whole book of Genesis and the creation story in particular serve as one long "introduction" for the sole purpose of explaining the background to the mitzvah of the Sabbath which would only be mentioned later in the Torah. The Sabbath was commanded to Israel because G-d created the world in six days and rested on the seventh. Had we not known the creation story we would not be able to fully appreciate the mitzvah of the Sabbath; therefore the story was elaborated on in the book of Genesis. From this comment we see how the Rashbam considers the narrative portion of the Torah as subservient to and as mere background to the legal/halachic portions of the Torah.

This is an example of the Rashbam's principle of "introductions." Rashbam draws on this principle often in his commentary to explain phrases that do not seem to be necessary. There is some similarity here to Rashi's first comment in Genesis where he gives a reason for the Torah not beginning with the first mitzvahs which are only recorded much later in the twelfth chapter of Exodus. But the Rashbam's interpretation is more radical.

RECONCILING APPARENT REDUNDANCIES

The Rashbam, like all Torah commentators, deals with apparent redundancies in the Torah, to explain why they are necessary and what they teach us. We choose the following example because of the interesting moral lesson the Rashbam draws from a redundancy.

Moses tells the people of his prayers on their behalf after the sin of the Golden Calf.

> *Deut. 9:25:*
> "I *threw myself down* before *Hashem* for the forty days and the forty nights that I *threw myself down*, for *Hashem* had intended to destroy you."

> **And I fell before *Hasehm* those forty days *etc.*:**
> *Rashbam:* Who is the wise man that will pay attention and understand: Why was there need to repeat this "falling down for forty days"? Is it the custom of the Scriptures to repeat and duplicate a matter and say 'When I fell down for forty days such and such happened and I fell down'? ...But there is much wisdom here. Its purpose if to reprove Israel. Perhaps they will think, 'Wasn't it so that for a terrible sin like the Golden Calf, the prayers of Moses helped save us? So too in the Land of Israel if we sin, then the prayers of the prophets will help us.' So Moses said to them 'Prayer will not help you in the Land of Israel because now it only atoned for you so as not to desecrate the Name ...for that is what it says 'Lest (Egypt) say "G-d was unable to bring them into the Land and because of His hatred of them He caused them to die in the wilderness." But once the thirty-one kings (of Canaan) are defeated and you inherit the Land, then (if you sin) He will evict you from the Land (and prayers won't help you) because there will no longer be a desecration of the Name. The nations will no longer say '*Hashem* was unable to bring them into the Land' rather they will say Israel has sinned and that is why they were driven out.

WHAT IS THE RASHBAM SAYING?

The Rashbam understands the Torah's repeating Moses' "falling down" as a way of emphasizing a point. The repetition is necessary to make the point that prayers protected the people in the wilderness, but prayer alone would help only in the wilderness, before they succeeded in entering the Land. After they arrive in the Land, only true repentance would save them. G-d can punish them for their sins, because no longer will Israel's defeat be considered a *Chillul Hashem*. It will rightly be seen by the nations of the world as fitting punishment for Israel's sins.

A powerful message in the Rashbam's day and all the more so in ours, when we have returned to the Land!

THE RASHBAM *vs* RASHI ON REPETITIONS

The Rashbam sees repetitions as a linguistic technique of emphasizing a point and considers it *p'shat*, as we saw above. Rashi, on the other hand, interprets repetitions as a *p'shat* method of teaching us something new. But for the Rashbam this is a familiar method of *drash* interpretation; it should not be considered *p'shat*.

Another example should further help clarify this point.

> *Exodus 22:21-23:*
> "Every widow and orphan you shall not afflict. If you truly afflict him lest he cry out to Me I will surely heed his outcry. And My anger will wax hot and I will kill you with the sword and your wives will be widows and your children, orphans."

Rashi asks the obvious. If a person is killed of course his wife will be a widow and his children, orphans. It is not necessary for the Torah to spell out the obvious. Why then is the Torah redundant in stating the obvious?

Rashi's answer is that this repetition hints at another painful, unmentioned, consequence of harming widows and orphans. The consequence is that husbands will be lost in war and their wives will be 'living widows' meaning they will be *agunos,* never able to remarry because they have no proof that their husband is dead.

The Rashbam, on the other hand, deals with these "unnecessary words" with a brief three-word comment:

מדה כנגד מדה

> "Measure for measure."

His meaning is that the Torah spells out the obvious for its literary and emotional impact. The words "and your wives will be widows, etc." are to ring in our ears; we are to be shaken by the measure-for-measure justice that will be meted out. Here, too, we see the difference between Rashi and the Rashbam. Rashi requires that every repetition teach us something new and this, for him, is considered *p'shat*. The Rashbam, on the other hand, feels this interpretation is *drash*. For the Rashbam literary considerations themselves (like emphasizing a point) are part of *p'shat.* So we can have a repetition, which teaches us nothing new, yet is necessary to emphasize a point.

Let us now look at another of the *Ba'alei haTosafos,* the Bechor Shor.

THE BECHOR SHOR

Rabbi Joseph Bechor Shor (1140-?) was a student of Rabbeinu Tam, the brother of the Rashbam, who was one the major *Ba'alei haTosafos.* Bechor Shor continued the Rashbam's tradition in Torah interpretation. He also contributed to the *Tosafos* in the Talmud. The Bechor Shor wrote a full Torah commentary, in addition to his Talmudic novellae. The name "Bechor Shor" most likely derives from the verse in Moses' final blessings. In Deut. 33:17 we read:

בְּכוֹר שׁוֹרוֹ הָדָר לֹו...

"His first born ox is a glory for him…"

Since this was part of the blessing to the tribe of Joseph, it is appropriate that Joseph Bechor Shor received this as his surname.

SOME CHARACTERISTICS OF BECHOR SHOR'S TORAH COMMENTARY

As is characteristic of the school of Rashi, the Bechor Shor strove for *p'shat* interpretation over *drash.* But like all *Rishonim,* he accepted as the final authority the *midrashic* interpretations of the Talmudic Sages. Within these boundaries we can note some characteristic aspects of his Torah commentary. I will mention three:

1) Originality in interpretation;

2) Naturalistic, rationalistic approach;

3) Psychological interpretations

ORIGINALITY IN INTERPRETATION

P'shat interpretation always tries to cut through difficult passages by seeing matters in the simplest (not simplistic) light possible. The following is an example from Bechor Shor's commentary which illustrates *p'shat* as well as it illustrates his originality.

Jacob has made a deal with Laban to work for him and as payment he would receive Rachel for his wife.

Genesis 29:20:
"And Jacob worked seven years for Rachel *and they were in his eyes as a few days in his love for her.*"

The question that begs to be asked is:

What does it mean that Jacob worked seven years for Rachel and these were in his eyes as *but a few days* because of "his love for her" ? One would have thought just the opposite — that if Jacob loved her, he would want to marry her as soon as possible; having to wait seven years would seem like an eternity and not like "a few days in his eyes" ?

The *Bechor Shor* comments: "You shouldn't wonder why he said seven years and not a year or two. This indicates that he loved her so much that even seven years seemed to him a good bargain and that he was out-smarting Laban, because he would receive such a beautiful woman for such little work."

When I first read this interpretation I was taken aback. I realized what I had never noticed before. It was Jacob — not Laban — who suggested the seven-year price tag. See verse 18. If Laban had been the one to make the seven-year stipulation, then Jacob would have been forced to accept it and probably would have felt it was like an eternity to wait for Rachel. But since Jacob himself made the suggestion of seven years, it was he who set the price-tag, we can understand that he felt it was a good bargain and Rachel was well worth it because "of his love for her."

Another example will illustrate the originality of the Bechor Shor, as well as how he strove to interpret the Torah's words in the simplest, most natural way.

Pharaoh dreamt two dreams and he called Joseph, the imprisoned slave, to interpret them.

Genesis 41:7:
"And the seven thin ears (of corn) *swallowed* ותבלענה the seven plump and full ears."
Bechor Shor: The thin ears grew tall until they covered ותבלענה the good ears, they were "swallowed" and hid-den under them. As it says (Numbers 4:20) "And they shall not come and look as the holy is covered — כבלע את הקדש." Because ears of corn cannot literally swallow any-thing, rather they covered; for it is not the custom to dream something that cannot exist in reality.

WHAT IS BECHOR SHOR SAYING

We should note three aspects of this comment which typify his commentary in general. 1) He strives for a naturalistic interpretation over a more fanciful one, even in the case of a dream, where one could imagine the dream did contain fanciful images. 2) He finds support for his interpretation by citing another verse in the Torah which has the same verb. In the verse in Numbers the verb בלע certainly means "covered" and not swallowed. 3) And he relies on a psychological principle (in dream interpretation).

NATURALISTIC APPROACH TO MIRACLES

The naturalistic approach which we have just seen in Bechor Shor's interpretation of Pharaoh's dream, we see, as well, in his interpretation of the miracles in the Torah.

His interpretation of the plague of Boils in Egypt exemplifies his approach.

> *Exodus 9:7,8:*
> "Take for yourselves handfuls of furnace soot and let Moses hurl it heavenward before Pharaoh's eyes. It will become dust over the entire land of Egypt and it will become boils erupting into blisters on man and beast throughout the land of Egypt."
> **And let Moses hurl it heavenward.** *Bechor Shor*: It will fall on man and animal and they will be scalded by it and it will cause boils to rise …but in fact a handful of fire wouldn't be enough to afflict all Egypt, so in reality the boils came of themselves. But G-d does not want to change the nature of the world, therefore He acts partially through natural means. That is why He commanded to throw burning soot. *And so too you will find with most of the miracles that the Holy One, blessed be He, does not change the natural order of the world. …*"

In this last phrase the Bechor Shor's expresses his view of miracles throughout the Torah. Miracles are miracles, but G-d always strives to make them seem as natural as possible.

Psychological Insight

The Bechor Shor frequently makes use of psychological interpretations to explain people's actions as recorded in the Torah. Some examples follow.

In the story of Cain and Abel, we read:

> *Genesis 4:7,8:*
> [*Hashem* said] 'Surely if you improve yourself you will be forgiven. But if you do not improve yourself, sin rests at the door . Its desire is toward you, yet you can conquer it.' **And Cain said to his brother Abel.** And it happened when they were in the field, that Cain rose up against his brother Abel and killed him.

The commentators all deal with the question, what did Cain say to Abel? The Torah only says "And Cain said to his brother Abel" but it tells us nothing of the conversation.

> **And Cain said to his brother Abel**: *Bechor Shor*: [He said] That which G-d had said to him. He did so with guile. Cain sensed that Abel was on his guard before Cain and therefore Cain said to him 'Such and such is what G-d said to me and we can now make peace for I am no longer distressed' . ...thus Abel thought that his brother was no longer angry with him and he let down his guard "and they were in the field and Cain rose up against his brother Abel and killed him." Because Abel paid no attention to Cain's knife.

Bechor Shor's interpretation not only fills in the missing links in this narrative, it also provides an inside, psychologically cogent, look into Cain's premeditated mental workings as he schemes to commit fratricide.

Here is yet another example of Bechor Shor's psychologically insightful commentary:

When Abraham's servant, Eliezer, sought a wife for Isaac, he made a plan to test the kindness of the maiden.

> *Genesis 24:13:*
> "Behold , I stand by the spring of water and the daughters of the men of the city go out to draw water."

Behold, I stand by the spring of water: *Bechor Shor*: How can I check the girl's character? If I enter the city and I stay over in one of the homes there and one of the maidens serves me, maybe her goodness is because her parents are around and her kindness would not be of her own doing. And if she didn't serve me, maybe that is due to her modesty and shyness. Therefore it is not wise to check her out while in her home. So I will wait here **by the spring** and if a maiden does act charitably, I will know she is doing it on her own motivation.

A beautiful insight. An original approach. And how psychologically true. Oh, that we could see in the Torah's words what these *Rishonim* saw!

The Bechor Shor has many such psychological flashes throughout his Torah commentary.

The *Das Zekeinim Ba'alei haTosafos*

The *Das Zekeinim* is a collection of comments by various of the *Ba'alei haTosafos*. It is printed in many editions of the *Mikraos Gedolos*.

Being an anthology of various contributors, it is not possible to categorize or characterize the commentary by any clear-cut stylistic traits. The commentary is characterized by a wide variety of interpretative styles — from *p'shat* to *drash* to *sode*. I will give some examples.

Das Zekeinim and *P'shat*

Following is an example of a simple interpretation intended to explain the Torah's linguistic style.

Genesis 1:3:

'Let there be light' and there was light. *Das Zekeinim:* The reason it didn't say 'And it was so' — ויהי כן — as it says by all the other creations (see for example 1:7; 1:9; 1:15 etc.) is because it said this in the other cases because this is a briefer way of saying it, instead of repeating all that was created and saying "and there was — and a listing of all that was created." But in our verse to say 'And there was light' is just as brief (in Hebrew) as it is to say 'and it was so.'

This is clearly a *p'shat* interpretation which answers a linguistic question.

Following is another example which illustrates further how this commentary can relate to questions in the Torah-text in a straightforward and insightful manner.

In *parashas Shelach*, the Torah names the Spies whom Moses sent to spy out the Land. There we find the following verse:

> *Numbers 13:11:*

"For the tribe of Joseph, for the tribe of Menasseh, Gaddi son of Susi."

The question asked by the *Das Zekeinim* is why is Joseph's name, who was the father of both Menasseh and Ephraim, associated here with Menasseh when elsewhere in the Torah he is always associated with Ephraim.

He answers that Joseph, himself, had delivered an evil report — הביא דיבה — to his father Jacob when he suspected his brothers of wrongful behavior (Genesis 37:2). Likewise, here, Menasseh together with the other the Spies also delivered an evil report — הביא דיבה — regarding their negative view of the Land. Therefore Joseph was linked to Menasseh in the list of names in *Shelach*. On the other hand, Joshua who was from the tribe of Ephraim, did not align himself with the Spies' report and was thus distanced from his grandfather's act.

A creative answer to a question of *p'shat*. Many such examples can be found in the *Das Zekeinim's* commentary.

On the other hand, the *Das Zekeinim* relies often on non-*p'shat* interpretations. His reliance on *gematrios* is an example of this.

GEMATRIOS – RASHI AND BA'ALEI HATOSAFOS

Gematria (which can be considered a *Remez* type-interpretation) is the numerical equivalent of the Hebrew letters.

א-ט = 1-9

י-צ = 10-90

ק, ר, ש, ת = 100, 200, 300, 400, respectively.

Words are decoded into their numerical equivalent and matched with other words with an equal *gematria*.

Use of *Gematria* can already be found in the Talmud, (*Makkos* 23b) but its extensive application was adopted by the *Reshonim*, among them the *Ba'alei haTosafos*. They relied on *gematria* interpretation to a much greater extent than Rashi did. While there are only five *gematria* interpretations throughout Rashi's Torah commentary, the *Ba'alei haTosafos* made use of them much more often. Following is a brilliant example of the use of *gematria* by the *Das Zekeinim*.

Jacob tells Joseph that he has adopted Joseph's two sons as his own.

Genesis 48:5:

"And now your two sons who were born to you in Egypt before my coming to you in Egypt, shall be mine; **Ephraim and Menasseh shall be mine like Reuben and Simeon**." אפרים ומנשה כראובן ושמעון יהיו לי

The *Das Zekeinim* points out that the *gematria* of אפרים ומנשה (726) is the same as that of the names ראובן ושמעון (725) plus one. This extra "one" accords with Jacob's promise later (48:22) "I have given you one portion more than your brothers."

While such interpretations do not teach us anything new, they do show the fascinating variety of aspects to the Torah's words.

Summary: In comparing Rashi to the *Ba'alei haTosafos* we can summarize by saying that Rashi's commentary is more focused and more concise than that of *Tosafos*. Regarding the emphasis on *p'shat*, Rashi stands somewhere between the Rashbam and Bechor Shor who were more *p'shat* oriented than Rashi and, on the other side, other *Ba'alei haTosafos* who were more eclectic in their choice of interpretive modes, including much *Drash* and *Remez*.

While Rashi's commentary often has the appearance of a simple commentary, that appearance is misleading. At first glance we might assume that *Tosafos* has more depth to it. That this is not the case is attested to by one of the most brilliant of the *Ba'alei haTosafos* – Rashi's grandson, Rabbeinu Tam. His evaluation of Rashi's Torah commentary is most fitting summation of this short essay on Rashi and the *Ba'alei haTosafos*.

"Regarding my master, my grandfather's commentary on the Talmud, I too could have made a comparable commentary. But his Torah commentary - that is beyond me. I could never have produced such a work !"

In Loving Memory

of my Mother

Yetta Pearl ע״ה

יעראל בת רי שלמה דוד ע״ה

and

Grandmother

Helen Pearl ע״ה

היתדא בת רי יעקב הלוי ע״ה

הנאהבים בחייהם ובמותם לא נפרדו

Tosafos questions Rashi's midrashic *interpretation.*

Deut. 1:1

אֵלֶּה הַדְּבָרִים אֲשֶׁר דִּבֶּר מֹשֶׁה אֶל־כָּל־יִשְׂרָאֵל בְּעֵבֶר הַיַּרְדֵּן בַּמִּדְבָּר בָּעֲרָבָה מוֹל סוּף בֵּין־פָּארָן וּבֵין־תֹּפֶל וְלָבָן וַחֲצֵרֹת וְדִי זָהָב.

> **אֵלֶּה הַדְּבָרִים:** לפי שהן דברי תוכחות ומנה כאן כל המקומות שהכעיסו לפני המקום בהן לפיכך סתם את הדברים והזכירם ברמז מפני כבודן של ישראל.
>
> **These are the words**: *Rashi:* Because these are words of rebuke and [because] he (Moses) intended to recount here all the places where they angered the Almighty he therefore said these words in an obscure manner and only mentioned them in hints out of respect for the honor of Israel.

QUESTIONING RASHI

A Question: Why does Rashi interpret these place names as symbolic terms for the sins of Israel? Why doesn't he accept them simply as actual places?

Hint: See the other Rashi-comments on this verse.

YOUR ANSWER:

WHAT IS BOTHERING RASHI?

An Answer: In his ensuing comments on this verse Rashi points out two difficulties with accepting these place-names at face value. First, he says "They were not in the Wilderness, they were in the Plains of Moab!" And further on in his comments Rashi cites Rabbi Yochanan who says "We have reviewed all the Scriptures and have not found places whose names were Tofel or Lavan!" If these were among the places where Moses had spoken to the People, why didn't the Torah mention these places when Moses spoke to them originally?

On the basis of these questions, Rashi searches for another interpretation of this verse.

How does his interpretation help matters?

YOUR ANSWER:

UNDERSTANDING RASHI

An Answer: With Rashi's comment we are to read this verse as follows: These are the words (of rebuke) that Moses spoke to the Children of Israel on the other side of the Jordan: (then follows a recitation of place-names which hint at their various sins committed while they wandered in the Wilderness). Thus the place-names do not necessarily denote actual geographical locations. So, in fact, they were in the Plains of Moab (on the other side of the Jordan); they were not presently in the Wilderness. The place-name "Wilderness" instead refers to the sin they did while in the Wilderness, i.e. complaining in the Wilderness about not having food to eat.

RESPECT FOR THE HONOR OF ISRAEL

Rashi tells us that the reason the sins were only hinted at, and not mentioned explicitly, was out of respect for Israel, so as not to openly criticize and embarrass them.

Can you think of a question on this interpretation?

Hint: Look further on in the sedra.

YOUR QUESTION:

TOSAFOS QUESTIONS RASHI

The *Moshav Zekeinim,* a compilation of comments by the *Ba'alei haTosafos,* asks the following question. If Moses was so respectful of their honor that he did not openly mention their previous sins, how come we find, further on (1:27ff), that he openly castigates them for the sin of the Spies? And later on (9:15) he criticizes them quite harshly regarding the Golden Calf that they made. From these verses and others, it does not seem that Moses was overly sensitive to their honor. How can we say that his concern for their honor caused him to just hint at their sins in our verse?

The *Moshav Zekeinim* does not offer any answer to this question and therefore says these place-names are, in fact, places.

Can you think of a defense for Rashi? Why would Moses only hint at their sins here, whereas later on he was most outspoken and direct?

YOUR ANSWER:

DEFENDING RASHI

An Answer: A commentary on Rashi, *Amar Nekai*, which was written by Rabbi Ovadia of Bartenura, the famous commentator on the mishna, suggests a very reasonable answer to Tosafos' question. He says that because this is the very first verse in the Book of Devarim, Rashi understood that Moses would be extra sensitive to the honor of the people. But, once Moses' oration began, he no longer felt the necessity to speak in hints. On the contrary, it was important to speak clearly and directly, so that his *musar* would be correctly understood.

Can you think of another place in the Torah where the idea of not beginning a Book of the Torah with criticism of Israel is found?

YOUR ANSWER:

SUPPORT FOR RASHI

An Answer: See Rashi on Numbers 9:1. There he explains that the Torah intentionally recorded events not in their chronological order so as not to begin the Book of Bamidbar with the story of the first and only Pesach offering that Israel made during their forty years in the wilderness. Because that would have reflected negatively on the People of Israel, it was not recorded at the beginning of the Book, when it actually took place.

A simple-looking comment turns out to be complex.

Deut. 1:1

אֵלֶּה הַדְּבָרִים אֲשֶׁר דִּבֶּר מֹשֶׁה אֶל־כָּל־יִשְׂרָאֵל בְּעֵבֶר הַיַּרְדֵּן בַּמִּדְבָּר בָּעֲרָבָה מוֹל סוּף בֵּין־פָּארָן וּבֵין־תֹּפֶל וְלָבָן וַחֲצֵרֹת וְדִי זָהָב.

בֵּין פָּארָן וּבֵין תֹּפֶל וְלָבָן: אמר רבי יוחנן "חזרנו על כל המקרא ולא מצינו מקום ששמו תופל ולבן אלא הוכיחן על הדברים שתפלו על המן, שהוא לבן, שאמרו (במדבר כ"א:ה') ונפשנו קצה בלחם הקלוקל' ועל מה שעשו במדבר פארן על ידי המרגלים."

Between Paran and Between Tofel and Lavan: *Rashi:* Rabbi Yochanan said 'We have gone through the whole Scriptures and we have found no place with the name Tofel or Lavan! But [the meaning is] he reproved them because of the calumnious statements (= 'tofel' in Hebrew) that they made regarding the Manna which was white (= 'lavan' in Hebrew) — they said (Num. 21:5) "And our soul loathes this light bread." And because of what they had done in the Wilderness of Paran in the matter of the Spies.'

WHAT IS RASHI SAYING?

Rashi is following the line he set out in his first comment, i.e. that these are not actual place names but rather hints at the sins of the People. Tofel and Lavan are not places that exist; they are code words for the Manna and the Spies. But as you look at the complete comment you should have a question.

Hint: Keep in mind the order of events described in Rashi's comment and compare this with the order of the words in the *dibbur hamaschil.*

YOUR ANSWER:

QUESTIONING RASHI

A Question: While our verse mentions Paran *before* Tofel and Lavan (as does Rashi's *dibbur hamaschil*) Rashi comments on Paran (the sin of the Spies) only *after* he interprets Tofel and Lavan. Why?

Can you see what's bothering Rashi and why he reversed the order in his comment?

Your Answer:

What Is Bothering Rashi?

An Answer: There is a difficulty here. If Tofel and Lavan are not places, then what does the word "between" mean here? "Between" would be appropriate if these were two places, but if they are not, what sense does it make to say "between" the Manna and the Spies?

Can you see how Rashi's comment deals with this?

This requires some complex reasoning.

Your Answer:

Understanding Rashi

An Answer: While Tofel and Lavan are not actual places, Paran is definitely a real geographic location.

In trying to make sense of the word בין in our verse, Rashi begins by telling us that Tofel/Lavan is not an actual place. This Rashi uses to point out that even though Paran is a real place, and we might have mistakenly thought that it means a place-name in this verse, nevertheless, he says that is not its meaning here. Here it refers to the sin of the Spies, which took place at Paran.

A Closer Look

But when we do some research, we find something interesting. See Rashi on Numbers 10:12. There we see that the people's complaint about the Manna also took place in a place called Paran. Rashi on that verse tells us that "*Kivros haTa'avah*" happened in Paran. *Kivros haTa'avah* refers to the punishment for the people's dissatisfaction with the Manna where they were punished by a Divine plague. In Numbers 11:34 we are told that this was called *Kivros haTa'avah* meaning "the graves of those that lusted."

So we see that *both* the sin of the Manna complaint and the sin of the Spies took place in the Wilderness of Paran.

Now we can better understand this *drash* and Rashi's ordering of his interpretation. The Hebrew word בין, which usually means "between" here carries a meaning less often used — "both." This meaning for the word בֵּין is common in the mishna, but rare in the Scriptures. Yet we do find this meaning also in the Torah. In Leviticus 27:12:

וְהֶעֱרִיךְ הַכֹּהֵן אֹתָהּ **בֵּין טוֹב וּבֵין רָע** כְּעֶרְכְּךָ הַכֹּהֵן כֵּן יִהְיֶה.

"And the Priest shall evaluate it, **both good or bad**, like the Priest's evaluation so shall it be."

Also in Numbers 26:56

עַל־פִּי הַגּוֹרָל תֵּחָלֵק נַחֲלָתוֹ **בֵּין רַב לִמְעָט**.

"According to the lottery you shall divide one's inheritance, **both the many or the few**."

Using this rare meaning of the word בֵּין, we are to read the verse as follows: "Both (בֵּין) the sin of the Spies (in Paran) and both (בֵּין) the sin of Manna (which also happened in Paran)."

SUPPORT FROM TARGUM ONKELOS

The interpretation that Paran refers to both the sin of the Spies and the sin of the complaints about the Manna, receives support from the Targum. On the Torah's words בֵּין פָּארָן וּבֵין תֹּפֶל וְלָבָן the Targum has: בפארן דאתפלו על מנא "And in Paran when they complained about the Manna." We see that he too connects the sin of Manna with Paran, because it took place there.

THE REVERSAL

We still have to understand why Rashi reversed the order of these sins in his comment, relating first to Tofel/Lavan and the Manna before the sin of the Spies.

The answer would be, that first Rashi had to establish that we weren't talking about actual places (Tofel and Lavan are not real locations) even though Paran is an actual place, Paran in this context would now be seen as a reminder of some sin done in that area. Once this was clarified, Rashi could go on to mention the other sin at Paran, that of the Spies.

(See *Be'er BaSadeh*)

A closer analysis of Rashi's words fortifies our faith in his depth and precision.

Deut. 1:5

בְּעֵבֶר הַיַּרְדֵּן בְּאֶרֶץ מוֹאָב הוֹאִיל מֹשֶׁה בֵּאֵר אֶת־הַתּוֹרָה הַזֹּאת לֵאמֹר.

> **הוֹאִיל**: הִתְחִיל, כְּמוֹ הִנֵּה נָא הוֹאַלְתִּי (בראשית יח).
>
> **Began**: *Rashi:* [This means] 'Began', as in "Behold now I have begun" (Genesis 18).

WHAT IS RASHI SAYING?

The word הואיל may have several meanings in the Torah. It can mean, "to begin" or it can mean "to be willing — to want." See for example Exodus 2:21 "and Moses was willing — ויואל משה — to dwell with man." (In Talmudic and Modern Hebrew this word may also mean "in as much as" or "since." But these are not Biblical usages.)

Thus Rashi is clarifying its meaning here.

QUESTIONING RASHI

A Question: By itself, this comment is not problematic. But if we look back to the verse Rashi cites in support of his translation (Genesis 18) we find something strange, indeed.

What did you find?

YOUR ANSWER:

An Answer: On Genesis 18:27 Rashi says:

הוֹאַלְתִּי: רָצִיתִי, כְּמוֹ לְשׁוֹן וַיּוֹאֶל מֹשֶׁה.'

Rashi: I was willing. As in "And Moses was willing."

Startling! Rashi seems to contradict himself. The verse that Rashi quotes here (Genesis 18:27) as proof that הואלתי means "to begin", Rashi himself, in its place, translates as "to be willing"!

How can we understand this? It is difficult to assume that Rashi forgot what he wrote in Genesis.

Can you figure it out?

Hint: Look at the verses in Genesis 18:27-31. What do you notice?

YOUR ANSWER:

UNDERSTANDING RASHI

An Answer: Actually in that section the words הנה נא הואלתי לדבר appear twice, one when Abraham begins his speech to *Hashem* in verse 27 and then a second time in verse 31. Did you notice that Rashi's comment in Genesis is on the word הואלתי in verse 18:31, but this same phrase word הנה נא הואלתי appears above in verse 18:27 and there Rashi has no comment. (Unfortunately there are some printed Rashi editions which erroneously confuse Rashi's comment on 18:31 with verse 18:27.) Now, when we think about the meanings of these two identical phrases, we can understand that only the first one of them can mean "to begin." When Abraham again uses this word in verse 31, it can no longer mean, "I have *begun* to speak" because he had already begun speaking several verses earlier. So only on the second occurrence of this word (in verse 31) does Rashi choose to translate it "I was *willing*." But when Rashi, on our verse here, cites the words הנה נא הואלתי he is referring to the words in verse Genesis 18:27 where its meaning is "Behold now, I have *begun* to speak." And for this meaning he refers us to Exodus 21:21 — 'Moses was willing.'

THE LESSON

The beauty and significance of this explanation is that it justifies our faith in Rashi. The question we had — the apparent contradiction between two Rashi-comments — appeared, before reflection, to be a very difficult one. But we have to give Rashi, at least, that much credit, that he would certainly remember what he wrote in his own commentary. If, in fact, there had been a contradiction, Rashi would have crossed out this comment. The fact that he didn't, is evidence enough that he had a method to his choice of words. When we are confronted with such a glaring contradiction in Rashi's words, we must pause and investigate to discover the correct meaning of his precisely chosen words.

(See *Divrei Dovid*)

P'shat and *Drash* again examined.

Deut. 1:6

הי אֱלֹקֵינוּ דִּבֶּר אֵלֵינוּ בְּחֹרֵב לֵאמֹר רַב־לָכֶם שֶׁבֶת בָּהָר הַזֶּה.

רַב לָכֶם שֶׁבֶת: כפשוטו. ויש מדרש אגדה, הרבה גדולה לכם ושכר על ישיבתכם בהר הזה – עשיתם משכן, מנורה, וכלים, קבלתם תורה, מניתם לכם סנהדרין שרי אלפים ושרי מאות.

You have dwelt too long: *Rashi*: [Understand it] as its Plain Sense. But there is an Aggadic explanation: He has given you much distinction and reward for your having dwelt at this mountain — you made the Tabernacle, the Candelabrum and the sacred articles, you received the Torah, you appointed the Sanhedrin, officers of thousands and officers of hundreds.

WHAT IS RASHI SAYING?

Rashi gives us *p'shat* and *drash* on this verse. The word רב is interpreted differently in both cases.

What are the two different meanings of the word in *p'shat* and in *drash*?

YOUR ANSWER:

UNDERSTANDING RASHI

An Answer: Rashi just says "as its Plain Sense" (כפשוטו) without telling us clearly what the "Plain Sense" is. We can assume that he means that the meaning of רב is "You have dwelt *too long* at this mountain." In this case, the word רב has the meaning of "too much."

The *drash* meaning of רב, on the other hand, is "You have received *a lot* at this mountain." In this case, רב means simply "much" or "a lot."

A CLOSER LOOK

The two versions of the word רב appear elsewhere in the Torah.

Do you remember where?

YOUR ANSWER:

An Answer: In *Parashas Korah* we find this word used with both these meanings.

Korah says to Moses (Numbers 16:3)

רַב־לָכֶם כִּי כָל־הָעֵדָה כֻּלָּם קְדֹשִׁים...

Rashi, on the verse, interprets his words as: "You have taken for yourselves *too much* for all the congregation is holy…"

Moses answers Korah, using Korah's own phrase, saying (Numbers 16:7):

...רַב־לָכֶם בְּנֵי לֵוִי.

Rashi comments on these words:

"A *great matter* have you taken upon yourself.."

Here too, we see the two interpretations of the word רב. Korah said רב and meant "too much" Moses said רב and meant "a lot."

(See *Nachlas Yaakov*)

So we see that the word 'רב' has two different meanings. Rashi's two interpretations, one *p'shat* and one *drash*, make use of them.

WHAT MAKES P'SHAT, P'SHAT?

The question can be asked: If both uses of the word רב have support in the Torah, then why does Rashi consider only his first interpretation to be *p'shat* and not the second one?

There are certain accepted criteria for *p'shat*. Can you see why only his first interpretation is *p'shat*?

YOUR ANSWER:

UNDERSTANDING P'SHAT

An Answer: Rashi's first interpretation translates רב as "too long." This fits in with the context, for the very next verse says "Turn and journey and come to the Amorite mountain…" Being "too long" at that place was the reason for G-d's command to them to journey from it. Context is one of the basic dimensions which differentiates *p'shat* from *drash. Drash* is not bound by context; *p'shat* is.

Rashi's interpretation teaches us the importance of seeing the verse in its larger context.

Deut. 1:14

וַתַּעֲנוּ אֹתִי וַתֹּאמְרוּ טוֹב־הַדָּבָר אֲשֶׁר דִּבַּרְתָּ לַעֲשׂוֹת.

> **ותענו אתי וגו':** חלטתם את הדבר להנאתכם היה לכם להשיב משה רבנו ממי נאה ללמוד ממך או מתלמידך? לא ממך שנצטערת עליה? אלא ידעתי מחשבותיכם הייתם אומרים עכשיו יתמנו עלינו דיינין הרבה. אם אין מכירנו אנו מביאין לו דורון והוא נושא לנו פנים.
>
> **And you answered me, etc.:** *Rashi:* You quickly agreed to the matter to your benefit. You should rather have replied: Moses, our teacher, from whom is it more fitting to learn, from you or from your student? Shouldn't it be from you who have taken such pains about it? But I knew your thoughts, you said 'Many judges will now be appointed over us, if he doesn't favor us, then we will bring him a gift and he will then show favoritism towards us.'

As you compare Rashi's comment with the Torah verse, what would you ask?

YOUR QUESTION:

QUESTIONING RASHI

A Question: Rashi's comment has Moses being critical of the People; while the verse itself conveys just the opposite, i.e., the People immediately agreed to Moses' request to have additional judges besides himself.

Why does Rashi inject a critical connotation to their words?

What lead him to this interpretation?

Hint: See the context of this remark.

YOUR ANSWER:

WHAT IS BOTHERING RASHI?

An Answer: If we read the previous verses and Rashi's comments on them, we get a picture of Moses as castigating the People. He was, as Rashi had said in his very first comment of the *parasha*, quite critical of their behavior during the years in the Wilderness. In that light, our verse which seems to relate the People's acquiescent behavior, rings a discordant note. When their words are understood as "good behavior" they don't fit in with the critical tenor and thrust of his speech.

How does his comment explain matters?

YOUR ANSWER:

UNDERSTANDING RASHI

An Answer: It is for this reason that Rashi saw these words, as well, as critical. Certainly Rashi has a point. Why should the People so readily allow Moses to relinquish his position as their exclusive judge. They should have considered it an honor for Moses, their teacher, to be personally involved in any disputes they may have. Why then did they so hastily agree to the arrangement of a system of judges? Rashi's comment helps us understand the human dimension involved in their acquiescence. As he points out, by having Moses as their sole arbiter, they couldn't be sure that they would always win their case, Moses being straight as an arrow. On the other hand, if they had a more fallible person as a judge, they could consider bribing him, then they would be more assured of getting the decision they desired.

(See *Sefer Zikaron*)

Simplicity – A basic rule in Torah interpretation.

Deut. 1:15

וָאֶקַּח אֶת־רָאשֵׁי שִׁבְטֵיכֶם אֲנָשִׁים חֲכָמִים וִידֻעִים וָאֶתֵּן אוֹתָם רָאשִׁים עֲלֵיכֶם, שָׂרֵי אֲלָפִים וְשָׂרֵי מֵאוֹת וְשָׂרֵי חֲמִשִּׁים וְשָׂרֵי עֲשָׂרֹת וְשֹׁטְרִים לְשִׁבְטֵיכֶם.

שָׂרֵי אֲלָפִים: אֶחָד מְמֻנֶּה עַל אֶלֶף.
Officers of thousands: *Rashi*: One who is appointed over a thousand.

Questioning Rashi

A Question: This comment seems totally unnecessary. It appears to say what the verse itself says.

Why does Rashi find the need to make this comment?

Your Answer:

What Is Bothering Rashi?

An Answer: The meaning of the words "officers of thousands," are unclear. Since the words "officers" and the word "thousands" are both in the plural, the verse can be interpreted to mean, many officers, each officer being in charge of many thousands.

How does Rashi's comment clear up matters?

Your Answer:

Understanding Rashi

An Answer: Rashi makes it very clear: *One* officer appointed over just one thousand soldiers.

But how does Rashi know that this is correct? Maybe, in fact, the verse means "officers each of which is in charge of thousands."

To know why Rashi chose this interpretation over the other, one must be familiar with a principle that Rashi relies on in interpretation.

What is that principle?

Hint: See Rashi on Genesis 21:34.

Your Answer:

A Fuller Understanding

An Answer: On the verse in Genesis 21:34 Rashi lays down a principle of interpretation. He says the Torah would not state things in an ambiguous way. Therefore, when we have two (or more) possible interpretations of a verse and we must choose between them, we should choose the least ambiguous; the one that gives us the clearest meaning. In our case, if the verse meant "officers of thousands" we would have no way of knowing how many officers were in charge of how many thousands of soldiers. On the other hand, if we say the verse means "one officer for one thousand" its meaning is very clear.

A shift in mind-set helps in understanding Rashi

Deut. 1:23

וַיִּיטַב בְּעֵינַי הַדָּבָר וָאֶקַּח מִכֶּם שְׁנֵים עָשָׂר אֲנָשִׁים אִישׁ אֶחָד לַשָּׁבֶט.

שנים עשר אנשים איש אחד לשבט: מגיד שלא היה שבט לוי עמהם.

Twelve men, one man per tribe: *Rashi*: This tells us that the tribe of Levi was not among them.

THE TWELVE TRIBES

The verse emphasizes the fact that there were only twelve Spies, representing the twelve tribes. But which twelve tribes are referred to here? There are actually thirteen tribes, when Ephraim and Menasseh are included (in place of the single tribe of Joseph) together with Levi. You will find throughout the Torah that, in spite of the fact, that the actual total is thirteen, the Torah always mentions only twelve tribes. Whether regarding the stones in the High Priest's breastplate, or the tribal encampments in the desert, or the Princes of each tribe who brought offerings at the dedication of the Tabernacle, or any other situation when the tribes were involved, the Torah mentions only twelve. Sometimes the twelve include Levi and Joseph, without Ephraim and Menasseh. Sometimes Joseph and Levi are excluded and Ephraim and Menasseh are included.

In our case, Rashi tells us that Levi was excluded, which means, incidentally, that Ephraim and Menasseh were included.

What would you ask on Rashi?

YOUR QUESTION:

Questioning Rashi

A Question: How does Rashi know that it was specifically the tribe of Levi that was excluded? Maybe this group of Spies included one representative from the larger tribe of Joseph as well as from Levi. That would also total twelve.

Can you think of an answer?

Your Answer:

Understanding Rashi

An Answer: The answer is too simple to be true! When we refer back to the story of the Spies in the Book of Bamidar, *parashas Shelach,* we find that the twelve Spies are listed by name and *by tribe*. Levi *is not* listed, Ephraim and Menashe *are* listed.

That's how Rashi knew that Levi was excluded. In light of this answer, your next question begs to be asked.

Your Question:

A Deeper Question

A Question: Since the Torah explicitly told us which tribes participated in the Spy venture, why does Rashi have to say here that *our verse* "tells us that Levi was not among them" ? It was not our verse that informed us of this; it was a verse in *parashas Shelach* that did. So our question is: What does Rashi mean by "*This* tells us, etc."

Can you think of an answer to this difficult question?

Hint: See the context of this verse.

Your Answer:

A Deeper Understanding

An Answer: The verse before our verse says:

"And you approached me and said 'Let us send men ahead of us and let them spy out the Land and bring a word back to us — the road on which we should ascend and the cities to which we should come.'"

Then Moses chose men "from you" meaning from the crowd that approached him.

That crowd was an unruly one, as Rashi says on that verse. It was from that crowd that Moses took the twelve Spies. Rashi's comment here tells us that Levi was not among *them* i.e. among the mob that asked for Spies. While we knew that the tribe of Levi didn't send a Spy, nevertheless they might have been among those that clamored for Spies. Rashi, therefore, tells us that the Torah's emphasis on twelve is meant to tell us that Levi *was not among them* i.e. among the unruly crowd that pressured Moses requesting Spies.

(See *Almosh'nino*)

The Lesson: A new approach and a new mind set are often necessary to understand Rashi.

❖❖❖

Careful comparing of texts explains a Rashi-comment

Deut. 1:42

וַיֹּאמֶר הי אֵלַי אֱמֹר לָהֶם לֹא תַעֲלוּ וְלֹא תִלָּחֲמוּ כִּי אֵינֶנִּי בְּקִרְבְּכֶם וְלֹא תִּנָּגְפוּ לִפְנֵי אֹיְבֵיכֶם.

לֹא תַעֲלוּ: לֹא עֲלִייָּה תְהֵא לָכֶם אֶלָּא יְרִידָה.
Do not go up: *Rashi:* It will not be an "ascent" for you, but only a "descent" (defeat).

WHAT IS RASHI SAYING?

This verse is ordinarily translated as "*Do not* go up and do not make war..." But Rashi takes the negative word לא not as a command but rather as a prediction, "you will not go up (succeed)..."

The question should be obvious.

YOUR QUESTION:

QUESTIONING RASHI

A Question: Why does Rashi abandon the more reasonable interpretation that these words mean "You shall not go up," and choose this less likely one, meaning "you will not go up"?

What's bothering him?

Hint: Look up the event as it is described in Numbers 14:41, 43.

YOUR ANSWER:

WHAT IS BOTHERING RASHI?

An Answer: When we compare what Moses said to the people in *parashas Shelach* with our verse, we can get an idea of Rashi's thinking.

Our verse	Numbers 14:41, 43
וַיֹּאמֶר ה'	וַיֹּאמֶר מֹשֶׁה
אֵלַי אֱמֹר לָהֶם	לָמָּה זֶּה אַתֶּם עֹבְרִים אֶת־פִּי ה'...
לֹא תַעֲלוּ וְלֹא תִלָּחֲמוּ כִּי אֵינֶנִּי בְּקִרְבְּכֶם	**אַל**־תַּעֲלוּ כִּי אֵין ה' בְּקִרְבְּכֶם
וְלֹא תִּנָּגְפוּ לִפְנֵי אֹיְבֵיכֶם.	וְלֹא תִּנָּגְפוּ לִפְנֵי אֹיְבֵיכֶם.

We see that where our verse has תעלו **לֹא**, the original verse in Bamidbar has תעלו **אַל**. One verse has **לֹא** and the other has **אַל**. This slight difference is what alerted Rashi and led to his comment. What is the significance of this difference and how does Rashi's comment deal with it?

YOUR ANSWER:

UNDERSTANDING RASHI

An Answer: The difference between **לֹא** and **אַל** is that **לֹא** can be either a command or a statement, while **אַל** is always a command. Rashi saw that our verse changed the original **אַל**, which meant a command, to **לֹא** which means a statement. Thus Rashi gave it the meaning of a statement — a prediction — "you will not go up" meaning "you will not succeed."

(See *Silbermann*)

The Torah teaches us an important rule in military self-restraint.

Deut. 2:4,5

וְאֶת־הָעָם צַו לֵאמֹר אַתֶּם עֹבְרִים בִּגְבוּל אֲחֵיכֶם בְּנֵי־עֵשָׂו הַיֹּשְׁבִים
בְּשֵׂעִיר וְיִירְאוּ מִכֶּם וְנִשְׁמַרְתֶּם מְאֹד.

אַל־תִּתְגָּרוּ בָם כִּי לֹא־אֶתֵּן לָכֶם מֵאַרְצָם עַד מִדְרַךְ כַּף־רָגֶל כִּי־יְרֻשָּׁה
לְעֵשָׂו נָתַתִּי אֶת־הַר שֵׂעִיר.

> **וְנִשְׁמַרְתֶּם מְאֹד. וּמַהִי הַשְּׁמִירָה? אַל תִּתְגָּרוּ בָם.**
> **And you shall be extremely careful**: *Rashi:* And what is
> this 'carefulness'? '**Do not incite them**.' (these are the
> first words of the next verse.)

WHAT IS RASHI SAYING?

Rashi explains that the word ונשמרתם "and you shall take care" or "be
careful" does not mean what we might have expected — "take care of
yourselves"(as it means in Deut. 4:15). Rather it means "take care not to
harm the sons of Esau." Rashi derives this by connecting the last words
of verse 4 with the first words of verse 5.

QUESTIONING RASHI

A Question: Why does Rashi prefer his interpretation of "be careful not to harm
others" to its more usual meaning "take care of yourselves"?

Hint: Look carefully at the verses.

YOUR ANSWER:

WHAT IS BOTHERING RASHI?

An Answer: Verse 4 says "You are crossing the border of your brothers, the
sons of Esau, who live in Seir. *They will fear you,* you must be
extremely careful." The question is, if *they fear us,* why should *we*
be careful?! *They* should be careful, since we can defeat them in
battle. This apparent *non sequitur*, is what is bothering Rashi.

Do you see how his comment deals with this?

YOUR ANSWER:

Understanding Rashi

An Answer: Israel should be extremely careful *precisely* because Esau fears them. Esau's fear of Israel could provoke Israel's aggression. History has too many cases where a strong nation senses the weakness — "smells blood" — of a neighboring state and is tempted to attack. Israel is forewarned not act in this way. The reason: For Mt. Seir belongs to Esau. And G-d says "I will not give you of his land."

See how Rashi connects the two verses to gain maximum effect of its meaning. What should Israel be careful about? — "Do not provoke them…."

(See *Sefer Zikaron*)

❖❖❖

Rashi pursues the reason behind the reason.

Deut. 3:18

וָאֲצַו אֶתְכֶם בָּעֵת הַהִוא לֵאמֹר הי אֱלֹקֵיכֶם נָתַן לָכֶם אֶת־הָאָרֶץ הַזֹּאת לְרִשְׁתָּהּ חֲלוּצִים תַּעַבְרוּ לִפְנֵי אֲחֵיכֶם בְּנֵי־יִשְׂרָאֵל כָּל־בְּנֵי־חָיִל.

לִפְנֵי אֲחֵיכֶם: הֵם הָיוּ הוֹלְכִים לִפְנֵי יִשְׂרָאֵל לַמִּלְחָמָה לְפִי שֶׁהָיוּ גִּבּוֹרִים וְאוֹיְבִים נוֹפְלִים לִפְנֵיהֶם שֶׁנֶּאֱמַר וְטָרַף זְרוֹעַ אַף קָדְקֹד׳ (דברים לג:כ).

Ahead of your brothers: *Rashi:* They were to go ahead of Israel in battle because they were mighty warriors and their enemies fell before them as it says "He (Gad) rips off the arm, even the head…." (Deut. 33:20).

If you recall Numbers Ch. 32 where the story of the Sons of Gad and the Sons of Reuben is recorded, you should have a question on Rashi's explanation.

Your Question:

QUESTIONING RASHI

A Question: In Numbers 32 we are told that the tribes of Gad and Reuben came forward to ask Moses for a special deal. They wanted to receive Trans Jordan as their inheritance and in turn they offered to go first, speedily before the Children of Israel in the battles to conquer the Land of Canaan.(32:17). Moses agreed and formalized this agreement by making their receiving Trans Jordan conditional on their going first before G-d to war (32:20). This is what Moses is referring to in our verse. But since Moses made this a precondition to receiving their inheritance, then the reason they went first in battle was because of this contractual agreement and not because they were mighty warriors, as Rashi says here. Why, then, does Rashi say this?

Can you think of an answer?

Hint: See Rashi's comment on Numbers 32:16.

YOUR ANSWER:

UNDERSTANDING RASHI

An Answer: Rashi himself comments in Numbers 32:16, that Gad and Reuben volunteered to go first into battle, precisely because they were warriors. In that comment, Rashi again quotes Deut. 33:20 as he does in his comment here. It is instructional to check out that verse and the one after it. In Deut. 33:20,21 it says:

20. "And about Gad he said: 'The Source of Blessing enlarges Gad. He dwells like a lioness and rips off the arm, even the head.

21. He saw his [portion] the first part of [the Land to be conquered] for there the plot of the Lawgiver was hidden. He came [to the Land] at the head of the people, he fulfilled his righteous [duty] before *Hashem* and his obligations to Israel."

We see clearly from these verses that Gad's strength (he "rips off the arm, even the head") is spoken of as being the cause of his leading the charge into the Promised Land ("He came [to the Land] at the head of the people.") So, when Rashi, here, attributes Gad's "going before the people" to his strength and not to his promise to Moses, he merely refers to the primary cause. Because they were strong, they volunteered to go first in battle; Moses then accepted this condition as part of their commitment.

(See *Liphshuto shel Rashi*)

לעילוי נשמות

ר׳ יעקב ב״ר אברהם ז״ל

זלדא רבקה בת ר׳ נתן נטע ע״ה

by

Mr. & Mrs. Yehuda Freeman

and

Family

What looks like a gross error on Rashi's part must be understood.

Deut. 3:24

אֲדֹנָי יֱהֹוִ-ה אַתָּה הַחִלּוֹתָ לְהַרְאוֹת אֶת־עַבְדְּךָ אֶת־גָּדְלְךָ וְאֶת־יָדְךָ הַחֲזָקָה אֲשֶׁר מִי־אֵל בַּשָּׁמַיִם וּבָאָרֶץ אֲשֶׁר יַעֲשֶׂה כְמַעֲשֶׂיךָ וְכִגְבוּרֹתֶךָ.

> **ה' אלוקים:** רחום בדין.
> ***Hashem G-d:*** *Rashi:* Merciful in judgement.

In order to understand Rashi's comment and the difficulties with it, we offer a brief introduction to the meanings attributed to the different names of G-d found in the Torah.

THE NAMES OF G-D: An INTRODUCTION

G-d is referred to by various names in the Torah. The more common ones are:

יהו-ה, אלוקים, אדוני, אל, שדי.

The Sages have informed us that each of these names reflects a different characteristic of the Divine entity. The unique and most holy name is יהו-ה. In English it is called the Tetragrammaton, meaning the name with four letters. This name is so holy it is not to be pronounced as it is spelled, except by the priests in the Temple service. Therefore, whenever we come across it in the Torah or in prayer we pronounce it as we would the word אדוני ("Adonoy") "my Lord." If you look at this name in a chumash or prayer book you will see that the Hebrew vowels under the letters י-ה-ו-ה are the vowels appropriate to the word אדוני "Adonoy." Which is our clue that we are to pronounce these letters as אדוני. Tradition has so scrupulously guarded the sanctity of this name that when we use it outside of prayer we say *"Hashem,"* meaning simply "the Name." The name יהו-ה, aside from being the unique name of the Jewish G-d, has a particular connotation as well. It is "the merciful G-d." This is derived from the verse in Exodus 34:6 where the thirteen attributes of G-d are enumerated.

וַיִּקְרָא יְהוָ-ה, יְהוָ-ה, אֵל רַחוּם וְחַנּוּן ...

And He called *"Hashem, Hashem,* the merciful and gracious G-d…"

The next most common name of G-d is אלוהים. This name has both a holy and a secular meaning. Its holy meaning is as a name of G-d. Its secular meaning is "judge," as in Exodus 21:5. It is also used as an appellation for pagan gods; then the term used is אלוהים אחרים, "other gods." When used to refer to the Jewish G-d, it reflects the judgmental aspect of G-d, His sitting in judgement of mankind.

With this in mind, we can begin to analyze Rashi's brief comment here.

WHAT IS RASHI SAYING?

Rashi tells us that since our verse has a combination of two Divine names, its meaning is a combination of the two attributes conveyed by these names. In our case that would mean "merciful (יהו-ה) in judgement (אלוקים)."

But as you look at our verse you should have a question for Rashi.

The Ramban asks the obvious question. Can you anticipate it?

What is it?

Hint: Compare Rashi's *dibbur hamaschil* with the Torah's words.

YOUR QUESTION:

QUESTIONING RASHI

A Question: The Ramban points out that our verse does *not* have the two names that mean "Judge and Merciful One." Our verse has the name אדוני and יהו-ה, and although Tetragrammaton is punctuated with the same vowels as אלוקים the actual name אלוקים "the G-d of Judgement" does not appear in the verse at all! So how can Rashi conclude that the names here mean "merciful in judgement"?

These are difficult questions.

Can you think of a defense for Rashi?

YOUR ANSWER:

UNDERSTANDING RASHI

An Answer: Two main answers have been suggested to explain Rashi's comment.

One is that the name ה-יהו in our verse does have the same vowels as the word אלוקים. Therefore, it is pronounced here as if אלוקים were written. While this is unusual, it is not unique. There are other places in Tanach where the special name of G-d is pronounced אלוקים. In the Book of Ezekiel we find this many times. See, for example, Ch. 4:14. In this case we have two names within one name, so to speak. The name written is ה-ו-יהו, the Merciful One, while the name pronounced is אלוקים, the Judgmental One. Thus we have, in one word, "Merciful in Judgement."

This is an ingenious interpretation but as an answer to our question on Rashi, there is still a problem. Can you spot it?

YOUR ANSWER:

A DIFFICULTY WITH THIS ANSWER

An Answer: A difficulty is that Rashi's *dibbur hamaschil* contains *both* names, אלוקים הי. If Rashi's comment were based just on the name ה-יהו, then why does he have both names in the *dibbur hamaschil*? This would seem to indicate that he is commenting on both words.

ANOTHER ANSWER

Another answer given to explain Rashi is that the word אדני, which means "the Lord", can also carry the connotation of judge or ruler, as in Genesis 42:33 ויאמר האיש אדני הארץ. The second name, ה-יהו, retains its sense of "Merciful One." So we have, using both names, "the Judge in Mercy." This suggests the same idea that Rashi tells us, but the order is reversed. Instead of "Merciful in judgement," this interpretation would mean "Judge with mercy." Some see this reversal as a weakness of this answer. Another problem is that the name אדני, although used in the verse cited above as "master," it is never considered to be a name of G-d which connotes the G-d of judgement.

We are left wondering what Rashi really had in mind. There is nothing better for the mind and for the soul than to be left thinking. Besides the intellectual challenge this offers us, it injects a little modesty into our souls and reminds us that our work in Torah study is never done.

❖❖❖

Tosafos sheds light on a basic concept.

Deut. 4:2

לֹא תֹסִפוּ עַל־הַדָּבָר אֲשֶׁר אָנֹכִי מְצַוֶּה אֶתְכֶם וְלֹא תִגְרְעוּ מִמֶּנּוּ לִשְׁמֹר אֶת־מִצְוֹת יְהֹוָה אֱלֹקֵיכֶם אֲשֶׁר אָנֹכִי מְצַוֶּה אֶתְכֶם.

> **לֹא תֹסִפוּ:** כגון חמש פרשיות בתפילין חמשה מינים בלולב וחמש ציציות וכן לא תגרעו.
>
> **Do not add**: *Rashi*: As five *parshios* (sections) in *Tefillin*, five species in the *Lulav* and five *Tzitzis*; and likewise "you shall not subtract."

WHAT IS RASHI SAYING?

The Torah tells us not to tinker with the mitzvos. This is referred to in Hebrew as בל תוסיף, *Bal Tosif*. Don't add to them, means don't "improve" upon them. The phylacteries contain four different sections of the Torah, which are placed in black boxes, one for the head and one for the arm. The four Torah sections are chosen because in each section there is mention of the mitzvah of *Tefillin*. One should not add another section and put it inside the *Tefillin*. Likewise, the mitzvah of *Tzitzis,* which requires fringes on the four corners of a garment, should not be "improved" upon to have five fringes. And certainly one must not subtract from the requirements of these, or other, mitzvos.

QUESTIONING RASHI

Although Rashi's comment is quite straightforward, yet when we examine his examples we can perhaps begin to question his approach.

A Question: Why were just these examples of "adding to the mitzvos" chosen? Aren't there other ways that one can add to the mitzvos?

Can you think of other examples?

YOUR SUGGESTIONS:

TOSAFOS EXPLAINS THE CONCEPT OF *BAL TOSIF*

An Answer: *Tosafos* asks (Talmud *Rosh Hashanah* 16b) why aren't the *Shofar* blasts that we hear on Rosh Hashanah considered as adding to the mitzvos. The Sages taught that the basic Torah command on Rosh Hashanah is to blow a sum total of nine *Shofar* blasts. Yet, in fact, in all synagogues today we blow one hundred blasts! Why is this not considered "adding to the mitzvos"?

If a person ate matzos on Passover for eight days, one more than the Torah requirement of seven days, would he be transgressing the command of "adding to the mitzvos"? The *halachic* answer is, no, he wouldn't be committing *Bal Tosif*.

Can you see a difference between these cases and the ones that Rashi cites?

YOUR ANSWER:

UNDERSTANDING RASHI

An Answer: *Tosafos* answers this question. He says that one does not transgress this command by doing a mitzvah twice (or more times); one transgresses it by changing the essential make-up of the mitzvah itself. Adding a species to the required four in the *Lulav*, is a change in the mitzvah itself; while taking the four species more than once a day, is not. Adding a Torah section to the *Tefillin* is a change in the essential make-up of the *Tefillin* and is prohibited, whereas putting the *Tefillin* on more than once a day, is not. Likewise, eating matzah an extra day, on the eighth day or hearing one hundred *Shofar* blasts — much more than the Torah's requirement — is not a transgression of *Bal Tosif,* because the essential mitzvah has not been tampered with. Because while we have added to the mitzvah, we have not actually changed the make-up of the mitzvah itself.

Now let us examine the latter part of Rashi's comment and question it.

"AND LIKEWISE 'YOU SHALL NOT SUBTRACT'"

This additional phrase in Rashi's comment is strange. The Torah itself says clearly "you shall not add…and you shall not subtract." Why does Rashi need to repeat this for us? By this time you certainly realize that Rashi does not make such seemingly unnecessary, self-understood comments for no reason. What is his reasoning here?

Can you think of what he intends to tell us with these words?

YOUR ANSWER:

A Fuller Understanding _____

An Answer: Actually, when given a little thought, the prohibition of subtracting from the commandments is strange. If this means that one should
not cross off one of the 613 commandments, one would think that
it is obvious. If, for example, the Torah says "You shall not steal"
and I cross that off my "don't-do list" and proceed to steal, of course
I have transgressed the prohibition by stealing. I need not be told
so again by telling me "do not subtract from the mitzvos." So that
cannot be the Torah's meaning here.

If, on the other hand, it means I shall not subtract from a mitzvah
itself, for example, by subtracting one of the four species from my
Lulav-mitzvah, then I might think that although I have not fulfilled
the mitzvah completely, I have fulfilled three-quarters of it; after
all, I did take a *Lulav* and an *Esrog*. So, perhaps, I should get par-
tial credit for the mitzvah.

Rashi's comment teaches us that this is not so. By likening the prohibition of subtracting from a mitzvah to the prohibition of adding to it,
Rashi shows us that just as we have not fulfilled the mitzvah of *Lulav* at
all if we have added a species to it, likewise we have not fulfilled the
mitzvah *at all* if we subtract any part from it.

(See *Maharsha*)

Making sense of the Targum gives us a better understanding of the verse.

Deut. 4:28

וַעֲבַדְתֶּם־שָׁם אֱלֹהִים מַעֲשֵׂה יְדֵי אָדָם עֵץ וָאֶבֶן אֲשֶׁר לֹא־יִרְאוּן וְלֹא
יִשְׁמְעוּן וְלֹא יֹאכְלוּן וְלֹא יְרִיחֻן.

> **ועבדתם שם אלהים:** כתרגומו, משאתם עובדים לעובדיהם,
> כאלו אתם עובדים להם.
>
> **And you will serve there gods:** *Rashi:* As the *Targum*
> ("and you will serve there the nations that worship idols").
> Since you will serve those (pagans) who worship them
> (idols) it is as if you are worshiping them (the idols).

What would you ask on this comment?

YOUR QUESTION:

QUESTIONING RASHI _____

A Question: Why does Rashi interpret this verse so differently from its apparent simple sense? The verse clearly says that the exiled Israelites
will worship foreign gods in the land of their captivity. Why did
Rashi wander so far from simple *p'shat*?

Can you see what led him to this interpretation?

What is bothering him?

Hint: Notice the context of this verse.

YOUR ANSWER:

WHAT IS BOTHERING RASHI? _____

An Answer: If we look at the previous verses, we can see what is bothering
Rashi.

> *Deut. 4:25-28:*
>
> "When you have children and have grown old in the Land…and
> you will make a statue…and do that which is evil in the eyes of
> *Hashem* your G-d …you will be swiftly removed from the Land
> and *Hashem* will disperse you among the nations …*and you will
> serve there man-made gods…*"

As we look at these verses, we see that our verse is part of G-d's punishment meted out to Israel *for worshipping idols!* So the simple meaning
cannot be that Israel will (again) worship idols. Is that a punishment!? It
makes no sense to say that worshiping idols will be the punishment for
worshiping idols.

It is for this reason that Rashi sought a different understanding of these
words.

How does Rashi's comment make sense out of this verse?

YOUR ANSWER:

UNDERSTANDING RASHI

An Answer: Rashi realized that this verse, as understood at first glance, did not fit in with the general tenor of the surrounding verses. It was a continuation of the dire consequences that the people would suffer in exile, one of them being their servitude to their gentile hosts. These gentiles would be idol worshippers and Israel will have to serve them as a punishment for serving the idols themselves. With a look backward over the centuries of Jewish Exile, we see that history unfortunately attests to the veracity of this prophecy!

(See *N. Leibowitz & Ahrand*)

❖❖❖

A one word comment reveals an amazing rule of Biblical linguistics.

Deut. 5:3

לֹא אֶת־אֲבֹתֵינוּ כָּרַת ה' אֶת־הַבְּרִית הַזֹּאת כִּי אִתָּנוּ אֲנַחְנוּ אֵלֶּה פֹּה הַיּוֹם כֻּלָּנוּ חַיִּים.

לֹא אֶת אֲבֹתֵינוּ: לבד כרת ה' וגו'.

Not with our fathers: *Rashi:* Alone, **did *Hashem* make [this covenant] etc**.

WHAT IS RASHI SAYING?

Rashi inserts his one word comment "alone", between the Torah's words. This usually means that Rashi is helping us avoid a misunderstanding. (I refer to this kind of Rashi-comment as a Type II comment.)

Which misunderstanding are we to avoid?

YOUR ANSWER:

WHICH MISUNDERSTANDING?

An Answer: The verse seems to say that G-d did not make a covenant with the fathers of the present generation. But this contradicts all we know. The generation that left Egypt, forty years previously, was the generation that stood at Sinai, received the Torah and entered into a covenant with G-d (see Exodus 24:8). When they sinned by accepting the disparaging report of the Spies, they were condemned to die in the wilderness. Now when Moses is speaking to the nation, the generation of the fathers had already died out. Moses is now addressing their children. But it was with their fathers, not the children, that G-d had made His covenant. Yet our verse seems to say just the opposite — it says "*not* with your fathers did I make this covenant." Rashi is telling us it is a misunderstanding to think that the verse means what it seems to say. Its meaning is rather "not *only* with your fathers did I make the covenant...." The verse now means that G-d certainly made a covenant with the fathers; He made it not *only* with them, but with all future generations as well.

QUESTIONING THE TORAH

But if the Torah means that G-d made His covenant *not only* with the fathers, why then does it say "Not with your fathers did I make the covenant"? Why does the Torah use such a misleading phrase?

This is a difficult question. This is also an excellent example of struggling to make sense out of an apparently senseless verse in the Torah.

UNDERSTANDING THE TORAH'S LINGUISTIC STYLE

An Answer: Before we go on to understand this anomaly let us cite other examples of similarly misleading verses.

1) Joseph reveals himself to his brothers (Genesis 45:8) and says:

"So now it was *not you* that sent me here, *but* G-d ..."

Indeed! Was it not they? Did they not throw him into the pit? Did they not sell him to the passing Ishmaelites? Joseph said so himself, just a few verses earlier,

"I am Joseph your brother *whom you sold into Egypt*..."(Genesis 45:4)!

This is truly a contradiction.

2) After Jacob's struggle with the angel (Genesis 32:24-29) he is told

"*Not Jacob* shall your name be called any more, *but Israel*, for you have contended with G-d and man ..."

Yet, later on G-d Himself calls Israel 'Jacob':

"And G-d said to Israel in a vision of the night and said '*Jacob, Jacob,* ...'"(Genesis 46:2).

Another contradiction!

3) A most striking example comes from the Book of Jeremiah when he makes the following startling statement:

"For I spoke *not unto your fathers* nor commanded them in the day that I brought them out of Egypt concerning burnt offerings and sacrifices. *But* this thing did I command them, saying, 'Listen to My voice and I shall be for you for a G-d and you shall be for Me for a nation...'" (Jeremiah 7:22-23).

Indeed! Did G-d not speak of sacrifices? He made a covenant at Sinai which was sealed with sacrifices. The Tabernacle was constructed in the wilderness as a place to offer sacrifices to G-d. The major part of the book of Leviticus is devoted to the laws of the sacrifices. What did Jeremiah mean by his puzzling statement?

Can you make sense out of these verses, which seem to make statements, which fly in the face of facts that we know to be true. Do you notice a similar linguistic pattern in these verses?

YOUR ANSWER:

THE DEEPER UNDERSTANDING

An Answer: You may have noticed that all these verses have a similar pattern. They all say "Not ...x, But...y." "Not you sent me here...but G-d ." "Not Jacob shall be your name be called ...but Israel." In all these verses, as Rashi tells us here, the meaning is rather "Not *only* Jacob shall be your name be called ...but also Israel." "Not *only* you sent me here...but *also* G-d ." The pattern is: "Not *only* x, but *also* y." If you go back to each verse and insert these words you will see that all the contradictions that troubled us are eliminated.

This rule is amazingly consistent and precise. See that Abram's name was changed to Abraham and he was never again called "Abram," not like Jacob whose name was changed to Israel, but nevertheless retained the name Jacob. This is because G-d's statement to Abram was significantly different (though with only one word changed) than His statement to Jacob.

"And your name shall *not be called* anymore Abram *and* your name shall be Abraham.." (Genesis 17:5).

Notice that here we *do not* have the "*not ..x, but...y*" formula. We have, instead, "*not Abram, and your name shall be Abraham.*" This slight change from "but" to "and" makes all the difference. Because G-d did not want Abraham ever to be called Abram, He phrased His command in a way that avoided the formula we have become familiar with. G-d was not saying to Abram that "Your name is not (*mainly*) Abram, *but* is Abraham." That would have meant — as it does in the case of Jacob — that the original name would remain together with the new name.

A LESSON

Glaring contradictions which posed difficult questions in the Torah have been explained away with a new insight into the Torah's way of speaking. One should never (never!) dismiss the Torah's words on the basis of our limited knowledge. Questions call for answers. But we are not necessarily always blessed with the ability to answer them.

Rashi shows the connection between the Sabbath and the redemption from Egypt.

Deut. 5:15

וְזָכַרְתָּ כִּי עֶבֶד הָיִיתָ בְּאֶרֶץ מִצְרַיִם וַיֹּצִאֲךָ הי אֱלֹקֶיךָ מִשָּׁם בְּיָד
חֲזָקָה וּבִזְרֹעַ נְטוּיָה עַל־כֵּן צִוְּךָ הי אֱלֹקֶיךָ לַעֲשׂוֹת אֶת־יוֹם הַשַּׁבָּת.

> **וזכרת כי עבד היית וגו':** על מנת כן פדאך שתהייה לו עבד
> ותשמור מצותיו.
> **And you shall remember that you were a slave, etc**.
> *Rashi:* On this condition He redeemed you, that you shall
> be His servant and you shall keep His commandments.

QUESTIONING RASHI

A Question: Why does Rashi comment here at all? The verse seems understandable without any commentary. What is bothering him?

YOUR ANSWER:

What Is Bothering Rashi?

An Answer: The verse connects the keeping of the Sabbath with the redemption from Egypt. But there does not appear to be any cogent connection between the two. Rashi searches for a connection.

How does his comment make the connection?

Your Answer:

Understanding Rashi

An Answer: Rashi's comment is meant to offer a coherent connection between the commandment to keep the Sabbath and the redemption from Egypt. The connection: The redemption of Israel from Egyptian bondage was solely for the purpose of obligating the people to keep their Redeemer's commandments. It is similar to the case where a person redeems a slave and takes him as his own slave. The new owner can rightfully claim that the only reason he freed the slave from his former master's control was so that he (the new master) could take the redeemed man as his own slave. So too, G-d freed Israel and thus has first claim on their service .

The *Divrei Dovid,* a commentary on Rashi, highlights the logic behind the relationship between keeping the Sabbath and the redemption from Egypt.

"Why was the redemption from Egypt especially tied to our becoming G-d's servants? Why is the Sabbath different from other mitzvos? It seems to me that this is to show how different *Hashem* is from human masters. A person who frees a servant from his master, certainly does so in order that the redeemed servant will work for him and will be his indentured servant, to do his work. But the Holy One, blessed be He, redeemed Israel from Egypt where they had performed harsh labor and He made them His servant with no obligation to work, or — more to the point — they were to cease all work on the Sabbath and that cessation from work, that rest, would be the sign that they were *His* servants!"

(See *Divrei Dovid*)

A deeper understanding of a familiar verse.

Deut. 6:4

שְׁמַע יִשְׂרָאֵל הי אֱלֹקֵינוּ הי אֶחָד.

> **הי אֱלֹוקֵינוּ הי אֶחָד:** הי שהוא אלקינו עתה, ולא אלהי האומות,
> הוא עתיד להיות הי אחד. שנאמר (צפניה ג:ט׳) ׳כי אז אהפך אל
> עמים שפה ברורה לקרא כלם בשם הי ונאמר (זכריה י״ד:ט׳)
> ׳ביום ההוא יהיה הי אחד ושמו אחד.׳
>
> **Hashem our G-d, *Hashem* is One**: *Rashi: Hashem* who
> is our G-d presently but not the God of the gentiles, He is
> destined to be the one G-d. As it says (Zephaniah 3:9)
> "For then I will change the peoples [to speak] a pure lan-
> guage that they may all call upon the name of *Hashem*."
> And it says (Zechariah 14:9) "On that day *Hashem* will
> be One and His name One."

WHAT HAS RASHI DONE?

Rashi has made some changes to this well-known verse. He inserted the
words "who is" between the words "*Hashem*" and "our G-d." He also
introduces the idea of the contrast between the present and the future.

QUESTIONING RASHI

An obvious question is: Why does he do this?

What's bothering Rashi?

YOUR ANSWER:

WHAT IS BOTHERING RASHI?

An Answer: The Ramban relates to Rashi's comment and shows what lies behind his words. Let us take our cue from him. In order to better
understand Rashi, he compares our verse with two other verses in
Deuteronomy, both of which also begin with "Hear Israel" as our
verse does.

Deut. 9:1-3

שְׁמַע יִשְׂרָאֵל אַתָּה עֹבֵר הַיּוֹם....וְיָדַעְתָּ כִּי הֹ׳ **אֱלֹקֶיךָ** הוּא־הָעֹבֵר
לְפָנֶיךָ....

Hear, O Israel, you are passing this day…. And you shall
know that **Hashem your G-d**, He passes before you…..

Deut. 20:3-4

שְׁמַע יִשְׂרָאֵל אַתֶּם קְרֵבִים הַיּוֹם לַמִּלְחָמָה....כִּי הֹ׳ **אֱלֹקֵיכֶם** הַהֹלֵךְ
עִמָּכֶם....

Hear, O Israel, you are drawing near to battle…..because
Hashem your G-d goes with you….

The Ramban points out a difference between our verse and these two
verses.

Do you see a difference?

YOUR ANSWER:

An Answer: Only our verse has "*Hashem, **our** G-d.*" The other two verses (and
many similar ones in Deuteronomy) have " *Hashem, **your** G-d .*"

This, the Ramban implies, is what Rashi is reacting to. What would you
say is the significance of the difference between the words "our G-d"
and "your G-d"?

YOUR ANSWER:

UNDERSTANDING RASHI _____

An Answer: In most of Moses' speeches to the nation he says "*Hashem,* your
G-d" making the point that he is speaking *to them.* Here he says
"*Hashem,* our G-d" implying that Moses stands together with the
nation Israel. Now, if he stands together with them, who is this
verse excluding? Right! The nations of the world. So that Rashi
understood this verse as a declaration which placed Israel on one
side and the other nations of the world on the other. Therefore he
emphasized that today Israel, but not the other nations, recognize
the one G-d.

How do you understand the simple message of the *Shema* declaration?
Is Rashi's interpretation similar to your understanding of the *Shema*?

YOUR ANSWER:

A Deeper Understanding

An Answer: Ordinarily we understand the *Shema* to mean, "The Lord, our G-d, is One." This is considered a declaration of G-d's "oneness," or indivisibility.

But if that were its message, the Torah could simply have stated "Hear Israel, *Hashem* is One." Why the extra words "*Hashem*, our G-d" ?

The *Mizrachi* suggests that this too was bothering Rashi. Rashi sought a way to make sense of these extra words. So he divided the verse in two. The first part of the verse refers to the present situation when the Jews alone believe in *Hashem*. This is the meaning of the words "*Hashem*, our G-d" (ours, but not your G-d!). Rashi emphasizes this by adding the words (in bold letters) "*Hashem*, **who is** our G-d **now**."

Then come the words "*Hashem* is One" this speaks of the future when all people will recognize *Hashem*.

On what basis do you think Rashi ascribed this phrase to a future time?

YOUR ANSWER:

A Closer Look

An Answer: We see that Rashi quotes the prophet Zechariah. "And it will be on *that* day and *Hashem* will be One and His name will be One." Notice that this verse stresses the words. "ה' אֶחָד" This semantic similarity to our verse is the basis for Rashi's associating the words in our verse with the verse in Zechariah which speaks of what will happen in the future, "on *that* day."

Why do you think Rashi cites two verses? Isn't the one from Zechariah sufficient? If Rashi cites more than one verse to make his point, there is a reason he cites each verse.

YOUR ANSWER:

Why Two Verses?

An Answer: As we said, the verse from Zechariah makes the point that *Hashem's* unity will be recognized some time in the future ("on that day"). But the idea that this recognition will be shared by all the nations, is absent from this verse. The verse from Zephaniah 3:9 makes this point as it says "I will change *the peoples* [to speak] a pure language that they may all call upon the name of *Hashem*."

So with the combined effect of these two verses Rashi substantiates his interpretation of the *Shema*.

Let us look at another aspect of this fascinating verse.

Hashem is One

The meaning of the above phrase is by no means transparently clear.

These words, more specifically, the word "one" can have at least two different meanings.

What are they?

Your Answer:

An Answer: "One" can mean "unity," an indivisible entity. That is, *Hashem* is indivisible, One, in the absolute sense.

Or it can mean, The "only One." That is, *Hashem* is the one and only G-d; He, and He alone, is the Ruler of the Universe. He has neither partners nor competitors.

Which of these two interpretations would you say Rashi opts for?

Your Answer:

Rashi's View of ה' אחד

An Answer: Rashi is saying that the verse means, *Hashem* is the only G-d. Granted that today He is recognized only by Israel, and not by other nations. But in the future *Hashem* will be the one and only G-d accepted by all. He alone will reign supreme without other gods being worshiped.

But Rashi's understanding of this verse is not the only one.

The Rambam offers a different interpretation.

THE RAMBAM'S VIEW OF ה' אחד

An Answer: Maimonides, the Rambam, relies on this verse to teach us G-d's unity. (See his Code, Laws of *Yesodei HaTorah* Ch 1 #7):

> "This G-d is One. He is not two or more than two. Rather He is one, whose oneness is not like any other oneness in the world…..Knowledge of this matter is a positive command. As it says "*Hashem, our G-d, Hashem is One*" (Deut. 6:4).

> The Rambam quotes our verse as the basis for the Torah's command to believe in the unity of G-d. The message of this verse, according to the Rambam, is G-d's unity, His indivisibility, more so than that He is the only G-d. Of course, the Rambam understood that *Hashem* is the one and only true deity in the world. But he sees this verse as the basis for the Jewish concept of the unique indivisibility of G-d.

In Summary: The *Shema* is a most versatile verse, which contains within it the two core concepts about the Divine Being. It is rightfully the verse which is pronounced daily by believing Jews and also the last words as he leaves this life on earth.

Rashi's unusual definition withstands Tosafos' question.

Deut. 6:7

וְשִׁנַּנְתָּם לְבָנֶיךָ וְדִבַּרְתָּ בָּם בְּשִׁבְתְּךָ בְּבֵיתֶךָ וּבְלֶכְתְּךָ בַדֶּרֶךְ וּבְשָׁכְבְּךָ וּבְקוּמֶךָ.

> **ושננתם:** לשון חדוד הוא, שיהיו מחודדים בפיך שאם ישאלך אדם דבר לא תהא צריך לגמגם בו אלא אמר לו מיד.
> **And you shall teach them:** *Rashi:* [The word ושננתם] is an expression of sharpness. [The words of the Torah] should be sharp in your mouth so that if a person asks you anything about them you will not stammer but tell him immediately.

WHAT IS RASHI SAYING?

The word ושננתם is an unusual word and Rashi helps us by telling us its meaning. He considers the word to be similar to the word שנונים "sharp" as in the verse (Psalms 120:4) חצי גבור שנונים, "the arrows of the mighty are sharp." Rashi then interprets the meaning of "sharpness" in our verse. The person is to learn the Torah and know it so well, that its words being sharp [precise] on his tongue, that when asked a question he can answer it immediately and to the "point".

THE BECHOR SHOR'S INTERPRETATION

Rashi's is not the only interpretation of this word offered by the commentators. The Bechor Shor, one of the *Ba'alei haTosafos*, offers an original idea. He says the word derives from the word שנים, "two." A paraphrasing of the verse, according to him, would be:

> You (first) learn them ("and these matters should be…on your heart"), then *repeat* them ושננתם לבניך (i.e., a second time) to your children ("and you shall teach them to your children") and they, in turn, will "thrice" teach them to their children.

The Bechor Shor's interpretation actually fits into the words of the verse better than Rashi's does.

Can you see a difficulty with fitting in Rashi's meaning in this verse?

YOUR ANSWER:

An Answer: The verse says ושננתם לבניך "*to* your sons." How does "they should be sharp in your mouth" connect with the words "to your sons"?

The word לבנך must be translated differently to have Rashi's meaning make sense.

How would you translate it?

YOUR ANSWER:

An Answer: A slight change must be made in the translation of the word לבניך. Instead of "*to* your sons," we would translate it "*for* your sons (students)." It now means "And you should learn them sharply for your sons' (sake)."

(See *Silbermann*)

TOSAFOS QUESTIONS RASHI

The *Moshav Zekeinim* (a collection of the *Ba'alei haTosafos* on the Torah) asks a question based on a statement in the Talmud.

In *Baba Metzia* 23b the Talmud says: "In these three matters the Rabbis were to change their words (tell a "white lie"): in the amount of Talmud they learned, in intimate matters and in matters regarding being a guest at someone's home."

Rashi on the Talmud explains what the issue is regarding Talmud.

Rashi: If you are asked if you learned a certain Talmudic tractate, answer 'No' (even though you actually did).

The question of the *Moshav Zekeinim* is, if a person, when asked if he learned a particular Gemora, is to deny he ever did, how can this be squared with what Rashi says here, that he should answer immediately "without stammering"?

Can you find a difference between the two cases?

YOUR ANSWER:

TOSAFOS ANSWERS FOR RASHI

Tosafos Answers:

He says that the Talmud tells us that we are to deny knowledge when we are asked a question just for "show" or just to test us. But if a person asks a question because he seriously wants to know a point of law or wants to learn, then our Rashi applies, i.e. a person should know his material so well that he answers "without stammering."

DOES RASHI CONTRADICT HIMSELF?

There is a curious contradiction in Rashi. Further on, in Deut. 28:37 the Torah says:

וְהָיִיתָ לְשַׁמָּה לְמָשָׁל וְלִשְׁנִינָה בְּכֹל הָעַמִּים אֲשֶׁר־יְנַהֶגְךָ הי שָׁמָּה.
"And you will be for an astonishment, a proverb and a byword in all the nations where *Hashem* shall lead you."

Rashi comments on this:

וְלִשְׁנִינָה: לשון יושננתם׳ ידברו בך וכו׳
And as a byword: *Rashi:* This is similar to ושננתם (our verse), meaning 'they will speak about you.'

In the above comment Rashi refers to our verse and to our very word, but here he says the word means "and they will speak." How can we understand this?

YOUR ANSWER:

UNDERSTANDING RASHI

An Answer: We have to try to understand Rashi's thinking here and his method in his commentary. It would appear that the word basically means "to speak" and that is how it is used in our verse — "and you shall speak about them to you children." But it has a more precise meaning, it is not speech in general, otherwise the more familiar word, ודברת, would have been used (as it is in the very next words). Its more precise meaning is related to, and derives from, the idea of sharpness, that is, one should speak sharply. When Rashi comments on our verse — ושננתם לבניך — he emphasizes the idea of sharpness, because that is its particular connotation here. However, when he comments on the word לשמה למשל ולשנינה since it is an unusual term, he wants to give us its basic meaning, which is "to speak." But here too, the idea of "sharp speech" is fitting, because the Torah is telling us that people will speak despairingly about Israel, in a "sharp", i.e., critical manner.

We get a glimpse of Rashi's method in his commentary. His is not a wooden, inflexible commentary. He is in the service of the student, and he wants to help the student how best to understand the words of the Torah in their context. In one place he tells us a word's precise nuance, because that is what is called for, while in another place he tells us its general meaning because that is all that is necessary.

(See *Be'er Besadeh*)

❖❖❖

Close reading of the Torah's words, helps us understand Rashi.

Deut. 6:7 (same verse as above)

וְשִׁנַּנְתָּם לְבָנֶיךָ וְדִבַּרְתָּ בָּם בְּשִׁבְתְּךָ בְּבֵיתֶךָ וּבְלֶכְתְּךָ בַדֶּרֶךְ וּבְשָׁכְבְּךָ
וּבְקוּמֶךָ.

> **לבניך:** אלו התלמידים מצינו בכל מקום שהתלמידים קרויים
> בנים שנאמר 'בנים אתם לה' אלקיכם' ואומר 'בני הנביאים
> אשר בבית אל' וכן בחזקיהו שלמד תורה לכל ישראל וקראם
> בנים שנאמר 'בני עתה אל תשלו' וכשם שהתלמידים קרויים
> בנים כך הרב קרוי אב שנאמר 'אבי אבי רכב ישראל' וגו'.

To your sons: *Rashi*: These are the students. We find in all places that students are called 'sons' as it says "You are sons of *Hashem* your G-d." And it (also) says 'the sons of the prophets who were in Beis El. And also in the case of Hezekiah who taught Torah to all of Israel and he called them 'sons' as it says "My sons be not negligent." And just as students are called 'sons' likewise the teacher is called 'father' as it says "Father, Father, Chariot of Israel, etc."

What Rashi says is clear, i.e. the Torah's term "sons" here actually means "students." The question is not *what* he says, but....

YOUR QUESTION:

QUESTIONING RASHI

A Question: Why does Rashi prefer interpreting the word בנים as students and rejects the simple meaning, which is "sons"?

Can you suggest why he would say this?

Hint: Compare our verse with Deut. 11:19.

YOUR ANSWER:

WHAT IS BOTHERING RASHI?

An Answer: To understand this we would do well to compare our verse with a very similar one in Deuteronomy 11:19 (from the second paragraph of the *Shema*).

Our verse	Deut. 11:19
וְשִׁנַּנְתָּם לְבָנֶיךָ וְדִבַּרְתָּ בָּם	וְלִמַּדְתֶּם אֹתָם אֶת־בְּנֵיכֶם לְדַבֵּר בָּם
בְּשִׁבְתְּךָ בְּבֵיתֶךָ וּבְלֶכְתְּךָ בַדֶּרֶךְ	בְּשִׁבְתְּךָ בְּבֵיתֶךָ וּבְלֶכְתְּךָ בַדֶּרֶךְ
וּבְשָׁכְבְּךָ וּבְקוּמֶךָ.	וּבְשָׁכְבְּךָ וּבְקוּמֶךָ.

Notice any similarities and differences between these two verses?

YOUR ANSWER:

An Answer: There are several important differences. First of all our verse (from the first paragraph of the *Shema*) is in the singular, "and *you* (singular) shall teach"; the second verse (from the second paragraph of the *Shema*) is in the plural, "and *you* (plural) shall teach..." The word ושננתם looks like a plural form but is really a singular form with a plural suffix — תם. It means "you (singular) shall teach *them*." It is a contraction of ושננת and אתם. The "them" refers to "these words" This is parallel to ולמדתם **אתם**.

A second difference is the obvious one between the words ושננתם and ולמדתם. The use of the unusual word ושננתם instead of the more common ולמדתם is what perks our interest — and Rashi's too.

How does Rashi's comment deal with this?

YOUR ANSWER:

UNDERSTANDING RASHI

An Answer: The word ושננתם means more than mere teaching (as we pointed out in the previous analysis); it means clear, precise teaching; teaching so that the student can understand with clarity. Such a word is more appropriate for a teacher/student relationship than it is for a father/son relationship, whose teaching may not be that exacting or pedagogically adept.

A closer look will show us another reason why Rashi sees this verse as referring to a teacher/student relationship.

Can you spot it? This is not easy.

YOUR ANSWER:

A Closer Look

An Answer: Another indication that we are talking about students and not sons is the word לְבָנֶיךָ itself. How do you translate it?

"Your sons," in the plural, not "your son," in the singular. The use of the plural is unusual, though maybe it does not appear so at first glance. While a man may have several sons, nevertheless, the Torah consistently refers to a man and his son in the singular. Look at a verse above (6:2):

לְמַעַן תִּירָא אֶת־יְהֹוָה אֱלֹקֶיךָ לִשְׁמֹר אֶת־כָּל־חֻקֹּתָיו וּמִצְוֺתָיו אֲשֶׁר אָנֹכִי מְצַוֶּךָ **אַתָּה וּבִנְךָ וּבֶן־בִּנְךָ** כֹּל יְמֵי חַיֶּיךָ וּלְמַעַן יַאֲרִכֻן יָמֶיךָ.

"You and your **son and your son's son**" — all in the singular.

Also Exodus 13:8:

וְהִגַּדְתָּ **לְבִנְךָ** בַּיּוֹם הַהוּא

"And you will tell **your son** on that day..."

And again, Exodus 13:14:

וְהָיָה כִּי־יִשְׁאָלְךָ **בִנְךָ** מָחָר וגו'

"And it will be when **your son** asks you tomorrow," etc.

So, while not readily apparent, the use of the word "sons" in the plural is unusual. Rashi was certainly aware of this. This supports the idea of a teacher and his students. A teacher usually relates to many students in class, while a father usually relates to one son, on an individual basis, even if he has several sons.

(See *Gur Aryeh*)

In Memory
of my beloved grandparents

Chana Sara bas Dovid Rosenblum ע״ה

Yerachmial Yisroel Yitzchak ben Moshe Avigdor Rosenblum ע״ה

and

Menachem Munish ben Avrohom Yehuda Mermelstein ע״ה

Whose love of *Yiddiskeit* and *ma'asim tovim* are
qualities that I continuously strive to emulate

and

in honor of my eighth grade Chumash teacher
at the Bais Ya'akov Academy of Queens

Who instilled a love of learning in me and remains
a constant source of inspiration

Dedicated by

Leah Mermelstein

We learn from Rashi's sensitivity to linguistic nuances.

Deut. 7:17,18

17) כִּי תֹאמַר בִּלְבָבְךָ רַבִּים הַגּוֹיִם הָאֵלֶּה מִמֶּנִּי אֵיכָה אוּכַל לְהוֹרִישָׁם.

18) לֹא תִירָא מֵהֶם זָכֹר תִּזְכֹּר אֵת אֲשֶׁר עָשָׂה ה׳ אלקיך לְפַרְעֹה וּלְכָל־מִצְרָיִם.

כִּי תֹאמַר בִּלְבָבְךָ: על כרחך לשון דילמא הוא שמא תאמר בלבבך מפני שהם רבים לא אוכל להורישם, אל תאמר כן...

לֹא תִירָא מֵהֶם: ולא יתכן לפרשו באחת משאר לשונות של ׳כי׳, שיפול עליו שוב ׳לא תירא מהם.׳

Perhaps you may say in your heart: *Rashi:* You must, perforce, say that [the word כי] is an expression of 'perhaps': "Perhaps you will say in your heart: 'Because they are many I will be unable to dispossess them.'" Don't say that…(instead)…

Do not fear them: *Rashi:* It is not possible to explain it [the word כי] by any of the other meanings of כי that would fit with the words לא תירא מהם "do not fear them."

WHAT IS RASHI SAYING?

To appreciate the import of Rashi's comment we must know the various meanings of the word כי. The Talmudic Sage, Reish Lakish said (*Gittin* 90a) "The word כי has four interpretations: 1) "If" or "when"; 2) "perhaps"; 3)"but (rather)"; and 4) "because." Rashi tells us that in our verse the word כי can only mean "perhaps."

What would you ask to clarify Rashi's intent?

YOUR QUESTION:

QUESTIONING RASHI

A Question: Why can't כי have any of the other meanings here? In particular, why can't it mean "if"? "If (or When) you will say in your heart: these nations are greater than I am, how can I dispossess them?" That seems to make sense. What is wrong with it?

YOUR ANSWER:

UNDERSTANDING RASHI

An Answer: If we were to choose the interpretation "*When* you say in your heart etc.," this would mean that the people are already fearful. The thoughts "they are many and I will not be able to dispossess them" are thoughts that express their fear. To tell a people who already are fearful, "Don't fear" is quite naive. Such "reassurance" does not help a person overcome his fear. So this apparently linguistically reasonable choice (כי meaning "if" or "when") is not psychologically realistic. That is why Rashi rejects it.

The other two possibilities ("rather" and "because") cannot be used meaningfully at the beginning of a sentence. Our verse begins with כי so these choices are also not viable. We are left with "*perhaps* you will say in your heart." This makes the connection between the two verses understandable. It is to read as this:

"Perhaps you will say in your heart: 'The nations are more numerous than I. How can I possibly drive them out?' (Don't say that) Do not be afraid of them…"

This is why Rashi repeats this in his second comment we cited above. He wants to reinforce the point that the connection between the two verses can only be understood with this translation. As he says, only "perhaps" makes the connection reasonable.

(See *Almishnino*)

Rashi shows us the importance of careful analysis of the Torah's words.

Deut. 9:4, 5

4) **אַל־תֹּאמַר בִּלְבָבְךָ** בַּהֲדֹף הי אֱלֹקֶיךָ אֹתָם מִלְּפָנֶיךָ לֵאמֹר בְּצִדְקָתִי הֱבִיאַנִי הי לָרֶשֶׁת אֶת־הָאָרֶץ הַזֹּאת וּבְרִשְׁעַת הַגּוֹיִם הָאֵלֶּה הי מוֹרִישָׁם מִפָּנֶיךָ.

5) לֹא בְצִדְקָתְךָ וּבְיֹשֶׁר לְבָבְךָ אַתָּה בָא לָרֶשֶׁת אֶת־אַרְצָם כִּי בְּרִשְׁעַת הַגּוֹיִם הָאֵלֶּה הי אֱלֹקֶיךָ מוֹרִישָׁם מִפָּנֶיךָ וּלְמַעַן הָקִים אֶת־הַדָּבָר אֲשֶׁר נִשְׁבַּע הי לַאֲבֹתֶיךָ לְאַבְרָהָם לְיִצְחָק וּלְיַעֲקֹב.

אל תאמר בלבבך: צדקתי ורשעת הגוים גרמו.

Don't say in your heart: *Rashi:* My righteousness and the wickedness of the nations caused.

What Is Rashi Saying?

Rashi is telling us that the verse says that we are not to think that both our righteousness and the nation's wickedness caused us to conquer the Land of Canaan.

What would you ask about this comment?

Your Question:

Questioning Rashi

Rashi's interpretation appears to be as we would have understood this verse on our own. What has he added? Why did he see the need to comment here at all?

What is bothering him?

Your Answer:

What Is Bothering Rashi?

An Answer: When we examine this verse closely it seems to say two separate things, two separate causes with two separate outcomes.

1) "Don't think that your righteousness (cause) allowed you to possess this Land. (outcome)

2) "Don't think that the wickedness of the gentiles (cause) allowed you to dispossess them." (outcome)

But this can't be its meaning. Why not?

Because the very next verse says that it was, in fact, the wickedness of the gentiles that caused them to be expelled. Does not verse 5 say "because of the wickedness of these nations *Hashem*, your G-d, is driving them out before you" etc.?

But this is what #2 above told us *not to* think.

This is what is bothering Rashi.

How does his brief comment deal with this?

YOUR ANSWER:

UNDERSTANDING RASHI

An Answer: Rashi's comment disabuses us of the idea that one cause lead to one result. This is an incorrect reading of these verses. Rather, the verse is telling us that we are not to think that *both of these factors* are the cause of *both of these results*. It was not our righteousness *together with* the gentiles' wickedness that lead to their expulsion. It was their wickedness alone that caused them to be expelled from the Holy Land.

Moses warns the People about another mistaken assumption that it was the righteousness of Israel that entitled them to possess the Land. This too was not so. Not their righteousness entitled them to the Land (for that generation was not righteous, as verse 6 says), but rather their rights to Land were due to G-d's promise to the Forefathers.

(See *Be'er Basadeh*)

THE "SIN OF THE AMORITES"

The Torah actually foretells this condition in Genesis. When G-d makes His "Covenant Between the Pieces" with Abraham, He explains the connection between the sins of the inhabitants and their expulsion. In Genesis 15:15 we read:

"And the fourth generation shall return here, because the iniquity of the Amorites is not yet complete."

We see that until the sin of the Amorites was complete, until their conduct in the Land of Canaan was so evil that the Land could no longer tolerate them, then and only then could the offspring of Abraham inherit the Land. Their evil ways together with G-d's promise to Abraham, were the necessary and sufficient conditions for Israel to take possession of the Land.

Tosafos *questions a well-known saying of the Sages.*

Deut. 10:12

וְעַתָּה יִשְׂרָאֵל מָה ה' אֱלֹקֶיךָ שֹׁאֵל מֵעִמָּךְ כִּי אִם־לְיִרְאָה אֶת־ה' אֱלֹקֶיךָ
לָלֶכֶת בְּכָל־דְּרָכָיו וּלְאַהֲבָה אֹתוֹ וְלַעֲבֹד אֶת־ה' אֱלֹקֶיךָ בְּכָל־לְבָבְךָ
וּבְכָל־נַפְשֶׁךָ.

> כי אם ליראה וגו': רבותינו דרשו מכאן: הכל בידי שמים חוץ
> מיראת שמים.
>
> **Except to fear etc.**: *Rashi*: Our Rabbis derived from this [verse] that all is in the hands of Heaven except for the fear of Heaven.

QUESTIONING THE RABBIS' TEACHING

How do the Rabbis derive this lesson from our verse?

YOUR ANSWER:

UNDERSTANDING THE DERIVATION OF THE LESSON

An Answer: The verse says that G-d requests Israel "only to fear" Him. If G-d must make this request of the people, it is clear that He has no control over the matter. Secondly, the fact that it says "only" to fear Him implies that this is the only thing that G-d demands of us — because it is the only thing He has to demand, since everything else is in His power. This would seem to be the basis of this *drash*.

TOSAFOS QUESTIONS RASHI

The *Moshav Zekeinim* finds another saying of the Sages, which seems to contradict our saying. They cite the Talmud (*Kesubos* 30a) which says:

הַכֹּל בִּידֵי שָׁמַיִם חוּץ מִצִּינִים וּפַחִים.

"All is in the hands of Heaven except for צינים ופחים."

The meaning of the Hebrew words "צינים ופחים" is based on the verse in Proverbs 22:5:

צִנִּים פַּחִים בְּדֶרֶךְ עִקֵּשׁ שׁוֹמֵר נַפְשׁוֹ יִרְחַק מֵהֶם.

"*Thorns* and *snares* are in the path of the perverse; he who guards his soul will distance himself from them."

(This is Rashi's interpretation in Proverbs).

The message of this proverb is that dangers exist in the world, particularly for those who are "perverse," that is, for those who don't try to avoid them; but the cautious person takes heed not to be harmed by them.

The Sages' statement can now be understood. These dangers are the individual's responsibility, he must guard himself against them; he should not be nonchalant and think they are a Divine decree and that there is nothing he can do. If he is not careful, there is no assurance that G-d will intervene to save him.

Now let us return to *Tosafos'* question: The contradiction between these two sayings of the Sages. If only the fear of Heaven is not in G-d's hand, then what of "thorns and snares"? And vice versa.

Can you suggest an answer?

YOUR ANSWER:

TOSAFOS' ANSWER

The *Tosafos* suggest that the two sayings represent two different areas of a person's life.

Regarding all matters of our material, worldly existence, such as health, wealth, and physical make-up, only "thorns and snares" i.e. harmful accidents that can be avoided, are not in G-d's hands. (The reckless or tired driver, take note.)

And of all matters related to the spirit, such as high or low intelligence, an angry or a pleasant personality, only the fear of Heaven is not in G-d's hands. This means that although we don't all begin our existence with the same physical, mental or psychological circumstances, nevertheless, we all can exert ourselves equally in the realm of the fear of G-d.

Thus, according to *Tosafos*, there is no contradiction. The two sayings relate to two different spheres of our life, the physical and the spiritual.

In each of these realms there remains one arena of behavior for which man, and man alone, is responsible for his fate; areas where Heaven allows man full freedom.

Tosafos adds that this idea is clearly expressed in the Tanach. The prophet Jeremiah said (9:22):

> "Let not a wise man glorify himself with his wisdom, and let not the strong man glorify himself with his strength, let not a rich man glorify himself with his wealth. For only with this may one glorify himself — contemplating and knowing Me, for I am *Hashem* Who does kindness, justice and righteousness in the land for this is My desire, says *Hashem*."

This means that since a man should only rightfully take credit for (and "glory in") accomplishments which he has achieved through his own efforts, there is no reason to glory in the accumulation of wealth, wisdom and strength, since these all are gifts from G-d. But only "knowing G-d," which is the same as fearing G-d, is an achievement that man can justifiably be proud of, since whatever he achieves in this area, he has achieved through his own efforts.

THE COMPARATIVE ANALYSIS OF *TOSAFOS*

This question and answer are typical of the comparative/analytical approach of the *Ba'alei haTosafos* in their Talmudic commentary. Frequently they uncover other citations in the Talmud which appear to contradict the text they are relating to. Their approach is to try to reconcile the divergent texts, just as they did in our case.

There is certainly an easier way to reconcile the contradiction between these two statements as to what is only in the hands of Heaven. It is reasonable to assume that two different Sages made these different statements. They might differ in their opinion as to what is and what is not in the hands of Heaven. We constantly find differences between Sages in the Talmud. That is the whole excitement of the Talmudic discourse. Why doesn't *Tosafos* simply say that these are two different and differing opinions? But this is not the approach taken by *Tosafos*. Characteristically their style of commentary, in the Talmud especially, is to prefer to reconcile matters in a way that avoids an argument and at the same time gives us an insight into the differing concepts.

There is a subtle linguistic nuance in our verse that lends support to the idea that the fear of G-d is a true accomplishment of the individual.

Can you spot it?

YOUR ANSWER:

THE TORAH'S PRECISE LANGUAGE

An Answer: The verse says מה ה׳ אלקיך שאל **מעמך**. It does not use the more common word ממך. The word ממך means "from you"; while the word מעמך, being formed from the word עמך "with you," conveys a meaning of "*of* that which is *with you.*" When this word is used in the Torah it means "of your own possession."

See for example Deut. 15:12 which speaks of freeing your servant. It says:

תְּשַׁלְּחֶנּוּ חָפְשִׁי מֵעִמָּךְ.

You shall send him away free **from you**.

Thus the use of מעמך in our verse and not ממך indicates that G-d is asking something of you which *you possess within yourself* and not just something external, which is among your possessions.

(See *Tosafos Berachah*)

Simple phrases in the Torah require in-depth understanding.

Deut. 10:17

כִּי ה׳ אֱלֹקֵיכֶם הוּא אֱלֹקֵי הָאֱלֹהִים וַאֲדֹנֵי הָאֲדֹנִים הָאֵ-ל הַגָּדֹל הַגִּבֹּר
וְהַנּוֹרָא אֲשֶׁר לֹא־יִשָּׂא פָנִים וְלֹא יִקַּח שֹׁחַד.

> **לֹא יִשָּׂא פָנִים:** אם תפקרו עולו.
>
> **וְלֹא יִקַּח שֹׁחַד:** לפייסו בממון.
> **Who does not show favor:** *Rashi:* If you throw off His yoke.
> **And Who does not accept a bribe:** *Rashi:* To appease Him with money.

The meaning of the Torah's verse is clear enough. G-d is a fair Judge; He does not show favoritism in judgement, He gives a man what he deserves. But in spite of the clarity of the verse, Rashi found the need to comment. It is our task to understand why he had to explain an apparently simple verse.

Let us examine each comment individually. What would you ask about his first comment?

YOUR QUESTION:

QUESTIONING RASHI

A Question: Why does Rashi make any comment here? And why does he choose "throwing off G-d's yoke" as the particular circumstance of this phrase?

What's bothering him?

Hint: Are there instances of G-d's showing favor in the Torah?

YOUR ANSWER:

WHAT IS BOTHERING RASHI?

An Answer: The Talmud (*Berachos* 20b) asks a question on our verse. Is this not a contradiction to the words of the third blessing of the Priestly blessings as written in Numbers 6:26? There it says:

יִשָּׂא הי פָּנָיו אֵלֶיךָ וְיָשֵׂם לְךָ שָׁלוֹם.

"May *Hashem* lift His countenance (i.e. show favor) to you…"

How then does Moses say here that G-d does not show favor? In fact, He does show favor and we even beseech Him to do so for our benefit.

This apparent contradiction is what is bothering Rashi.

How does his comment mend matters?

YOUR ANSWER:

UNDERSTANDING RASHI

An Answer: Considering that G-d is a Merciful G-d, it is reasonable to expect Him to judge us at times "beyond the letter of the law." But this is understandable as long as the issue is one of a moral or religious lapse. But if the individual has thrown off the yoke of Heaven, has divested himself of all responsibility for following G-d's ways, then it is not reasonable to expect G-d to show His favor to such an individual. It is for this reason that Rashi pointed out that only those who "throw off His yoke" of commandments will not be beneficiaries of G-d's favors.

(See *Be'er BaSadeh*)

Let us now look at Rashi's second comment.

QUESTIONING RASHI

A Question: Why does Rashi say "to appease Him with money"? How, in heaven's name, does one give money to G-d ? He is not a human judge who could pocket the cash for personal benefit. A "bribe" usually means giving an official money in order to find favor in his eyes, but is this in any way applicable to G-d? What has money got to do with Him? And, in any case, how would one make the transfer?! No hand will come out of the sky to take it.

We should also note Rashi's words "appease him." This connotes the desire to avoid punishment.

Oh, but you say: Rashi doesn't really mean "money," as we know it, rather he means any sort of a favor-finding in G-d's eyes. But, if this is so, why need Rashi say anything? Let Rashi remain silent and I would understand the meaning from the Torah's words on my own. Why then did he say "to appease Him with money"?

BEGINNING TO UNDERSTAND RASHI

As we think of "bribing" G-d, we can think of several possibilities.

1) Doing mitzvos in order to atone for and hopefully nullify our sin. This might appease G-d so that He wouldn't punish us.

2) Giving money to charity. This is a mitzvah which, in a sense, is like giving money to G-d, since this act of kindness (חסד) is one of G-d's mitzvos.

The first possibility is how both the Rambam and the Ramban understand our verse.

THE RAMBAM ON AVOS

The Rambam in his commentary on Pirkei Avos (Ch.4: 28) writes:

"This does not mean: He doesn't take a bribe to pervert justice, because such an interpretation is absurd, such a thing is far removed from G-d. It is something that cannot even be imagined, for how could He take a bribe? And what could possibly be the bribe? Rather the meaning is, He does not accept good acts (mitzvos) as compensation; for example, if a person has done a thousand mitzvos and one evil deed, *Hashem* will not forgive him his one sin because of all his mitzvos, as if to deduct one mitzvah in place of that one sin. Instead He will punish him for his one sin and reward him for all of his mitzvos. This is the meaning of 'He takes no bribery.'"

RAMBAN'S INTERPRETATION

The Ramban offers an identical interpretation of "bribery" in relation to G-d to that of the Rambam. (The Ramban was thoroughly conversant with all of the Ramban's writings, so he likely adopted this interpretation.) He says on this verse:

"Even if a truly righteous man has transgressed, [G-d will not] accept from him, as bribery, one of His mitzvos in order to atone for the man's transgression. Instead He will punish him for his sin and likewise reward him with all His good (for the mitzvos he has performed)."

QUESTIONING THE RAMBAM AND THE RAMBAN

One wonders why this is considered bribery. The Rambam himself writes in the Laws of Repentance that if a person has more mitzvos than sins he is considered a righteous person. So why shouldn't the fact that the person has more mitzvos than sins allow him to gain atonement for his sin?

But let us first return to Rashi's comment, which differs from the Rambam/Ramban answer.

Rashi's comment seems closer to the second possibility above, since it involves money. We must understand why Rashi rejects the first possibility and why the second (giving charity) is not an acceptable means of obtaining atonement for one's sins.

This is not easy!

Can you understand Rashi's comment that G-d cannot be "appeased with money"?

YOUR ANSWER:

UNDERSTANDING RASHI

An Answer: Rashi's comment may be better understood when seen in light of a verse in Proverbs (16:6):

בְּחֶסֶד וֶאֱמֶת יְכֻפַּר עָוֹן, וּבְיִרְאַת הי סוּר מֵרָע.

"Through kindness and truth will sin be forgiven, and with the fear of *Hashem* one turns from evil."

Here we have the formula for really "appeasing G-d" and having our sins forgiven — the crucial factors: "kindness and truth." By kindness may be meant acts of charity (giving money to a charitable cause). But what does "truth" mean here? The answer would seem to be that complete atonement and the achieving of appeasement from G-d, requires "truth." In the case of a sinner who seeks the revocation of his sins, the elemental truth would be to admit one's sins. "This above all, to thine own self be true." This is the first step in doing *tshuvah*. Rashi is telling us that bribery for G-d is to think that doing more of His commandments without at the same time confessing and regretting one's sins, will achieve G-d's favor. But G-d takes no bribery. No matter how much money is given for a good cause, no matter how many good deeds one has in his account, unless and until a man asks forgiveness for his sin, G-d is not appeased. Unless and until he is "truthful" about his actions and does not try to sweep them under the rug by "appeasing G-d" with additional mitzvos, he is not entitled to G-d's favor.

(See *Oznayim L'Torah*)

A brief comment leads to insights in psychology and the Torah.

Deut. 10:19

וַאֲהַבְתֶּם אֶת־הַגֵּר כִּי־גֵרִים הֱיִיתֶם בְּאֶרֶץ מִצְרָיִם.

כי גרים הייתם: מום שבך אל תאמר לחברך.
Because you were strangers : *Rashi:* A blemish that you possess, do not attribute to your friend.

What Is Rashi Saying?

Rashi's comment seems simple enough. It recalls similar Rashi-comments in Exodus 22:20 and Leviticus 19:34 which also refer to strangers (i.e., converts).

Let us compare these comments and see a question that arises from such a comparison

<table>
<tr><td>Our verse</td><td>Exodus 22:20</td></tr>
<tr><td align="right">וַאֲהַבְתֶּם אֶת־הַגֵּר
כִּי־גֵרִים הֱיִיתֶם בְּאֶרֶץ מִצְרָיִם.</td><td align="right">וְגֵר לֹא תוֹנֶה ולֹא תִלְחָצֶנּוּ
כִּי־גֵרִים הֱיִיתֶם בְּאֶרֶץ מִצְרָיִם.</td></tr>
</table>

Leviticus 19:33-34

וְכִי־יָגוּר אִתְּךָ גֵּר בְּאַרְצְכֶם לֹא תוֹנוּ אֹתוֹ...
וְאָהַבְתָּ לוֹ כָּמוֹךָ כִּי גֵרִים הֱיִיתֶם בְּאֶרֶץ מִצְרָיִם.

As you compare these verses and Rashi's comment here, what would you ask?

Your Question:

Questioning Rashi

A Question: While all three verses contain the same phrase "Because you were strangers in the land of Egypt" and on these verses Rashi also comments "a blemish you possess, do not attribute to another," yet these verses differ from ours. In the other two verses there is a prohibition to harm the stranger. Exodus 22:20 says "Don't taunt or oppress a stranger." In Leviticus 19:34 it says "Don't taunt him." Our verse, on the other hand, only says "Love the stranger." There is no prohibition to taunt him. To use Rashi's phrasing, there is no mention of "blemishes" in our verse.

The question is: Why does Rashi mention blemishes? Rashi's warning is appropriate when there is a prohibition to taunt him, but our verse says nothing about acting disrespectfully towards the stranger. Ours speaks of loving him. Why does Rashi repeat the aphorism "a blemish you possess, do not attribute to another"?

Can you see what prompted this comment?

Your Answer:

WHAT IS BOTHERING RASHI?

An Answer: Our verse enjoins us to love the stranger "because we were strang-ers in Egypt." What sense does that make? It is understandable that we should love someone because he did us a favor. But to love someone just because we had similar experiences? Because both he and we were strangers? Why? It makes as much sense to say, Love basketball players because you too were once a basketball player!

How does Rashi's comment deal with this difficulty?

YOUR ANSWER:

UNDERSTANDING RASHI

An Answer: Rashi is telling us that since the Torah reinforces the command to "love the stranger" with the reminiscence of our Egyptian experi-ence, the point of the verse must be: do not inflict on the stranger what we went through when we were strangers in Egypt. In this light, "love" consists of not doing evil towards the stranger; of not taking advantage of the stranger because he is less powerful than us as we were less powerful than our Egyptian taskmasters.

This is reminiscent of Hillel's interpretation of "Love your neighbor as yourself" which he gave to the gentile who professed interest in con-verting to Judaism. His words "What is hateful to you, do not do to another" are a way of rendering the Torah's positive command of "lov-ing" as a negative prohibition not to harm another.

In our verse as well, Rashi transposes the Torah's positive command to love the stranger into a negative admonition "don't ascribe to him your faults."

PSYCHOLOGICAL DEFENSE MECHANISMS

It is interesting to note in this regard, that psychologists have under-stood the dynamics underlying negative, racist stereotypes, the preju-dices people hold for certain minorities in their midst, to be, in reality, projected images of their own weaknesses. They project onto others those traits which are distasteful to them and which they cannot accept as part of themselves. This projection ascribes to the other their own "wicked-ness," thereby accomplishing two psychological maneuvers at once — denial of one's own imperfection as well as projecting the anger one has for oneself onto another. This is exactly the meaning of "A blemish you have do not attribute to another." The Torah's psychological astuteness predates Freudian defense mechanisms by a few years.

A Closer Look

As I pondered this verse and the Rashi-comment on it, I wondered why the Torah had to use the idea of Love to begin with. If the verse means the avoidance of doing harm to the stranger, why say "you shall love the stranger"? That seems a bit much.

Then I noticed the context of the verse and I saw something interesting.

The Seven Code and the Torah's Message

This *parashah* begins with verse 10:12, and continues until the end of the sedra. Verse 10:12 begins with "Now Israel, what does *Hashem,* your G-d, ask of you? — only to fear *Hashem,* your G-d, to go in all of His ways, to *love* Him" etc.

After Moses tells us to "go *in all* of His ways" it continues with verse 10:19, which tells us of His ways:
"He does justice to the orphan and the widow and *He loves the stranger* to give him bread and clothes."

We see that this whole *parashah* is a lesson in *Imitatio Dei,* to imitate G-d's ways. He *loves* the stranger, so you too shall *love* the stranger. That is probably why this language was used here.

The idea of love — G-d's love for Israel, Israel's love for G-d and G-d and man's love of others — is a central theme in this *parashah.* This is attested to by the fact that the word "love" appears seven times in this *parashah* – from verse 10:12 till the end of the sedra. (Count them: Verses 10:12, 15, 18, 19; 11:1, 13, 22). This is a telltale sign that the Torah wants to emphasize this idea of love. (For a fuller discussion of the significance of the Seven Code in the Torah, see "*Studying the Torah: A Guide to In-depth Interpretation.*")

Rashi shows us the dimensions of devout service to G-d.

Deut. 11:13

וְהָיָה אִם־שָׁמֹעַ תִּשְׁמְעוּ אֶל מִצְוֹתַי אֲשֶׁר אָנֹכִי מְצַוֶּה אֶתְכֶם הַיּוֹם לְאַהֲבָה אֶת־יְהֹוָה אֱלֹקֵיכֶם וּלְעָבְדוֹ בְּכָל־לְבַבְכֶם וּבְכָל־נַפְשְׁכֶם.

לְאַהֲבָה אֶת ה': שלא תאמר הרי אני לומד בשביל שאהיה עשיר, בשביל שאקרא רב, בשביל שאקבל שכר, אלא כל מה שתעשה עשה מאהבה וסוף הכבוד לבוא.

To love *Hashem*: *Rashi:* You should not say "Behold I will learn in order that I will be rich; in order that I will be called 'Rabbi'; in order that I will get reward." Rather do all that you do out of love and in the end, the honor will come.

WHAT IS RASHI SAYING? _____

The command to love G-d is problematic on several points. How can we be *commanded* to love Him? Love is a spontaneous emotion, how can it be ordered by fiat? And, even if it were possible, how is one to love G-d, a totally spiritual Being who can neither be seen nor much less approached? Rashi's comment is meant to show us how this "love of G-d" can be practically accomplished. His answer is that when we do His mitzvahs for no ulterior purpose except for the love of G-d, we are manifesting the love of G-d. Such a request can indeed be commanded of man, for it is an act that can be willfully striven for.

That said, there are several questions that can be asked on Rashi's educational comment.

What would you ask?

YOUR QUESTION(S):

QUESTIONING RASHI _____

A Question: Why does Rashi (the *midrash* actually) choose learning as the example of a mitzvah that a person should not do for ulterior motives? Why not any of the other 612 mitzvos?

Another Question: Why does Rashi say "in order *to be* rich" but when he speaks of being a Rabbi he says "in order *to be called* Rabbi"? Why doesn't he use parallel wording "in order *to be* a Rabbi"?

And a last Question: Why does Rashi add at the end of this comment "and in the end, the honor will come"? Aren't we talking about learning for the love of *Hashem* — לשמה? Why the need to tack on the reward of "honor"? That no longer looks like a "non-profit" mitzvah.

Do you have answers (or other questions!)?

YOUR ANSWER(S):

UNDERSTANDING RASHI

Some Answers:

1) Rashi chooses learning Torah as the mitzvah because our verse begins with "And it will be if you hear diligently" this seems to mean learning. On this basis Rashi speaks of studying the Torah, more so than any other mitzvah. Although certainly a person should do all the mitzvos for the sake of G-d alone.

2) Rashi is pointing out motives of questionable value as life goals. Being rich as an ultimate life-goal, is not a true-value goal. *Being a Rabbi*, on the other hand, is. Being a teacher in Israel is an admirable occupation. But if one does this mainly for the honor he is given by being *called 'Rabbi,'* then he has missed the point and has exploited Torah for personal gain.

3) Serving G-d for love would seem to be its own reward. Nevertheless, the Torah itself suggests rewards here. See the following verse (14): "And I will give the rains in their time" etc. So rewards are promised even though we are enjoined to serve G-d out of love. This is similar to the lesson from the Sayings of the Fathers (1:3) "Be not like servants who serve their master in order to receive reward; rather be like servants who serve their master *not in order to receive* reward." Note that it does not say "in order *not to receive* reward." That would mean that we relinquish all consideration of reward. If we do a mitzvah we are entitled to reward, but that should not be our motivation for doing it in the first place.

(See *Divrei Dovid*)

"AND IN THE END, HONOR WILL COME"

We should note a nuance of Rashi's phrasing. He says

וסוף הכבוד לבוא

"And in the end, honor will come."

He does not say:

והכבוד יבוא בסוף

"And honor will come in the end."

These two versions say essentially the same thing. But there is a subtle difference. What is the difference between them?

An Answer: "And honor will come in the end" implies that honor (the first word in the phrase is the emphasized word) is upper most in the individual's mind. He is waiting patiently. When will it come? In other words, he still has the mindset of receiving something for his mitzvah — he looks forward to the honor he will gain, albeit after a while.

On the other hand the phrase "And in the end, honor will come" has a different emphasis. Honor is almost an afterthought. It comes *after* "the end", after the mitzvah has been completed and the person is ready to move on to something else. The implication being that the honor he receives at the end, is anticlimactic, it is something he has neither expected nor striven for — an afterthought.

An interesting insight by one of the famous Ba'alei haTosafos.

Deut. 11:15

וְנָתַתִּי עֵשֶׂב בְּשָׂדְךָ לִבְהֶמְתֶּךָ וְאָכַלְתָּ וְשָׂבָעְתָּ.

Following is the comment of Rav Joseph Bechor Shor:

וְאָכַלְתָּ וְשָׂבָעְתָּ: רבותינו דרשו מכאן שצריך אדם לתת תבן לבהמתו קודם שיאכל משום דכתיב ונתתי עשב בשדך לבהמתך והדר יואכלת ושבעתי וכן (תהילים קד:יד) ׳מצמיח חציר לבהמה ועשב לעבודת האדם להוציא לחם מן הארץ׳. וכן הקב״ה עושה: מקדים שחת בשדה שהוא לבהמות ואחר כך הגרגיר שהוא לצורך האדם. לפי שאין הבהמה יודעת לקצור ולאסוף כמו האדם, הקב״ה מקדים לה מאכלה, כי ירחמיו על כל מעשיו.׳ (תהילים קמה: ט)

And you will eat and be satisfied: *Bechor Shor:* Our Rabbis learned from here that a man must first give straw to his animals before he himself eats because it says "And I will give grass in your field for your animal." And only afterwards does [it say] "and you will eat and be satisfied." Likewise [we find in Psalms 104:14] "He makes grow fodder for the animal and grass for the working of man in order to bring forth bread from the land." And so does the Holy One, blessed be He, do: First He places fodder in the field which is for the animals and only afterwards, the grain, which is for the needs of man.[This is so] because the animal does not know how to harvest and gather as does man, therefore the Holy One, blessed be He, precedes for it (the animal) its food, because "His mercy is on all His creatures." (Psalms 145:9)

BECHOR SHOR SEES G-D'S WISDOM IN NATURE

See how the Bechor Shor cleverly combines a description of the natural phenomenon — how grain is grown — with the nuances of the Scriptural passages. All to show the Divine wisdom in His creation which is manifestation of mercy to all His creatures — man and animal alike.

An apparent contradiction disappears with further study.

Deut. 11:16

הִשָּׁמְרוּ לָכֶם פֶּן־יִפְתֶּה לְבַבְכֶם וְסַרְתֶּם וַעֲבַדְתֶּם אֱלֹהִים אֲחֵרִים וְהִשְׁתַּחֲוִיתֶם לָהֶם.

אֱלֹהִים אֲחֵרִים: שהם אחרים לעובדיהם, צועק אליו ואינו עונהו נמצא עשוי לו כנכרי.

Other gods: *Rashi:* They are "other" to those who worship them; he cries out to it (the god) but it does not answer him. Turns out that it (the god) is to him as a stranger.

WHAT IS RASHI SAYING?

We should be aware that the words אלהים אחרים can be translated in various ways.

1) "Other gods" meaning, gods other than *Hashem,* the G-d of the Jews.

2) "Others' gods" meaning, the gods of the gentiles.

3) "Other-like (alien, estranged) gods" meaning, gods who act estranged from their worshippers.

Rashi has chosen the third possibility.

What question would you ask?

YOUR QUESTION:

QUESTIONING RASHI

A Question: Of these three choices, why does Rashi choose #3 above; why does
he reject the other two choices?

YOUR ANSWER:

WHAT IS BOTHERING RASHI?

An Answer: Choice #1 above is definitely unacceptable to Rashi. If the phrase
"other gods" means that there are other gods in addition to *Hashem,*
this is certainly not true. "Hear O Israel, *Hashem,* our G-d, *Hashem*
is One." It is for this reason that Rashi rejects this option.

But why does he reject option #2? This question becomes even more
puzzling when we note the following inconsistency in Rashi's commentary.

An INCONSISTENCY IN RASHI'S COMMENTS?

Compare this Rashi-comment with what he writes on "other gods" in
the verse in Exodus 20:3.

לֹא־יִהְיֶה לְךָ אֱלֹהִים אֲחֵרִים עַל פָּנָי.

אֱלֹהִים אֲחֵרִים: שֶׁאֵינָן אֱלֹהוּת אֶלָּא אֲחֵרִים עֲשָׂאוּם אֱלֹהִים
עֲלֵיהֶם. וְלֹא יִתָּכֵן לְפָרֵשׁ אֱלֹהִים אֲחֵרִים זוּלָתִי, שֶׁגְּנַאי הוּא
כְּלַפֵּי מַעְלָה לִקְרֹאותָם אֱלֹהוּת אֶצְלוֹ. דָּבָר אַחֵר, אֱלֹהִים אֲחֵרִים
שֶׁהֵם אֲחֵרִים לְעוֹבְדֵיהֶם צוֹעֲקִים אֲלֵיהֶם וְאֵינָם עוֹנִין אוֹתָם,
וְדוֹמֶה כְּאִילוּ הוּא אַחֵר שֶׁאֵינוֹ מַכִּירוֹ מֵעוֹלָם.

Other gods: *Rashi:* Which are not actually gods, but "others" made them gods over them. It would be incorrect to
interpret אלהים אחרים "other than Myself." For it would
be disrespectful towards the One Above to call them gods
in relation to Him. Another explanation of אלהים אחרים is

that they are אחרים — alien — to those who worship them.
They cry out to them but they do not answer them, and it
is as if it is a stranger, who has never known him.

What inconsistency do you see?

YOUR ANSWER:

An Inconsistency

An Answer: In this comment Rashi mentions choices #2 ("Which are not actually gods, but "others" made them gods over them") and #3 ("they
are אחרים — alien — to those who worship them.") However, on
our verse Rashi does not mention option #2. Why does he mention
it in the verse in Exodus but not here?

Can you think of a reason?

Hint: Look at the context of both verses.

YOUR ANSWER:

Understanding Rashi's Precise Choice

An Answer: If you looked at the context of our verse, you saw that our verse is
among verses that speak of the rewards G-d gives those who follow His mitzvahs. The verses preceding our verse say:

> "And it will be if you thoroughly heed My commandments....I
> will give rain in its time …and grass in your field …and you will
> eat and be satisfied."

This means that G-d is sensitive and responsive to our actions; He rewards our right acts and punishes our evil acts. This is not true of the
"alien" gods. They are unresponsive to man's actions. So it was important for Rashi to emphasize this particular characteristic of the false gods
(he cries out to it (the god) but it does not answer him) to show the
difference between them and the G-d of Israel.

On the other hand, the verse that Rashi comments on in the Ten Commandments says:

> "You shall have no other gods before Me."

"*No other gods*" includes all possible meanings of this phrase, both those
that others consider gods as well as those who are "alien" to their fol-

lowers. Rashi therefore includes these two interpretations of the words אלהים אחרים in his comment in Exodus. It is appropriate.

The Prophet's View of "gods who are broken cisterns"

In spite of the fact that the Torah forewarned Israel not to forsake *Hashem* for alien gods, the nation was nevertheless unmindful of this. Let us listen to Jeremiah's castigation of the people on this matter.

Jeremiah 2:11:

> "Has a nation ever exchanged its gods, though *they* are not gods? Yet My people has exchanged its Glory for something of no avail. …My people has committed two evils: They have forsaken Me, the source of living waters, to dig for themselves cisterns, broken cisterns that cannot hold water."

Jeremiah condemns the people precisely on this point. G-d who can give them life ("the source of living waters ") in reward for fulfilling His mitzvos, was abandoned for alien gods who are not responsive nor capable of sustaining life ("broken cisterns that cannot hold water.")

Rashi presents a radical idea, which offers a new look at the purpose of the mitzvos in Exile.

Deut. 11:18

וְשַׂמְתֶּם אֶת־דְּבָרַי אֵלֶּה עַל־לְבַבְכֶם וְעַל־נַפְשְׁכֶם וּקְשַׁרְתֶּם אֹתָם לְאוֹת עַל־יֶדְכֶם וְהָיוּ לְטוֹטָפֹת בֵּין עֵינֵיכֶם.

ושמתם את דברי: אף לאחר שתגלו היו מצוינים במצות הניחו תפילין עשו מזוזות כדי שלא יהיו לכם חדשים כשתחזרו. וכן הוא אומר, הציבי לך ציונים (ירמיהו לא:כא)

And you shall place My words: *Rashi*: Even after you have been exiled make yourselves distinctive by means of My commandments: put on *Tefillin*, attach *Mezuzos* [to your door posts] so that these shall not be new (i.e. unfamiliar) to you when you return (to the Land of Israel). Similarly it says (Jeremiah 31:21): "Set up, for yourself, distinguishing signs."

This is an unusual comment, any way you look at it. But let us first try to understand why Rashi mentions the idea of exile when the verse is speaking about the mitzvah of *Tefillin*.

What's bothering him?

Can you see what lies behind this comment?

YOUR ANSWER:

WHAT IS BOTHERING RASHI?

An Answer: Did you notice that the phrase which immediately precedes our verse says, "And you will be lost quickly from off the good Land which *Hashem* gives you." This is the punishment of exile. Rashi's implicit question is: What connection is there between the threat of exile (verse 17) and the commandments to wear *Tefillin* and to attach *Mezuzos* to our doorposts (verse 18-20)?

The Torah, in an earlier *parashah* (Deut. 6:8-9) also prescribed these commandments, yet there, there was no mention of exile. What is its place here?

How does Rashi's comment make sense of this strange juxtaposition?

YOUR ANSWER:

UNDERSTANDING RASHI

An Answer: Rashi connects the observance of these — and other — mitzvos, with the expulsion from the Land of Israel. This juxtaposition is intended to enjoin us, Rashi says, to continue to keep these mitzvos even though we no longer live in the Land. That is the meaning of the relatedness of these two themes.

What would you ask about Rashi's statement?

I believe the question is glaring.

YOUR QUESTION:

QUESTIONING THE *DRASH*

A Question: Are we supposed to keep these mitzvos in Exile only so that we won't forget them once we return to the Land? Certainly not?! The

613 mitzvos can be divided into two broad categories: Those, which obligate the individual personally, irrespective of where he lives and those which are dependent on, and connected to, the Land. The first category includes observing the Sabbath; the second includes observing the Sabbath of the Land (*Shemitah*). The first includes eating only kosher food; the second includes giving tithes from our crops. The first includes wearing *Tefillin*; the second includes building the Temple. In view of this most basic knowledge (which Rashi was also aware of !!) how can Rashi say that *Tefillin* is observed in Exile *only* so that we will not forget it? Strange, to say the least.

Can you explain this? This has stumped the best Jewish minds.

YOUR ANSWER:

THE RAMBAN'S VIEW

An Answer: The Ramban asks this question and teases us by saying this is a hidden matter — סוד. In this way he hides more than he reveals. It is clear from other comments he makes in other places in his Torah commentary that the Ramban means that the Torah was essentially intended to be practiced in the Land of Israel. This is a truth of a higher, theoretical level. Practically, the division we spoke of previously, between mitzvos related to the Land and those not so related, is to be considered halachically in force.

THE K'SAV V'HAKABALAH'S PARABLE

The *K'sav v'haKabalah* explains the deeper idea here. He cites a *midrash, Sifri*, which uses a parable to explain the idea in Rashi's comment.

> "A king became angry with his wife and he sent her out of his home and she returned to her father's house. Her father advised her to dress nicely every day while she was living at his home, with her jewelry, so that "when you return to your husband you will not have forgotten (it will be customary) to dress this way." Likewise, G-d advised His people to continue with their same behavior (keeping the mitzvos) in exile as they had done in their own home (the Land)."

The parable, which seems simple enough (as are most parables), in fact, shines new light on the whole concept of exile. The wife who is banished from her home by her angry husband, the king, cannot be sure that he will ever take her back. He may finally decide to end their relationship and divorce her. Likewise the Jew during the long, dark, painful Exile, could reasonably imagine that there is no hope, no redemption and no return to the Land will ever materialize. It may just be a wish-propelled fantasy. Thus when the Jew continues to keep the mitzvos in Exile, it is his proclamation that he believes that his connection with G-d has not been severed. G-d's promise of redemption and return will be fulfilled — albeit at some unknown time in the future.

For us, who live in a period after the modern State of Israel came into existence, who, after nearly two millenium of exile, have now come home, it is difficult to imagine how sorely the Jew's faith was tested during that long, dark, degrading Exile.

This is what I think Rashi means when he says "continue to keep these mitzvos so that when you return they will not be forgotten." What will not be forgotten? Not just the mitzvos, but the whole concept that the Jew has a unique relationship with G-d. During those years "away from home" the Jew could easily have lost faith that he was G-d's partner in the "Covenant between the Pieces." Today we see exactly this reality. Some Jews have returned to Israel and that Return has validated their belief in that Covenant, because during the years of Exile they continued to keep G-d's mitzvos. But others, who have also returned to the Land, do not see this as a fulfillment of a Divine promise; and this is because they lived in Exile without keeping G-d's Torah. Unfortunately during the long Exile they have forgotten His mitzvos and, while they have been returned to the Land, they have forgotten the Sanctity of the Land.

The parable sheds a completely new light on Rashi's comment. We see that while the mitzvos are certainly an individual obligation, and are to be fulfilled wherever the Jew finds himself, they also contain within them a separate message when performed during the long Exile.

The message: By continuing to keep His commandments, we bear testimony to our abiding trust in the irrevocability of His Covenant with His People — even though our being in Exile is a clear sign of His disfavor with our behavior.

(See *the K'sav v'haKabalah*)

עולת תודה

With gratitude to *Hashem yisbarach*
and to all the school children
and friends whose *tefillos* helped me
through a difficult time.

May *Hashem* grant them
all the blessings of the Torah.

מרים בת רחל

A small comment with large implications.

Deut. 11:27

אֶת־הַבְּרָכָה אֲשֶׁר תִּשְׁמְעוּ אֶל־מִצְוֹת הי אֱלֹקֵיכֶם אֲשֶׁר אָנֹכִי מְצַוֶּה אֶתְכֶם הַיּוֹם.

אֶת הברכה: על מנת **אֲשֶׁר תשמעו.**
The blessing: *Rashi:* On condition **that you will heed**.

This short comment is of the style of the Type II Rashi comment. A few words are inserted in between the Torah's words. But, I would say, in spite of the style, I believe that Rashi is bothered by something.

What would you ask here?

YOUR QUESTION:

QUESTIONING RASHI

A Question: What has Rashi told us here and why the need to comment at all?

What prompted his comment?

What is bothering Rashi?

Hint: Compare our verse with the next verse.

YOUR ANSWER:

WHAT IS BOTHERING RASHI?

An Answer: Verses 27 and 28 speak of the blessing and the curse that will follow as a consequence to those who follow G-d's word and those who do not. Let us look again at the two verses and compare them.

27) אֶת־הַבְּרָכָה **אֲשֶׁר** תִּשְׁמְעוּ אֶל־מִצְוֹת הֹ' אלֹקֵיכֶם אֲשֶׁר אָנֹכִי מְצַוֶּה אֶתְכֶם הַיּוֹם.

28) וְהַקְּלָלָה **אִם** לֹא תִשְׁמְעוּ אֶל־מִצְוֹת הֹ' אֱלֹקֵיכֶם וְסַרְתֶּם מִן־הַדֶּרֶךְ אֲשֶׁר אָנֹכִי מְצַוֶּה אֶתְכֶם הַיּוֹם לָלֶכֶת אַחֲרֵי אֱלֹהִים אֲחֵרִים אֲשֶׁר לֹא יְדַעְתֶּם.

"The blessing **that** you will heed etc.."

"And the curse **if** you will not heed ….."

We see that our verse, speaking of the blessing, uses the word "that" אֲשֶׁר. The next verse, speaking of the curse, uses the word "if" אִם.

Why the change of wording in the two verses? And why doesn't our verse have the more fitting, conditional "if" אִם?

The difference in wording in these two verses is what is bothering Rashi.

How does Rashi's two-word comment help matters?

YOUR ANSWER:

UNDERSTANDING RASHI

An Answer: Rashi's use of the words על מנת has a precise meaning in the Talmud.

The Sages (*Gittin* 75b) tell us:

כל האומר "על מנת" כאומר "מעכשיו" דמי.

"Whoever says 'on condition that' is like he said 'from now.'"

This can be illustrated when we compare two sentences.

I can say to a mechanic "I am giving you $100 **on the condition** that you repair my car."

Or I can say:

"I will give you $100 **if** you repair my car. "

In the first case the money is given up front with the condition that the mechanic do the work. In the second case, no money is given unless and until the work is done.

With this in mind, let us look at these verses and see what difference this verbal nuance makes.

What difference do you see?

YOUR ANSWER:

An Answer: The blessing is given "on condition," says Rashi. This means that G-d gives His blessing even *before* we have fulfilled His conditions. G-d is willing to give us of His bounty on credit; on the understanding that we will, in the future, fulfill His conditions. The curse, on the other hand, is not given "on condition," it is not inflicted unless and until the people transgress G-d's commandments.

THE LESSON

This is an encouraging view of G-d's benevolent ways. His blessings of food, shelter and security are basic givens of this world. He has placed them here for us to enjoy. Only if and when we transgress His Torah — which is a Torah of Life — are we in danger of losing these blessings. The blessings are given unconditionally; but they are sustained only upon fulfillment of His conditions. The punishments, on the other hand, come only **if** (when) we don't follow His ways. We could say the punishments are inherent, natural outcomes of straying from His path, from His Torah of life and from His life of Torah.

This idea is, in fact, built into these verses. You may have noticed that even though we are talking about conditional phrases, nowhere are the consequences mentioned.

> "The blessing, that you will heed the commandments of *Hashem*, your G-d…"

Notice that the blessing is "that you will heed the commandments." It is not an extrinsic reward (for example: becoming rich) which is granted when we fulfill G-d's word. The blessing is rather identified with "heeding the commandments of *Hashem*." The Torah is saying clearly: Doing good is its own reward.

Likewise regarding the curse, the Torah says:

> "And the curse: If you do not heed the commandments of *Hashem*.."

The curse, itself, is identified with not heeding the commandments. Again, the message is that doing evil is its own punishment.

The Sages in *Pirkei Avos* (Ch. 4:2) put it succinctly: "The reward of a mitzvah is a mitzvah; the reward of sin is sin."

(See N. Leibowitz, Iyunim b'sefer Devarim)

Rashi alerts us to subtleties in syntax.

Deut. 12:2

אַבֵּד תְּאַבְּדוּן אֶת־כָּל־הַמְּקֹמוֹת אֲשֶׁר עָבְדוּ־שָׁם הַגּוֹיִם אֲשֶׁר אַתֶּם
יֹרְשִׁים אֹתָם אֶת־אֱלֹהֵיהֶם עַל־הֶהָרִים הָרָמִים וְעַל הַגְּבָעוֹת וְתַחַת
כָּל־עֵץ רַעֲנָן.

> אֶת כָּל הַמְּקֹמוֹת **אֲשֶׁר עָבְדוּ שָׁם וְגוֹ'**: וּמַה תְּאַבְּדוּן מֵהֶם? **אֶת
> אֱלֹהֵיהֶם** אֲשֶׁר עַל הֶהָרִים.
>
> **All of the places where the nations worshipped etc:**
> *Rashi:* What must you obliterate from them? "**Their gods
> who are on the mountains.**"

This comment has all the signs of a Type II comment. It is short and
Rashi's few words are interspersed between the Torah's words. This clues
us in that Rashi is relating to a possible misunderstanding.

What would you ask?

YOUR QUESTION:

QUESTIONING RASHI

A Question: The verse says to "destroy all the places where the nations
worshipped…their gods." Rashi changes this to "destroy their gods
who are on the mountains." Why does he do this? What possible
misunderstanding is he helping us avoid?

YOUR ANSWER:

WHAT MISUNDERSTANDING?

An Answer: You do not destroy a place — you cannot destroy a place. You can
destroy a building, but not a natural, geographical location. How
would they destroy a mountain?! Therefore Rashi finds a different
meaning of this verse. How does his comment instruct us to read
the verse differently?

YOUR ANSWER:

UNDERSTANDING RASHI

An Answer: Rashi does a neat trick. He connects the first words in the verse,
אבד תאבדון, with the last words, את אלהיהם אשר על ההרים.

He, in effect, skips over all the intermediate words: את כל המקמות
אשר עבדו שם הגוים אשר אתם ירשים אתם.

The new word order, according to Rashi, is:

אבד תאבדון את אלהיהם [אשר] על ההרים הרמים ועל הגבעות
ותחת כל עץ רענן את כל המקמות אשר עבדו שם הגוים אשר
אתם ירשים אתם.

"You shall surely destroy their gods [which are] on the
high mountains and on the hills and under every leafy
tree, all the places that the nations served there, whom
you are dispossessing."

But there is something awkward about the construction of the verse in
this way.

What looks awkward?

YOUR ANSWER:

A CLOSER LOOK

An Answer: The last part of the verse "all the places that the nations, etc." seems
out of place. If Rashi implied that you could not destroy a geographic location, then what do these words mean? They do not
connect smoothly with the words that precede them nor do they
seem to make sense.

Can you make the words

את כל המקמות אשר עבדו שם הגוים אשר אתם ירשים אתם

fit better in this verse?

An Answer: The little word את in את כל המקומות does not ordinarily have a
literal counterpart in English. It is the silent word which comes
before the direct object "all the places." But את can also mean
"from," as in Exodus (9:29) when Moses says to Pharaoh:

כְּצֵאתִי אֶת־הָעִיר

When I go out **from** the city."

So in our verse it would mean "on the high mountains and on the hills and beneath every leafy tree **from** all the places that the nations served there." This makes perfect sense. Not the places are to be destroyed, rather the idols which are *from* those places, are to be destroyed.

(See *Almoshnino, Mizrachi*)

Analyzing Rashi-comments that offer more than one interpretation.

Deut. 12: (2,3) 4,5

2) אַבֵּד תְּאַבְּדוּן אֶת־כָּל־הַמְּקֹמוֹת אֲשֶׁר עָבְדוּ־שָׁם הַגּוֹיִם אֲשֶׁר אַתֶּם יֹרְשִׁים אֹתָם אֶת־אֱלֹהֵיהֶם עַל־הֶהָרִים הָרָמִים וְעַל־הַגְּבָעוֹת וְתַחַת כָּל־עֵץ רַעֲנָן.

3) וְנִתַּצְתֶּם אֶת־מִזְבְּחֹתָם וְשִׁבַּרְתֶּם אֶת־מַצֵּבֹתָם וַאֲשֵׁרֵיהֶם תִּשְׂרְפוּן בָּאֵשׁ וּפְסִילֵי אֱלֹהֵיהֶם תְּגַדֵּעוּן וְאִבַּדְתֶּם אֶת־שְׁמָם מִן־הַמָּקוֹם הַהוּא.

4) **לֹא תַעֲשׂוּן** כֵּן לַה' אֱלֹקֵיכֶם.

5) כִּי אִם־אֶל־הַמָּקוֹם אֲשֶׁר־יִבְחַר ה' אֱלֹקֵיכֶם מִכָּל־שִׁבְטֵיכֶם לָשׂוּם אֶת־שְׁמוֹ שָׁם לְשִׁכְנוֹ תִדְרְשׁוּ וּבָאתָ שָׁמָּה.

> **לֹא תַעֲשׂוּן כֵּן:** להקטיר לשמים בכל מקום כי אם במקום אשר יבחר. דבר אחר, 'ונתצתם את מזבחתיהם וגי' ואבדתם את שמם — לא תעשון כן' אזהרה למוחק את השם ולנותץ אבן מן המזבח או מן העזרה. אמר ר' ישמעאל וכי תעלה על דעתך שישראל נותצין את המזבחות? אלא שלא תיעשו כמעשיהם ויגרמו עונותיכם למקדש אבותיכם שיחרב.
>
> **Do not do thus***: Rashi:* To bring burnt-offerings for the sake of Heaven anywhere except in the place that He will choose. Another explanation, "Smash their altars, etc. and obliterate their name — do not do thus." This is a prohibition for erasing the [Divine] Name and for breaking a stone from the altar or from [the Temple] courtyard. Rabbi Ishmael said "Is it conceivable that an Israelite would smash the altars? Rather, (its meaning is) do not act as they (the Canaanites) do, so that your sins will cause the Temple of your forefathers to be destroyed."

WHAT IS RASHI SAYING?

The word "thus" in our verse is ambiguous. "Do not do thus — *what?*" It is not clear what "thus" refers to. Rashi offers three interpretations for the possible referent.

The first is: Don't do as the gentiles do; they make offerings in *any place* that suites them; you are to bring your offerings *only to the place* G-d has chosen. This means that "thus" refers back to verse 12:2, which speaks of idol worship on the mountains and under every leafy tree.

The second explanation focuses on smashing their altars. You are commanded to smash *their* altars; but don't smash G-d's altars. This means that "thus" refers back to the immediately previous verse 3.

Rabbi Ishmael can't accept this interpretation. To him, it seems too far-fetched that Jews would have to be warned against willfully destroying their own holy places. His interpretation is an indirect reference: Don't act as the gentiles acted, which eventually lead to the destruction of their temples. Act in accordance with G-d's wishes and your Temple will not be destroyed.

What would you ask on this three-part comment?

YOUR QUESTION:

QUESTIONING RASHI

A Question: Whenever Rashi offers more than one interpretation, we can ask why he wasn't satisfied with just one. The Rashi super-commentators use this questioning approach to find the weaknesses and strengths of each interpretation. They reason that if a second interpretation is necessary this indicates that the first was deficient in some way. But if the first was problematic, why does Rashi offer it at all? And if the first did have merit, why offer the second one? So maybe both have their merits. We therefore look for the strengths and weaknesses of both interpretations.

Appropriate questions are: Why are other interpretations necessary? What is weak and what is strong about each of the interpretations?

Let us apply the same method here. What is weak with Rashi's first explanation? And what is its strength?

Hint: From whence does Rashi derive the idea of "To bring burnt-offerings ... anywhere, except in the place" etc.?

Your Answer:

Understanding the First Interpretation _____

An Answer: The first interpretation is based on the words in verse 2, which say that the nations "make offerings on the mountains, on the hills and under every leafy tree." That is, almost everywhere. This is what "thus" refers to. Meaning that we should not be so casual as to bring offerings to G-d any and everywhere, except in the place which He has designated. This seems to be a reasonable interpretation, because right after the words "Do not do thus to *Hashem* your G-d" the Torah says "except in the place that *Hashem* your G-d will choose…" So our verse would be saying, in effect, "Do not do thus (*viz.* offer sacrifices anywhere) except in the place that G-d will choose."

But it must have a weakness, otherwise Rashi would not suggest another interpretation. What is its weakness?

An Answer: The two verses, which Rashi connects, are not next to each other. One is verse 2 the other is verse 4. Verse 3 separates them. We have to assume that the word "thus" refers back to a clause, which is not adjacent to it. For this reason this is not a preferred interpretation.

So Rashi offers his second interpretation. How does the second interpretation avoid the difficulty of the first one?

Your Answer:

Understanding the Second Interpretation _____

An Answer: The second interpretation remedies that weakness as it does connect two adjacent verses. Verse 3 says "Destroy and burn their holy places," and verse 4 says: "Don't do thus to *Hashem*." Don't erase the Divine Name nor break part of the altar or the Temple.

But this too has its weakness.

What is it?

Your Answer:

An Answer. The weakness has been pointed out by Rabbi Ishmael. Could anyone conceive of a Jew tearing down their own Temple or altar, making it necessary for the Torah to warn him not to do this!?

But with a little thought, we can also question Rabbi Ishmael's question.

Questioning Rabbi Ishmael's Interpretation

A Question: Rabbi Ishmael is amazed that Jews have to be warned not to tear down their Temple, it is such a sacrilegious act that one cannot imagine a Jew doing such a thing. But there are many commandments in the Torah, which enjoin Jews not to do terrible things. Among them are rape, murder, stealing, incest, taking advantage of the powerless widow etc. So the dastardliness of a transgression does not seem to be reason enough for the Torah not to warn us against doing it.

Why then is Rabbi Ishmael surprised here?

YOUR ANSWER:

Understanding Rabbi Ishmael's Interpretation

An Answer: Keep in mind that our verse says "Do not do thus to **Hashem, your G-d.**" Certainly the Jew has an evil inclination, as do all human beings. Therefore he may be tempted to steal, he may, in the throes of passion, murder, rape or commit incest. But if he already accepts the Temple as *his* G-d's Sanctuary ("*your* G-d") , why would he willfully tear it down? The verse could have simply said "Do not do thus to *Hashem*," without adding the words "*your* G-d." This is what is strange, in Rabbi Ishmael's opinion, about the second interpretation.

In order to avoid such an unreasonable interpretation, Rabbi Ishmael suggests a metaphoric approach, which he believes is more reasonable. That is, since the gentiles were driven out of the Land and their places of worship were destroyed because they worshiped idols and became debased, so the Jew must be extra careful not to fall into the same sinful ways. For if he does, G-d will have no more mercy on him than He did on the gentile. The Jew will also be evicted from the Land and his Temple will also be destroyed. (As unfortunately actually did transpire — twice!)

(See *Maskil L'Dovid*)

❖❖❖

Rashi cites evidence for the antiquity of the Oral Law Code.

Deut. 12: 21

כִּי־יִרְחַק מִמְּךָ הַמָּקוֹם אֲשֶׁר יִבְחַר הי׳ אֱלֹקֶיךָ לָשׂוּם שְׁמוֹ שָׁם וְזָבַחְתָּ
מִבְּקָרְךָ וּמִצֹּאנְךָ אֲשֶׁר נָתַן הי׳ לְךָ כַּאֲשֶׁר צִוִּיתִךָ וְאָכַלְתָּ בִּשְׁעָרֶיךָ
בְּכֹל אַוַּת נַפְשֶׁךָ.

> **וְזָבַחְתָּ וְגו׳ כַּאֲשֶׁר צִוִּיתִךָ:** לִמְּדָנוּ שֶׁיֵּשׁ צִוּוּי בִּזְבִיחָה הֵיאַךְ יִשְׁחוֹט
> וְהֵן הִלְכוֹת שְׁחִיטָה שֶׁנֶּאֶמְרוּ לְמֹשֶׁה בְּסִינַי.
> **And you shall slaughter etc. as I have commanded you**:
> *Rashi*: This teaches us that there is a command regarding
> slaughtering [animals to be eaten], how one should slaugh-
> ter, and these are the laws of slaughtering which were
> told to Moses at Sinai.

SOME BACKGROUND

The laws of *shechita*, ritual slaughter, are an important part of daily
Jewish living. The fact that meat must be prepared in a specifically kosher manner is something every traditional Jewish household is familiar
with. These laws are quite complex and precise. Yet, in spite of their
centrality in Jewish life, these laws are nowhere to be found in the Written Torah. Why something so basic to the Torah way of life should be
missing from the Torah, is answered in our verse.

WHAT IS RASHI SAYING?

Rashi bases his comment on the fact that this verse tells us that we are to
slaughter an animal "as I have commanded you." Since we do not find
such a commandment in the Torah, Rashi concludes that these laws were,
in fact, commanded to us. But, rather than being incorporated explicitly
into the Written Torah, they were given by G-d to Moses orally at Mount
Sinai.

THE SIGNIFICANCE OF THIS COMMENT

I have chosen this Rashi-comment, not because of any difficulty in interpretation, but rather because it teaches a very important concept about
the Oral Tradition of the Torah law. The *halachic* corpus in Judaism is
comprised of different levels of authority. There are the 613 mitzvos
that are taught to us in the Written Torah and explained in finer detail by
the Sages in the Talmud. These explanations, based on argumentation

and analysis, comprise a substantial part of what is called the Oral Law. It is assumed that the sources of these laws were also given to Moses at Sinai together with the Written Law. There are other laws that the Talmudic Sages themselves promulgated; they are of a lesser authority than the Written Law. Some examples of these: The laws of *muktza* on the Sabbath; taking the Four Species on *Sukkos* for the seven days of the holiday in the synagogue; and the writing of a marriage contract (*kesuba*).

There is yet another category of laws called הלכה למשה מסיני, "a law given to Moses at Sinai." These are laws that do not appear in the Written Torah nor are they laws decreed by the Sages. And while there is no hint of them in the Written Torah they, nevertheless, have the same authoritative level as the laws found in (or derived from) the Written Law. Rashi is telling us that the laws which regulate the slaughtering of animals belong to this latter category.

THE IMPLICATION OF RASHI'S COMMENT

The implications of Rashi's statement are quite significant from an historical and a theological perspective. What this means is that together with the Written Law, an accompanying codex of laws was received by Moses from G-d and imparted by him to the people at Sinai. It must be emphasized that these laws existed *at the time of Moses* (as is implied by our verse). They were not later accretions to the basic Sinai laws.

Thus when the Torah says "and you shall slaughter *as I have commanded*" this indicates clearly that we are not to slaughter the animal any way we see fit, but rather only "as I have commanded." Meaning, that G-d commanded Moses the laws of slaughtering animals, even though we find no hint of these laws in the Written Torah.

The whole question of the existence of a corpus of Oral Law, which accompanied the Written Law, is a matter of dispute between traditional Jewish philosophy and more modern interpretations of Judaism. Our verse offers validation for the belief that the Oral Law Tradition did indeed exist side-by-side, contemporaneously, with the laws found in the Written Torah.

This comment affords us a look at different interpretations of the Sages and of the Rishonim *as well.*

Deut. 12:23

רַק חֲזַק לְבִלְתִּי אֲכֹל הַדָּם כִּי הַדָּם הוּא הַנָּפֶשׁ וְלֹא תֹאכַל הַנֶּפֶשׁ עִם הַבָּשָׂר.

רק חזק לבלתי אכל הדם: ממה שנאמר יחזק' אתה למד שהיו שטופים בדם לאכלו לפיכך הוצרך לומר יחזק', דברי רבי יהודה. רבי שמעון בן עזאי אומר לא בא הכתוב אלא להזהירך וללמדך עד כמה אתה צריך להתחזק במצות אם הדם שהוא קל להשמר ממנו שאין אדם מתאוה לו, הוצרך לחזקך באזהרתו קל וחומר לשאר מצות.

Only be strong not to eat the blood: *Rashi:* From the fact that it says "be strong" you may learn that they had a predilection to blood, to eat it, therefore it was necessary to state "be strong!" This is the view of Rabbi Yehuda. Rabbi Shimon, son of Azai says the verse only comes to admonish and teach you the extent to which you must exercise will power with mitzvos. If blood, which is easily avoided, as a man has no craving for it, yet it is necessary to strengthen you in admonishing against it; then certainly this is so for the other mitzvos.

WHAT IS RASHI SAYING?

Rashi offers two opinions about the meaning of the word "be strong" in this verse. His starting point is the fact that it is strange to be told "be strong not to eat blood." As if we are ordinarily overwhelmed with an irresistible urge to be vampires!

Two diametrically opposed views are cited for understanding these words. Rabbi Yehuda's understanding is based on an historical perspective. He says: In those days, people did have this strange desire to drink blood; a desire, which to us today, seems quite vile and unnatural.

Rabbi Shimon differs and says, that if the Torah must strongly warn us against eating blood, an act for which man has a natural disgust, then we can learn a psychological lesson about the nature of man and his relationship to mitzvos. Once G-d commands us *not to* do something, we automatically feel a desire to do it. Maybe our all-too-human need to remain independent may even create within us the unnatural urge to eat blood. Thus, Rabbi Shimon derives the idea that if we have to be strongly urged not to eat blood, then how much more so do we need to be cautious when the Torah commands us to overcome desires which are natural, like stealing or prohibited sexual acts.

It is interesting to see how two Sages view these same words, which relate to human psychology, in two opposite ways.

RASHBAM AND BECHOR SHOR'S INTERPRETATION

A new interpretation to the meaning of "just be strong" has been offered by both the *Rashbam* and the *Bechor Shor*. They point out that while we are permitted to eat meat, yet we are prohibited from eating the blood contained within it. This creates a serious technical problem – how are we to separate the blood from the meat ? This undoubtedly requires us to be very stringent when it comes to "kashering" the meat. Much diligence is necessary for us to be sure that all the blood is drained from the meat, before we are able to use it for human consumption. This is what "be strong not to eat the blood" means — be strong and scrupulous to remove all the blood, even if it requires concerted effort on your part.

This is an interpretation that can be appreciated by housewives (in the "old days" when women "kashered" their meat at home). It understands חזק ("be strong") — not as a moral strength but rather as strength in determination in execution of the mitzvah.

RASHBAM & RASHI: INTERPRETIVE STYLES

The different approaches of Rashi as opposed to that of the *Rashbam* and *Bechor Shor* to this verse is characteristic of their different approaches to interpreting the Torah. Although *Rashi* proclaimed his interest in *p'shat* as opposed to the Sages' *drash*, yet he hasn't broken completely with their view of interpretation. He frequently relies on the Talmudic Sages' interpretations. In this respect, the *Rashbam* and *Bechor Shor* are much more independent of Talmudic influences in their approach to *p'shat*.

THE RAMBAN'S INTERPRETATION

It is appropriate to note that the *Ramban*, of the same period as the *Bechor Shor*, often strikes a middle ground between these two positions. He will often offer quite original *p'shat* interpretations, but he will also add the view of the Sages in interpreting a verse. When he does, he clearly designates which is *p'shat* and which is an interpretation of the Sages.

On our verse as well we see the *Ramban*'s characteristic approach. He cites the midrash of the Sages and then explains further the appropriateness of the word חזק in the prohibition to eat blood. He says:

> "It seems to me that "strength" was mentioned here due to the fact that in Egypt they had been attached to blood-rites. They had often offered sacrifices to the *Seirim* as it says (Leviticus 17:7)...and this rite included eating the blood. This has been discussed in the Rambam's Guide to the Perplexed."

See how the Ramban strikes a middle ground. He affirms the Sages' *midrash* that the people desired to eat the blood, but he explained this as part of the idol worship which they had "lusted" after.

Rashi, Rashbam and Bechor Shor and the Ramban, three views of *p'shat* by the early Torah commentators. They showed the way to the diversity possible in Torah interpretation.

Rashi chooses one drash *from among other possibilities.*

Deut. 12:28

שְׁמֹר וְשָׁמַעְתָּ אֵת כָּל־הַדְּבָרִים הָאֵלֶּה אֲשֶׁר אָנֹכִי מְצַוֶּךָ לְמַעַן יִיטַב לְךָ וּלְבָנֶיךָ אַחֲרֶיךָ עַד־עוֹלָם כִּי תַעֲשֶׂה הַטּוֹב וְהַיָּשָׁר בְּעֵינֵי ה' אֱלֹקֶיךָ.

הטּוֹב: בעיני השמים.

והישׁר: בעיני אדם.

The good: *Rashi*: [Behaviors that are proper] in the eyes of Heaven.
The right: *Rashi*: [Behaviors that are proper] in the eyes of man.

These two brief comments seem to have significance, but their meaning is not easily grasped.

What would you ask?

Your Question:

QUESTIONING RASHI

A Question: Why does Rashi align "the good" with G-d and "the right" with man? The opposite combination would seem to fit just as well. The good "in the eyes of man; the right "in the eyes of G-d."

A second question: In our verse *both* "the good and the right" are actions done "in the eyes of *Hashem,* your G-d." No mention is made of anything that refers to actions done "in the eyes of man"! Why does Rashi mention it?

Before you attempt an answer, let us look at Rashi's source.

RASHI'S *MIDRASHIC* SOURCE

It is only fair to give the student some background as to Rashi's source. This interpretation is found in the *midrash Sifrei* (the *midrash halacha* on Bamidbar and Devarim). Rashi's comment is Rabbi Akiba's view. Rabbi Ishmael argues with him and holds the opposite view. He says "The good, in the eyes of man. The right in the eyes of G-d." This is precisely what we suggested above, so it wasn't such an outlandish idea. Since this is a dispute between Rabbi Akiba and Rabbi Ishmael, we can understand why Rashi preferred Rabbi Akiba's opinion. There is a rule in the Talmud that in disputes between Rabbi Akiba and one other Sage, the decision goes according to Rabbi Akiba. But when more than one colleague argues with Rabbi Akiba, then the decision goes with majority. Rashi's choice follows this rule, because here Rabbi Akiba has only one opponent, Rabbi Ishmael.

But our question remains, only now it is directed to Rabbi Akiba. Why does *he* make the connection between "the good and G-d" and between "the right and man"?

Can you make sense of it?

YOUR ANSWER:

UNDERSTANDING RABBI AKIBA'S VIEW

An Answer: We could reason as follows: The Good has an objective and absolute sense to it. The human view of the Good is neither permanent nor absolute. If something seems good to us today, it may turn out to have bad consequences tomorrow. So one really needs a long perspective to determine if something is ultimately "good" or not. This absolute perception of the Good can only come from an eternal

Divine perspective. This is G-d's domain. Remember, it was G-d who made the judgements at Creation when the Torah says "and G-d saw that it was good." On the other hand, "the right" has a moral sense about it and morality is usually associated with actions between man and man.

This may be the thinking behind Rabbi Akiba's interpretation and its soundness may be another reason that Rashi chose it over Rabbi Ishmael's opinion.

In Defense of Rabbi Ishmael

In his defense, Rabbi Ishmael cites a previous verse (Deut. 12:25) which says:

...כִּי־תַעֲשֶׂה הַיָּשָׁר בְּעֵינֵי הי.

....when you do the *right in the eyes of Hashem*."

Here "the good" is not mentioned at all. It is "the right" that is unequivocally associated with "in the eyes of G-d." This is Rabbi Ishmael's opinion.

What can you say in defense of Rabbi Akiba?

Your Answer:

In Defense of Rabbi Akiba

An Answer: Rabbi Akiba could say: "Granted, when only "the right" is mentioned, as in this verse, then we are certainly referring to "actions before G-d." It is only when both "the good" and "the right" are juxtaposed in the same verse (as we have in our verse here) that we must make a choice and choose the best-fit association with either man or G-d. In such a case, Rabbi Akiba's choice still makes the best sense.

Our Second Question

But we asked another question above: Our verse only says "when you do the good and the right *in the eyes of Hashem*." No mention of "in the eyes of man." Why does Rashi (and Rabbis Akiba and Ishmael) mention it?

Your Answer:

An Answer to the Second Question _____

An Answer: Doing good "in the eyes of *Hashem*" includes both man's action between himself and G-d as well as his actions between man and man.

This is clearly spelled by Rabbi Chanina son of Dosa when he says (*Avos* 3:10):

כל שרוח הבריות נוחה הימנו רוח המקום נוחה הימנו, וכל **שאין** רוח הבריות נוחה הימנו אין רוח המקום נוחה הימנו.

"He who is pleasing to his fellow man, is also pleasing to G-d; and he who is not pleasing to his fellow man, is not pleasing to G-d."

So when our verse says on "in the eyes of *Hashem*" this necessarily includes both realms of man's behavior — between man and G-d and between man and man.

Keep this comment in mind for further investigation.

Deut. 15:3

אֶת־הַנָּכְרִי תִּגֹּשׂ וַאֲשֶׁר יִהְיֶה לְךָ אֶת אָחִיךָ תַּשְׁמֵט יָדֶךָ.

> **אֶת הנכרי תגש:** זו מצוה עשה.
> **You should demand payment from the stranger**: *Rashi:*
> This is a positive commandment.

Brief Background _____

This section deals with the laws of release of loans at the end of the Seventh year. All loans between Jews are to be nullified when the Seventh year ends, if they have not been repaid until then. Loans by Jews to Jews are to be released. Our verse says that loans to gentiles are not nullified.

Rashi seems to be saying that our verse teaches that claiming your debt from a non-Jew is one of the positive mitzvos of the Torah. This has puzzled the commentators.

For an understanding of this comment see our analysis further on to Deut. 23:21.

P'shat *and* Drash *and the need for both.*

Deut. 16:13

חַג הַסֻּכֹּת תַּעֲשֶׂה לְךָ שִׁבְעַת יָמִים בְּאָסְפְּךָ מִגָּרְנְךָ וּמִיִּקְבֶךָ.

> **בְּאָסְפְּךָ:** בזמן האסיף שאתה מכניס לבית פרות הקיץ. דבר אחר, באספך מגרנך ומיקבך למד שמסככין את הסכה בפסלת גורן ויקב.
>
> **When you gather in:** *Rashi*: At the time of the harvest when you bring the summer fruits into your house. Another interpretation, באספך מגרנך ויקבך [these words] teach that one should cover the *sukkah* with the twigs of the threshing floor and the wine-press.

Rashi offers two interpretations to this verse. Each has its own emphasis and its own focus within the verse.

What would you ask here?

YOUR QUESTION:

QUESTIONING RASHI

Several questions can be asked here.

1) Why does Rashi need to tell us the *p'shat*? Isn't that obvious from the verse itself?

   What's bothering him?

2) What is the basis for the *drash*? It must have some reasonable anchor in the verse.

3) Why does Rashi need to give two interpretations, *p'shat* (the first) and *drash* (the second) ?

WHAT IS BOTHERING RASHI?

An Answer: Taken at face value the verse says: "When you gather in your crops, then make the holiday of *Sukkos*." This is reasonable, since the holiday is an agricultural celebration. But what if there was a drought that year and you didn't harvest any crops? Or what if you're an accountant and you "harvest your crops" at tax season? In such circumstances, are we not supposed to celebrate the holiday of *Sukkos* in the Fall? A simple reading of this verse might lead us to think that, when a season does not have crops, we would not cel-ebrate *Sukkos* in the Fall. This incorrect implication is what Rashi is reacting to.

How does his *p'shat* interpretation explain matters?

YOUR ANSWER:

UNDERSTANDING RASHI

An Answer: In his first comment, the *p'shat* interpretation, Rashi takes the ב in the word באספך to designate "at the time of", i.e., the time of the harvest when fruits are *ordinarily* gathered in. Rashi's point is that the Fall (harvest) *season* of the year is essential to the celebration of *Sukkos,* not the actual harvesting activity. For if Rashi meant literally "when you bring the summer fruits into your house" he would not have prefaced those words with "*at the time* of the harvest."

Let us now examine the second part of Rashi's comment and its textual base.

THE TEXTUAL BASIS FOR THE *DRASH*

Let us look at our second question. What is the textual basis for this *drash*?

Can you see it?

Hint: Comparing our verse with other verses in the Torah about *Sukkos* will help.

Exodus 23:16

וְחַג הָאָסִף בְּצֵאת הַשָּׁנָה בְּאָסְפְּךָ אֶת־מַעֲשֶׂיךָ מִן הַשָּׂדֶה...

"...and the Festival of the Ingathering at the close of the year when you gather in your work from the field."

Leviticus 23:39

אַךְ בַּחֲמִשָּׁה עָשָׂר יוֹם לַחֹדֶשׁ הַשְּׁבִיעִי בְּאָסְפְּכֶם אֶת־תְּבוּאַת הָאָרֶץ תָּחֹגּוּ אֶת־חַג־ה' שִׁבְעַת יָמִים וְגוֹ'

"But on the fifteenth of the seventh month when you gather in the crops of the Land you shall celebrate *Hashem's* festival seven days " etc.

While the verses are not identical, all three mention the harvest. Both our verse and the one in Exodus mention באספך and the one in Leviticus says באספכם, in plural. But our verse has two points which differ from the other verses. Do you see them?

YOUR ANSWER:

A Closer Look

An Answer: Only our verse mentions *Sukkos* by name and only our verse is specific about the types of crops, when it says מגרנך ומיקבך, "from your threshing floor and from your winepress." Considering these two distinctive aspects of our verse, Rashi's deduction is easily made. Our verse mentions the *Sukkah* and mentions also the threshing floor and winepress, so we deduce that the *Sukkah* roof, the *s'khakh* (the most distinctive part of the *Sukkah*), is made from the remnants of the threshing floor and the winepress.

You will remember that in the *p'shat* interpretation the ב in the word באספך meant "at the time of." In the *drash* interpretation, the ב means "with" — "*with* your ingathering from the threshing floor and winepress" you are to make your *Sukkah*.

A comment which teaches us much about the Torah's subtle language.

Deut. 16:15

שִׁבְעַת יָמִים תָּחֹג לַה' אֱלֹקֶיךָ בַּמָּקוֹם אֲשֶׁר־יִבְחַר ה' כִּי יְבָרֶכְךָ ה' אֱלֹקֶיךָ בְּכֹל תְּבוּאָתְךָ וּבְכֹל מַעֲשֵׂה יָדֶיךָ וְהָיִיתָ אַךְ שָׂמֵחַ.

> והיית אך שמח: לפי פשוטו אין זה לשון צווי אלא לשון הבטחה, ולפי תלמודו למדו מכאן לרבות לילי יום טוב האחרון לשמחה.
>
> **And you will be only joyous**: *Rashi:* According to its Simple Meaning (פשוטו) this is not a command but rather a promise. And according to its Talmudic interpretation they learn from here that the last night of the Holiday is also included [in the command] to be joyous.

WHAT IS RASHI SAYING?

Rashi has *p'shat* and *drash* in this comment. Let us examine each in turn.

Rashi tells us that the correct *p'shat* meaning of the words והיית אך שמח is as a promise, not as a command. We needn't look for "What's bothering Rashi" here, because he tells us exactly what he wants us to know. He tells us we should exclude the possible, but incorrect, interpretation of commanding that we be joyous.

But, as we have pointed out before, whenever Rashi chooses one interpretation over another, we should always question him.

YOUR QUESTION:

QUESTIONING RASHI

A Question: How does Rashi know this is a promise and not a command?

Can you see what led him to this *p'shat*? In other words, how does Rashi know that והיית means "you *will be* joyous" and not "you *shall be* joyous"?

YOUR ANSWER:

UNDERSTANDING RASHI

An Answer: A search in a Biblical concordance or on a CD-ROM file will show that whenever G-d uses the word והיית in the Torah, it is always a promise and not a command. See the following examples:

When *Hashem* promises Abraham (Genesis 17:4):

וְהָיִיתָ לְאַב הֲמוֹן גּוֹיִם
"And you will be the father of a multitude of nations."

When *Hashem* speaks to Jacob (Genesis 28:3):

וְהָיִיתָ לִקְהַל עַמִּים
"And you will be a community of peoples."

And on the negative side, as well, we see the predictive use of the word והיית.

When *Hashem* speaks of the punishments that will follow those who do not uphold the Torah, He says (Deut. 28:37):

וְהָיִיתָ לְשַׁמָּה לְמָשָׁל וְלִשְׁנִינָה....

"And you will be an astonishment, a proverb and a by-word…"

And for a final example that clinches the proof that והיית is a prediction and not a command (Deut. 28:34):

וְהָיִיתָ מְשֻׁגָּע

"And you will be insane…"

Certainly it is not a mitzvah to be "*meshuga*"! It is a sad prediction of what will occur if we do not keep G-d's Torah.

A Deeper Look

But there is another fallacy with interpreting the word והיית here as a command.

How can we be *commanded* to be joyous? Joy is an emotion. An individual cannot be commanded to have an emotional feeling as he could be commanded to act in a certain way. Therefore Rashi says, this is not a command, rather it is a promise.

But can you ask a question on this latter point? Does the Torah, in fact, not command us to be joyful?

Hint: Look several verses above.

YOUR ANSWER:

An Answer: In verse 16:11 it says:

וְשָׂמַחְתָּ לִפְנֵי ה' אלקיך...

"And you shall rejoice before *Hashem* your G-d…"

Also verse 16:14:

וְשָׂמַחְתָּ בְּחַגֶּךָ...

"And you shall rejoice in your holiday…"

So we have two verses that do command us to be joyous.

Can you differentiate between them and our verse?

YOUR ANSWER:

A Deeper Understanding

An Answer: These two verses designate where we are to be joyous — ושמחת
לפני ה׳ ("before *Hashem*") — and when — ושמחת בחגך ("on your
holiday"). In this way these verses contain within them the behavioral prescription for producing this joy. "Before *Hashem*" means
in His Temple and His City, by partaking of the Holiday sacrifices.
Likewise, by designating "on your Holiday," the Torah tells us that
the joy is expressed in a behavioral way, not just as an internal,
phenomenological state.

Notice that the word והיית, "and you will be," is absent from these verses.
That word connotes a state of being — you *will be* happy, more so than
a state of doing. These verses say simply "and you shall rejoice." The
precision of the Torah's choice of words never fails to amaze.

So much for Rashi's *p'shat* interpretation. Let us now turn to the *drash*
and its difficulties.

"And According to its Talmudic Interpretation..."

In his second interpretation Rashi says: "according to its Talmudic interpretation, they learn from here that the last night of the Holiday is also
included [in the command] to be joyous."

What Talmudic question would you ask here?

Your Question:

Questioning Rashi

A Question: There is a Talmudic rule of Biblical linguistics which states:

כל אכין ורקין מיעוטים הן

"The words "but" and "only" (in the Torah) always exclude something."

So, how can our verse *include* the eighth day of the holiday to be joyous,
since it says,

וְהָיִיתָ אַךְ שָׂמֵחַ

"And you will be **'only'** joyous" ?

The word אך indicates we are to *exclude* something, not *include* something.

Can you think of an answer?

Your Answer:

Understanding the Drash

An Answer: To answer this conundrum we need the brilliance of the Gaon of Vilna's insights. He points out that even though the word אך always excludes, in our case it includes the last evening of the Holiday for joy. How so? Since each of the previous days of *Sukkos*, the Jew rejoiced with his *Esrog* and *Lulav* and by sitting in his *Sukkah*. But on the eighth day, these mitzvos were no longer relevant. The Jew therefore had *"only* to rejoice" — his joy was exclusively dependent on the Holiday and on no other artifacts. Thus, the word אך remains an exclusive term — it excludes all other mitzvos and *only* Joy remains — in its full, unadulterated splendor on the last night of the Holiday!

(See *D'var Eliyahu*)

Rashi leads us to some profound insights into the Torah's judicial system.

Deut. 16:19

לֹא־תַטֶּה מִשְׁפָּט לֹא תַכִּיר פָּנִים וְלֹא־תִקַּח שֹׁחַד כִּי הַשֹּׁחַד יְעַוֵּר עֵינֵי חֲכָמִים וִיסַלֵּף דִּבְרֵי צַדִּיקִם.

> וְלֹא תִקַּח שֹׁחַד: אפילו לשפוט צדק.
> **You shall not accept a bribe**: *Rashi*: Even in order to judge justly.

What would you ask here?

YOUR QUESTION:

QUESTIONING RASHI

A Question: Bribes are usually given to influence the judge to decide in a dis-honest way, to swing his verdict. If the person giving the bribe thought he was in the right and justice was on his side, he would have little need to bribe the judge. And if, in spite of this, he did give a bribe and the judge thought his case was just, why would this be considered "bribery"? And what is so wrong with it?

Why then does Rashi stipulate that the prohibition of bribery here refers even to the case where one "bribes" the judge to judge justly?

There are really two questions here:
1) What's bothering Rashi, that lead him to opt for an interpreta-tion different than simple *p'shat*?
2) Why is giving money — and accepting it — so that the judge will decide justly, considered a sin?

YOUR ANSWERS:

What Is Bothering Rashi?

Let us take each question separately.

An Answer to #1: The verse already says "Do not pervert judgement," which is the same as swinging a judgement in favor of the one who gave a bribe, if, in fact, he was not in the right. So, if we interpret "You shall not accept a bribe" to mean "don't take money in order to pervert the judgement" then we would have the same prohibition repeated twice in the same verse.

It is for this reason that Rashi interpreted these words in the unusual way he did.

Rashi's Interpretive Approach

Actually, Rashi is quite consistent in this regard. He sees each phrase in this verse as a different commandment. Look at his comment on another phrase in this verse:

לֹא תַכִּיר פָּנִים: אַף בשעת הטענות. אזהרה לדיין שלא יהי רך לזה וקשה לזה, אחד עומד ואחד יושב, לפי שכשרואה זה שהדיין מכבד את חברו מסתתמין טענותיו.

Do not show favoritism: *Rashi:* Not even during the deliberations. This is a warning to the judge that he should not be considerate with one and harsh with the other; making one stand and while the other sits, because when he (the defendant) sees that the judge defers to his fellow, his arguments are stifled (i.e. he is not at his best in defending himself).

Obviously, the simple meaning of "showing favoritism," is to decide the case in favor of the disputant that you favor, even though justice is not on his side. Yet, Rashi does not accept this as *p'shat.* We see here, as we did above, that Rashi searches for an interpretation that is not identical to "distorting judgement" (its obvious meaning), in order to avoid having the verse repeat the same prohibition, but in different words.

This, by the way, is a basic principle in Torah interpretation. There are no unnecessary repetitions in the Torah. Therefore, when the Torah appears to repeat itself unnecessarily, the commentators, frequently on the basis of the teachings of the Talmudic Sages, search for additional meanings. (For a fuller discussion, see my *Studying the Torah: A Guide to In-Depth Interpretation,* published by Jason Aronson.)

THE SECOND QUESTION: ACCEPTING MONEY TO JUDGE FAIRLY _____

Now let us return to our second question. What is wrong with accepting money to judge justly?

To accentuate the question, I would begin with the following apocryphal tale. A judge talked with two attorneys who were representing two feuding corporations. Turning to attorney A, he said "You have given me $50,000 to judge in your favor. But attorney B has given me $100,000 to judge in his favor. So, I think it only fair that you should give me an additional $50,000, so that I can judge this case on its merits and without bias!!"

This judge was accepting money to judge fairly. Can you fault him?

Hint: Think through logically what it means to decide to judge a case justly.

YOUR ANSWER:

UNDERSTANDING RASHI _____

An Answer: Let us think this through. Who gave this bribe? If it was one of the disputants, then what sense does it make to say that he gave it so the judge would "judge justly"? We would reasonably assume that even if he didn't give any bribe, the judge would also have judged justly. But now that he received money from one side, his chances of being objective and judging without bias are close to zero.

Another possibility is that the judge received money from a third party in order to judge the case justly. As is done today, judges are paid by the government or by some Rabbinical organization. But if such is the case, what is wrong with receiving money in this way? Is this a bribe in any sense of the term?

The Talmud deals with this question explicitly in Tractate *Kesubos* (105a). Pay close attention to their insightful analysis:

"Karna (a Babylonian Sage of the third century) used to take one *istra* from the innocent party and one *istra* from the guilty party. And then he informed them of his decision. But [the Talmud asks] does it not say 'you shall not accept a bribe'? Perhaps you will answer that the verse applies only where he does not take from both parties since he might be biased towards the party he received from, but Karna took from both parties and he would thus not be biased. But is even this permitted? Have we not learned: What

117 —

does the verse 'You shall not accept a bribe' refer to? Does it mean one should not acquit the guilty nor condemn the innocent? But the Torah already says 'You shall not distort judgement.' So this verse must refer even to a case where he proclaims the innocent to be innocent and the guilty to be guilty (Note: this is the basis for our Rashi comment). Therefore it says 'You shall not accept a bribe.' You may answer [the Talmud continues] that this only applies where the judge took the money as a bribe (before deciding the case) but Karna took the money as a fee (after deciding the case). But is even this permissible [to take money as a fee for serving as a judge]? Have we not learned that the legal decisions of one who takes a fee are null and void? [Answers the Talmud:] This applies only when one takes a fee for pronouncing judgement, while Karna was only taking compensation for loss of work."

The upshot of this passage is a startling and profound condition of the Jewish judicial process. That is, that a judge may not take payment even to perform faithfully the task of an honest judge. This means even if the payment comes from a third party or from both litigants. All he is entitled to is compensation for loss of work (income) that he could have earned, had he not been occupied judging this case.

This is what Rashi means when he says that the command "you shall not take a bribe" is intended even in cases where the judge is asked to judge fairly.

But what would you ask on this law?

YOUR QUESTION:

A Deeper Understanding of the Torah's Law

An Answer: Why should a salary for a judge, if it comes from the government or from a disinterested third party, be considered a "bribe"? This certainly sounds strange.

Can you think of an explanation for this strict rule?

YOUR ANSWER:

The Torah's Psychologically Profound Sensitivity to Justice

An Answer: This law shows us the profound psychological sensitivity of the Torah's judicial process. A judge is only human, after all. If he receives a comfortable salary for his work, he will be cautious to do the "right" and the "politically correct" thing in his legal pronouncements. His advancement within the system is dependent on how his superiors evaluate his work and the leanings of his judgements. Is he politically "Right" or "Left"? Do his decisions square with the legal outlook of his superiors? In such a case, his salary would have hidden strings attached. This would turn his salary into a "bribe" because his legal decisions would not be free of bias.

This is truly an amazing insight. The Talmud is replete with stories of Jewish judges who refused to accept cases because one of the litigants had some innocent, even commonplace, dealing with the judge(Talmud *Kesubbos* 105b). We learn from this Rashi-comment that a judge's bias can come from many quarters, not just from one of the disputants; he can be influenced to judge unfairly in order to keep his job. How then can a Jewish judge support himself, if he is not to take a salary? The Talmudic passage above makes it clear that he is entitled to receive the same salary that he could have earned in the free market doing any other work that he is actually capable of doing. When the judge earns no more money than he could earn otherwise, we can understand that he will feel no threat to his income if he judges a case fairly, even if it goes against the grain of those who pay his salary. If he is fired as a judge because of his judgements, he can always take on a job in his alternative vocation, with no loss in salary. He can truly be objective in judgement.

Such standards are hard to find even in today's enlightened, human-rights sensitive, secular courts. Truth to tell, even our own Jewish courts today could learn much from the morally sensitive standards set by our Sages' laws, as well as by their own personal behavior.

An Even Deeper Understanding _____

This insight helps us understand a question that has puzzled the Rashi-commentators. Rashi's very next comment seems to contradict our comment here. Rashi's next comment is:

כי השחד יעור: משקבל שחד ממנו אי אפשר שלא יטה את לבו
אצלו להפוך בזכותו.

Because the bribe blinds: *Rashi*: Once he accepts a bribe from him, it is impossible that his (i.e. the judge's) heart would not be inclined towards him to search for his merits (in this case).

The question asked is: If Rashi had previously said that our verse is speaking of a case when the judge is bribed to judge justly, then why should we fear that he would be inclined to search out the "briber's" merits. Has he not already stipulated that, in spite of the bribe, he will judge the case justly?

In light of our comment above, we can understand the psychological subtlety that is involved here. Let us take this analysis step by step. The judge has agreed to accept a bribe with the clear proviso that he would nevertheless judge the case justly. Our verse says "bribery blinds the eyes of the wise…" If the bribe was taken consciously and intentionally to decide in favor of the bribe giver, whether he is deserving or not, then there is no "blindness" here. The judge is doing this injustice with his eyes wide open. Therefore we have to interpret the verse as speaking of a case where the judge *becomes* "blind," that is, he does not see the truth and he is unaware that he is "blinded." Because, as we said, if he were aware of his distortion he wouldn't be considered to be "blind."

To answer our question: The judge may have "honestly" thought that he could maintain his objectivity and, in spite of receiving a bribe, he could offer a fair and unbiased decision. But as Rashi here points out, once he accepts the bribe, he is already on the way to becoming blinded. This transformation is natural and inevitable. Once the bribe has been accepted, its subjective influence on one's perception cannot be controlled. It's human nature.

(See *Nachlas Yaakov*)

We learn of Rashi's style in commentary.

Deut. 17:19,20

(19) וְהָיְתָה עִמּוֹ וְקָרָא בוֹ כָּל־יְמֵי חַיָּיו לְמַעַן יִלְמַד לְיִרְאָה אֶת־הֹ׳ אֱלֹקָיו לִשְׁמֹר אֶת־כָּל־דִּבְרֵי הַתּוֹרָה הַזֹּאת וְאֶת־הַחֻקִּים הָאֵלֶּה לַעֲשֹׂתָם.

(20) לְבִלְתִּי רוּם־לְבָבוֹ מֵאֶחָיו וּלְבִלְתִּי סוּר מִן הַמִּצְוָה יָמִין וּשְׂמֹאול לְמַעַן יַאֲרִיךְ יָמִים עַל־מַמְלַכְתּוֹ הוּא וּבָנָיו בְּקֶרֶב יִשְׂרָאֵל.

(19) (כֹּל) דִּבְרֵי הַתּוֹרָה: כְּמַשְׁמָעוֹ.

19) (All) The words of the Torah: *Rashi:* As its Literal Meaning.

As you look at this comment, what would you ask?

Your Question:

Questioning Rashi

A Question: If we are to understand the words in Rashi's *dibbur hamaschil*, "The words of the Torah" in its Literal Meaning, then why the need for him to comment at all?

Rashi's Style in Commentary

An Answer: When Rashi interprets a part of a verse *not to be understood* according to its Literal Meaning (as he does in the very next comment, see below), he will frequently emphasize that a nearby phrase *is to be understood* simply. That is what he has done here. We will now turn to his next comment to see how and why his does not accept a *p'shat* interpretation of it.

> **20)** ולבלתי סור מן המצוה: אפילו מצוה קלה של נביא.
> **20) And he does not stray from the commandments:**
> *Rashi:* Even an easy mitzvah from a prophet.

Your Question:

Questioning Rashi

A Question: On what basis does Rashi conclude that the mitzvah referred to here is "even an easy mitzvah of the prophets"? Maybe it is one of the 613 mitzvos of the Mosaic Torah.

    Hint: See our words on Rashi's style above.

Your Answer:

What Is Bothering Rashi?

An Answer: The previous verse had just said that "he should keep *all the words* of the Torah." If "*all the words* of the Torah" are already mentioned, what else could the words "turn aside from the mitzvah" allude to? This is what Rashi is relating to.

Understanding Rashi

We now understand why Rashi, above, interpreted the words *"the words of the Torah"* literally, while here he is forced to find a *midrashic*, interpretation of these words.

But it is curious that Rashi identifies this mitzvah as "an easy mitzvah from a prophet." This seems quite specific. Why does Rashi choose such a "mitzvah"? Why not, for example, a Rabbinical decree or a Law to Moses from Sinai? And if it must be from the prophets, why specifically "an easy mitzvah"? What does Rashi have in mind?

Hint: See a Rashi comment near by.

Your Answer:

The Reason for Rashi's Choice

An Answer: The very next Rashi-comment says:

> **So that the days [of his reign] will be prolonged:** *Rashi:*
> Implicit in the positive is the negative. (i.e. if he "strays
> from the mitzvah," his days *will not be prolonged*). We
> find this with Saul whom Samuel told "Wait seven days
> until I come to you, etc." to offer sacrifices. And it is
> written "He waited seven days but he did not keep his
> commitment to wait the entire day. He had hardly com-
> pleted sacrificing the offering when Samuel arrived and
> told him "You have been foolish! You have not heeded,
> etc. so now your reign will not endure." You learn from
> this, that because of an easily fulfilled mitzvah of a prophet
> he was punished.

The proof-text is an excellent one. Here we have "an easy mitzvah,"
namely, just to wait a full day and not jump the gun by offering the
sacrifice early, before Samuel arrived. And the consequence was just as
our verse (or the negative image of it) predicted "the days of his reign"
were shortened and not prolonged. Why? Because he failed to heed an
easy mitzvah of the prophet.

A subtle grammatical point leads to conflicting views.

Deut. 19:5

וַאֲשֶׁר יָבֹא אֶת־רֵעֵהוּ בַיַּעַר לַחְטֹב עֵצִים וְנִדְּחָה יָדוֹ בַגַּרְזֶן לִכְרֹת הָעֵץ וְנָשַׁל הַבַּרְזֶל מִן הָעֵץ וּמָצָא אֶת־רֵעֵהוּ וָמֵת הוּא יָנוּס אֶל־אַחַת הֶעָרִים־הָאֵלֶּה וָחָי.

> **וְנָשַׁל הַבַּרְזֶל מִן הָעֵץ:** יש מרבותינו אומרים נשמט הברזל מקתו ויש מהם אומרים שישל הברזל חתיכה מן העץ המתבקע והיא נתזה והרגה.
>
> **And the iron slips from the wood:** *Rashi*: Some of our Rabbis say that the iron (ax) flew off its handle; while there are those who say that the iron caused a splinter to fly off the wood being axed and it sprang off and killed.

WHAT IS RASHI SAYING?

Rashi here is just trying to give us the simple meaning of these words, which is by no means clear. We see that the Talmudic Rabbis have a dispute as to the basic meaning of these words. Looking at both interpretations, what would you ask?

YOUR QUESTION:

QUESTIONING RASHI

A Question: The word וְנָשַׁל (NOTE: with the Kamatz vowel) means "to fly off" while the word וְנִשֵּׁל (NOTE: With chirik vowel) means "to cause to fly off." How can the second opinion translate the word וְנָשַׁל as if it were written וְנִשֵּׁל? The verse says clearly וְנָשַׁל, which means "it flew off"?

This is a difficult question, knowledge of the Talmud on which this is based is necessary.

But you should ask the question in any event.

Your Answer:

UNDERSTANDING RASHI

Look closely at the two interpretations and see which words they disagree on.

List the words in dispute and the two different meanings they give to each word.

Here are the two opinions:

	First Opinion	**Second Opinion**
1) The word ונשל: Read וְנָשַׁל	Read וְנִשֵּׁל
	(intransitive verb)	(transitive verb)
Meaning:	It (the iron head) flew off	It caused to fly off
2) The word עץ		
Meaning:	the wood of the ax handle	the wood of the tree being axed

According to the first opinion, the iron ax head flew off its wooden handle and killed someone.

According to the second opinion, the iron ax head caused the wood of the tree to fly off and kill someone.

SUPPORT FOR EACH VIEW

What textual support could you bring for the first opinion?

Hint: Look closely at the words in the verse.

YOUR ANSWER:

SUPPORT FOR THE FIRST OPINION

An Answer: Did you notice that the verse begins with גרזן, "ax", and then proceeds to say "and the *iron* flew off." Why the switch in words? The change is significant because both words refer to the same object, both refer to the same ax head. Perhaps the change of wording was meant to emphasize the lethal potential of the *iron* and the damage it could cause. This would support the first view, which says it was the (iron) ax head that caused the death of the bystander.

Now can you find support for the second opinion?

Hint: Once again look closely at the verse and how it is translated.

YOUR ANSWER:

Support for the Second Opinion _____

An Answer: Did you notice that the word עץ is repeated twice in this verse? According to the first opinion this word has two different meanings within the same verse. First it means "tree" then it means "ax handle." This is inconsistent and potentially confusing. But according to the second opinion, the word עץ has the same meaning in both instances — it means the "tree" being cut. This is more consistent and in no way is it confusing. This may be the reasoning behind the second opinion. We should add that since the Torah is written without vowels, the word ונשל can actually be read in either way — either as וְנָשַׁל, meaning "it flew off," or as וְנִשֵּׁל, meaning "it caused to fly off" — as long as it makes sense with the rest of the verse.

❖❖❖

Introduction to the Laws of "Conspiring Witnesses" _____

In this section (Deut. 19:16-20) the Torah teaches us the laws regarding the "conspiring witnesses", עדים זוממים. This is a unique case where witnesses testify against another person and then other witnesses come and testify that they are lying. Ordinarily when two sets of witnesses offer conflicting testimony, the law is that the court discounts both groups of witnesses and the accused is let off, for lack of unequivocal testimony. However the case of "Conspiring Witnesses" is different. In this case the witnesses are accused of lying by other witnesses who claim that the accusing witnesses were with them at the time of the crime and therefore could not have been present at the scene when the alleged crime took place. These latter witnesses say nothing about the actual crime itself, whether it happened or not, just that the accusing witnesses could not have witnessed the alleged crime. In such a case the law is that the "Conspiring Witnesses" are not only discredited in court, but, in addition, are given the same punishment that they had intended the accused to receive. For example, if they say the accused had murdered someone, and then were found to be "Conspiring Witnesses," then they themselves are put to death by the court. This is quite unusual, since in the final analysis it is two witnesses against two witnesses. In the ordinary case of contradictory testimony we disqualify both groups, but punish neither. In this case we accept the honesty of one group over the other. This is what is called a גזירת הכתוב meaning "a decree of the Scripture." We accept the law as fiat, whether we understand it or not. We should add another point: In all cases of capital punishment, the witnesses whose testimony formed the basis for the guilty decision are the first to partici- pate in the execution of the guilty person's death — יד העדים תהיה בו בראשונה (Deut. 17:7).

This Rashi comment adds an unusual twist to the laws regarding the "Conspiring Witnesses."

Deut. 19:19

וַעֲשִׂיתֶם לוֹ כַּאֲשֶׁר זָמַם לַעֲשׂוֹת לְאָחִיו וּבִעַרְתָּ הָרָע מִקִּרְבֶּךָ.

> **כַּאֲשֶׁר זָמַם:** ולא כאשר עשה. מכאן אמרו 'הרגו, אין נהרגים.'
>
> **As he conspired [to do]:** *Rashi:* But not as he actually did. From here they (the Sages) say: "If they (the court) already killed him (the falsely accused), then they (the witnesses) are not killed."

WHAT IS RASHI SAYING?

Rashi (on the basis of the Talmud in *Makkos* 5b) teaches us a strange, paradoxical law. The "Conspiring Witnesses" may be put to death if, and only if, the court had not yet put the falsely accused one to death. If, on the other hand, the falsely accused person had already been executed by the court, then these Conspiring Witnesses would get off free. Strange, to say the least.

YOUR QUESTION:

QUESTIONING RASHI

A Question: What logic is there in such a paradoxical law? If the witnesses succeed in getting the accused executed by the court, then they *are not* to be punished. However, if they are not yet successful, (i.e. the accused has not yet been put to death) then they *are* punished!

Can you see what in the verse lead Rashi to such a conclusion?

YOUR ANSWER:

WHAT IS BOTHERING RASHI? _____

An Answer: The verse says clearly "Do to him as he had *conspired to do* to his brother…" He is to be punished for conspiring, not for doing. For if he had succeeded in bringing the falsely accused person to execution, then the verse should have said "Do unto him as he caused to be done to his brother." That is, execute him as he had caused the execution of his brother. But this is not what the verse says; it speaks only of conspiring but not of implementing.

How does Rashi's comment deal with this?

YOUR ANSWER:

UNDERSTANDING RASHI _____

An Answer: This is exactly what Rashi says "But not as *he did*" meaning the verse does not say "as he did," so he is only punished if he conspired to do, but did not actually do, his wicked plan.

Granted, this is what the verse implies, but what would you ask about this law?

YOUR QUESTION:

QUESTIONING THE LAW _____

A Question: If a man is punished for only planning to cause a man's execution, then he should certainly be punished for planning *and succeeding* at getting an innocent man executed. Why does the Torah allow such a man to go free?

Many commentaries have struggled with this question, so don't be surprised if it stumps you, but give it a try.

Hint: Read through our introduction and keep in mind the disturbing reality, that the validity of all testimony is ultimately uncertain.

YOUR ANSWER:

Understanding the Law

An Answer: Several answers have been suggested to this question.

> The Ramban offers a somewhat mystical answer. He says that since G-d is present in all court proceedings conducted according to Torah law, then if the court's decision was actually implemented, this itself is evidence that it was right. Since G-d would not allow His Name to be defiled by having one of His courts kill an innocent man.
>
> Another answer given: The laws regarding accepting witnesses' testimony as valid is always a matter of judgement. The judges always interrogate the witnesses to see if their words are both honest and accurate (see verse 19:18). The decision to accept or reject their testimony depends on a sensitive weighing of the evidence. The Jewish judge never approaches these decisions as either/or issues, in black or white terms. Here too, in our case of Conspiring Witnesses, the judges remain sensitive to any indication which would support or detract from the veracity of the witnesses.

In light of the ambiguity inherent in ferreting out the truth in any legal case, the Torah commentary, *haKesav V'haKabbalah,* points out several aspects of the situation of Conspiring Witnesses which sets it apart from other cases of contradictory testimonies. First of all, he says, we must remember that the second set of witnesses claims that the first, accusing, set were (for example) in Los Angeles with them at the time the alleged crime took place in New York City and therefore they couldn't possibly have witnessed the crime. Now, says *haKesav V'haKabbalah,* it certainly takes a lot of guts to make such a claim. For if they were lying, it would be quite easy for the first set of witnesses to obtain people to attest to the fact that they were, in fact, in New York on the day of the crime. So the second set would be taking a big risk if their own testimony were not true because it could be so easily disproved.

He offers another brilliant insight. If the accused man was actually put to death, this means that those Conspiring Witnesses stood there and "threw the first rock" in his execution, for the Torah requires that "the hand of the witnesses shall be against him first." In light of this, the Sages may have concluded that if these witnesses had the emotional fortitude not only to testify falsely (risking being caught for perjury) but also to personally participate in the execution of this man, then maybe they deserve our trust. Therefore if, and only if, the accused was killed, do we not kill the Conspiring Witnesses, because their testimony has gained another ounce of validity by their having personally participated in the accused's death.

SURPRISING EVIDENCE FOR THE UNUSUAL LAW OF CONSPIRING WITNESSES

The *haKesav V'haKabbalah* doesn't rest with that. He points out other subtle and surprising support for the idea that only if the witnesses did not cause the death of the accused, are they put to death.

Notice that our section ends with the following words (19:20):

וְהַנִּשְׁאָרִים יִשְׁמְעוּ וְיִרָאוּ וְלֹא־יֹסִפוּ לַעֲשׂוֹת עוֹד כַּדָּבָר הָרָע הַזֶּה בְּקִרְבֶּךָ.

"And those who remain *shall hear and fear and will not again commit any such evil thing among you.*"

This formula "they will hear and they will fear" is repeated several times in the Torah.

In the case of the Rebellious Elder זקן ממרא who decides an *halachic* question against the opinion of the Great Sanhedrin. When describing his punishment the Torah says (Deut. 17:13):

וְכָל־הָעָם יִשְׁמְעוּ וְיִרָאוּ וְלֹא יְזִידוּן עוֹד.

"And all the people *will hear and fear and they will not act presumptuously any more.*"

And likewise in the case of the Prodigal Son, who rebels against his parents' teachings, who is a glutton and a drunkard. The Sages point out that although the young child (legally a minor) has not committed a crime which is punishable by death, he nevertheless is punished by stoning to death. In this case as well, the Torah ends with the formula we have seen in the previous cases (21:21):

וּרְגָמֻהוּ כָּל־אַנְשֵׁי עִירוֹ בָאֲבָנִים וָמֵת וּבִעַרְתָּ הָרָע מִקִּרְבֶּךָ וְכָל־ יִשְׂרָאֵל יִשְׁמְעוּ וְיִרָאוּ.

"And all the men of the city shall stone him with stones and he shall die; and you shall remove the evil from your midst and *all Israel shall hear and they shall fear.*"

Do you see any similarity between these three cases? And why they are the only capital punishment cases that have the formula phrase "and they will hear and they will fear"?

Hint: Think!

YOUR ANSWER:

THE TORAH'S SUBTLE MESSAGE

An Answer: These words, which say that the punishment is to serve as a lesson and a warning to the people, are only used when the punishment "does *not fit* the crime," so to speak. Only when the punishment is given as a *preventative* measure and not exclusively as a *punitive* measure directed at the sinner. Neither the Prodigal Son nor the Rebellious Elder has committed a capital-punishment crime. The Prodigal Son, being a minor, is even under punishable age. So the punishment is actually intended to send a message to the community, more than to punish the sinner. In all other capital crimes in the Torah, the Torah prescribes death as the punishment, but does not say "and the people shall hear and shall fear." This is because that is not the main reason this man is being punished. In the other cases, he is punished since he deserved punishment because of his criminal act.

Here, in the case of the Conspiring Witnesses the *"Israel shall hear and they shall fear"* formula is also used, indicating that they have committed an act that demands punishment in order to instill fear in the community more than to punish them for the actual crime they committed (remember, the Conspiring Witnesses had not yet succeeded in having the accused killed by the court). If, on the other hand, they had succeeded in having him executed, this formula phrase would not be appropriate. Instilling fear in the community regarding the matter of Conspiring Witnesses makes much sense, because if people will readily perjure themselves in court, the whole judicial system collapses. Certainly this is a central issue; it is the bedrock for upholding the righteousness of the community as a whole.

The exclusive use of this phrase in the Torah again affords us the opportunity to witness (not as conspiring witnesses, but as inspiring witnesses!) the Torah's subtle and precise use of language.

(See *haKesav V'haKabbalah*)

Much can be learned from an arcane ceremony.

Deut. 21:7,8

7) וְעָנוּ וְאָמְרוּ יָדֵינוּ לֹא שפכה (שָׁפְכוּ) אֶת הַדָּם הַזֶּה וְעֵינֵינוּ לֹא רָאוּ.

8) כַּפֵּר לְעַמְּךָ יִשְׂרָאֵל אֲשֶׁר־פָּדִיתָ הי וְאַל תִּתֵּן דָּם נָקִי בְּקֶרֶב עַמְּךָ יִשְׂרָאֵל וְנִכַּפֵּר לָהֶם הַדָּם.

> **ידינו לֹא שפכה:** וכי עלתה על לב שזקני בית דין שופכי דם הם, אלא לא ראינוהו ופטרנוהו בלא מזונות ובלא לויה. הכוהנים אומרים **כפר לעמך ישראל** וגו'
>
> **Our hands have not shed** : *Rashi:* Is it possible to imagine that that the Elders of the court committed murder? Rather, "We did not observe him and dismiss him, without food and without escort." The Priests say: **Forgive your people Israel**, etc.

WHAT IS RASHI SAYING?

What is bothering Rashi is clear, he begins his comment with the question. Why should the Elders of the City need to absolve themselves of this murder? They are not the accused party. Therefore, Rashi reinterprets these words to mean 'We, the Elders, have not neglected this stranger, letting him off without food or letting him leave without accompanying him." The implication is that since we took good care of him when he visited our city, his unfortunate demise cannot, even indirectly, be attributed to us.

We should point out that Rashi mentions two points in the Elders' statement. First, that they didn't see him and second, that they didn't let him go without food. The meaning is that had they seen him they would have provided him with food and escort. It should be noted that the two parts of this statement are parallel to the two parts in the Torah verse. The Torah's words "Our hands did not shed this blood" are paralleled in Rashi by "we did not dismiss him without food and escort." And the Torah's words "Our eyes did not see" are paralleled in Rashi by "We did not see him."

Looking at this comment, do you have a question?

YOUR QUESTION:

131 —

Questioning Rashi

A Question: It is understandable that had the victim been escorted, his murder might have been prevented. But what does going without food have to do with being murdered? If he had had food, would that have prevented his murder?

YOUR ANSWER:

Understanding Rashi

An Answer: Rashi himself, in his Talmud commentary on *Sota* 45b, says that being without food led the man to attack others to obtain food. His aggressive and illegal behavior may have brought him into physical confrontation, which then resulted in his being murdered. Had he been given food by the city people, he never would have gotten into trouble. And this is the significance of the Elders' denial "we did not dismiss him without food."

   But we can ask another question, regarding the last words in this Rashi-comment:

YOUR QUESTION:

The Priests say: Forgive your people Israel, etc.

A Question: Why does Rashi add these words? Actually these are the Torah's words. Why does the Torah add them? After the Elders have claimed total innocence, of either directly or indirectly, being party to this man's death, why is there any need for atonement? Atonement means a sin has been atoned for? What sin?

YOUR ANSWER:

Understanding the Torah's Words

An Answer: There is a *corpus delicti*, the murdered body is lying in front of us. So a murder was committed. There's no denying that. The Elders of the city have proclaimed their innocence; as leaders of the community they acted responsibly. But nevertheless, someone did commit a murder. It is for this crime that the Priests have to request atonement from G-d.

EGLAH ARUFA: A MITZVAH WITH MEANING

The *Eglah Arufa* ceremony is quite strange. A young calf is taken to a stony valley that has never produced crops. There it is killed by breaking its neck and the Elders and Priests make their public declarations. There is much symbolism here (see Rashi on 21:4). But can the ceremony as a whole be rationalized?

The Abarbanel explains that this public ceremony, with it dramatic center piece of breaking the calf's neck followed by short public statements by community leaders is meant to awaken people's attention and cause public outrage to this humanly caused tragedy. Modern society knows only too well, how inured we can become to even the most shattering obscenities, if they happen often enough. We are aware how the crime-filled newspapers that we read daily, contribute to our growing insensitivity and to our moral paralysis. As has been said about the Holocaust, one death is a tragedy, six million is a statistic. The Torah, aware of the human inclination towards habituation, created the shocking *Eglah Arufah* ceremony to shake us and shock us out of our moral slumber. So that we don't conduct business as usual when a human being's life has been snuffed out through violence.

(see *Abarbanel*)

פרשת כי תצא

A psychological principle at work in the mitzvos

Deut. 21:11

וְרָאִיתָ בַּשִּׁבְיָה אֵשֶׁת יְפַת־תֹּאַר וְחָשַׁקְתָּ בָהּ וְלָקַחְתָּ לְךָ לְאִשָּׁה.

> **ולקחת לך לאשה:** לא דברה תורה אלא כנגד יצר הרע שאם אין
> הקב"ה מתירה, ישאנה באיסור אבל אם נשאה סופו להיות
> שונאה שנאמר אחריו כי תהיין לאיש וגו' וסופו להוליד ממנה
> בן סורר ומורה. לכך נסמכו פרשיות הללו.
>
> **And you will take her for a wife:** *Rashi:* The Torah
> speaks only in deference to the evil inclination. For if the
> Holy One blessed be He, would not permit her, he would
> live with her illicitly. However if he does marry her he
> will ultimately hate her, as it says later on "if a man has
> [two wives] etc." And in the end he will father from her a
> wayward and rebellious son. That is why these chapters
> are joined to one another.

WHAT IS RASHI SAYING?

Rashi gives us the psychological underpinnings of this unusual law. He
seems to say that the Torah allows the soldier in battle to marry a gentile
woman (who may also be a married woman; see Rashi 21:11) which
under ordinary circumstances is forbidden. In this case it is permitted
because, Rashi explains, if the Torah would prohibit the union, the man
might go ahead and marry her anyway.

The question here should be obvious.

What would you ask on the comment?

YOUR QUESTION:

QUESTIONING RASHI

A Question: How can we understand such logic? If the Torah permitted other prohibitions because they were difficult for a person to keep, we would have no Torah. We would have the *Ten Suggestions* and not the *Ten Commandments*! This would seem to put the Torah in the category of "Relative Ethics." G-d's contract with His people Israel given to them at Sinai is certainly not a relative contract. What does Rashi mean here?

Hint: What does the term כנגד יצר הרע ("in deference to the evil inclination") mean? The words are literally translated "against the evil inclination."

YOUR ANSWER:

THE *BECHOR SHOR* EXPLAINS RASHI

An Answer: An insightful, psychological answer is suggested by *Rabbi Joseph Bechor Shor*. The Torah does in fact speak to the evil inclination; it speaks to it in order to outwit it. By permitting the soldier to take the beautiful captive home and eventually allow him to marry her, his burning desire will be cooled down. This is accomplished by what the Talmud calls פת בסלו, "bread in one's basket." This is a psychological concept which means that if a person goes on a trip, for example, and takes no food with him, he will soon feel hunger pangs. If however, he takes a few sandwiches in his basket, he may make the whole trip without even touching his provisions. Psychologically, knowing that you have what you need makes you not need what you have. So too in our case, knowing that he can eventually take this beautiful woman home and take her legally as his wife, causes his evil inclination to cool down and thus enables him to control it. We see that the Torah has indeed spoken "*against* the evil inclination." The same idea is expressed in Proverbs (9:17) when it says "Stolen water is sweet." Although water ordinarily has no taste, but if it is stolen, that itself gives it a sweet taste! The woman gains attractiveness by the mere fact that she is forbidden to the soldier. Once she is no longer forbidden, her attractiveness loses much of its attraction.

This is a worldly-wise understanding and shows how psychologically attuned the Torah's laws are.

(See *Moshav Zekeinim*)

P'shat *and* Drash *are both necessary*

Deut. 22:1

לֹא־תִרְאֶה אֶת־שׁוֹר אָחִיךָ אוֹ אֶת־שֵׂיוֹ נִדָּחִים וְהִתְעַלַּמְתָּ מֵהֶם הָשֵׁב תְּשִׁיבֵם לְאָחִיךָ.

> **לֹא תִרְאֶה ... וְהִתְעַלַּמְתָּ:** לא תראה אותו שתתעלם ממנו. זהו פשוטו, ורבותינו אמרו פעמים שאתה מתעלם (כגון זקן ואינו לפי כבודו או כהן והוא בבית הקברות) וכו'.
>
> **You may not see…and you will hide yourself:** *Rashi:* You shall not see it so that you will hide yourself from it. This is its Plain Sense. Our Rabbis however said that there are times when you may hide yourself from it. (For example, an elderly person and it is not befitting his honor [to deal with the animal], or a priest in a cemetery [where he is forbidden to enter]).

A Clarification: The word והתעלמת has been translated in most *Chumashim* as "you will hide yourself." This is done because the Hebrew word is in the reflexive construct. But in English this is a bit clumsy. The simple meaning is "you will ignore."

What would you ask on this comment?

YOUR QUESTION:

QUESTIONING RASHI

A Question: Rashi gives us *p'shat* and *drash* interpretations on this verse. What is the need of two interpretations?

What's bothering him?

YOUR ANSWER:

WHAT IS BOTHERING RASHI?

An Answer: The verse seems to say contradictory things. First it seems to say: "You shall not see the ox of your brother or his sheep wandering; you should ignore it." Then it concludes "You shall surely return them to him." If you ignore the lost animal, how will you return it? This is what is troubling Rashi.

How does Rashi deal with this?

Your Answer:

UNDERSTANDING RASHI'S *P'SHAT* INTERPRETATION

An Answer: Rashi resolves the contradiction, on a *p'shat* level, by making a slight change in the verse. He accomplishes this by changing one letter. Look carefully.

Which letter does he change?

An Answer: Rashi changes the ו "and" in והתעלמת to a ש in שתתעלם which now means "so that." It now reads "you shall not see.... **so that** you will ignore." Rashi has dealt with an apparent contradiction by making this slight change in wording. In this way he has clarified the actual intent of the verse. To understand what logical steps are involved here we must remember that you cannot ignore someone or something without first noticing it. Paradoxically, ignoring always implies first seeing and only then ignoring. With this in mind, we can understand Rashi's new reading of the verse. "Do not (first) see your brother's ox or his sheep wandering so that (then) you will ignore it, rather return it to him."

If such a slight change remedies matters and explains the verse's meaning, why the need for a *drash* interpretation?

Can you see why a *drash* is needed?

YOUR ANSWER:

UNDERSTANDING THE NEED FOR *DRASH*

An Answer: The *drash* takes the word והתעלמת — "and you shall ignore" — at its face value. The word literally means "*and* you shall ignore it," and not, "*so that* you will ignore it" as the *p'shat* has it. If the Torah wanted to tell us not to ignore the lost article, it could have simply said "you are not allowed to ignore it" as it does in verse 3. But by putting it in the positive term והתעלמת the *drash* has a foothold in the verse.

The *drash* separates the two clauses — "Don't see" from "and you shall ignore." And in order to understand the phrase "and you shall ignore," the Sages sought a situation where one would be required not to retrieve the lost animal. The cases cited in the parentheses are ones where a law-abiding Jew (Priest or Elder) is not allowed to retrieve the animal. Nevertheless this remains *drash,* because the simple meaning of the verse is to require the Jew to return the animal and "not ignore it."

Notice how the *drash* interpretation takes the word והתעלמת at its literal meaning, while *p'shat* strays, somewhat, from the simplest meaning of this word, by turning it into "so that you will ignore." This illustrates that *p'shat* and literal translation are not always identical, while *drash* may be based on the literal meaning even more so than the *p'shat.*

DRASH AND HALACHA

It is important to realize the significance of *drash* interpretations. One type of *drash* is called *midrash halacha,* which teaches laws, and our verse is an example of this type of *drash.* Even though this is not *p'shat,* nevertheless, it is the guiding law for the Jew. *P'shat* and *drash* do not contradict each other, they complement each other.

A sensitive reading of the Torah's words teaches us a new law.

Deut. 22:2

וְאִם־לֹא קָרוֹב אָחִיךָ אֵלֶיךָ וְלֹא יְדַעְתּוֹ וַאֲסַפְתּוֹ אֶל תּוֹךְ בֵּיתֶךָ וְהָיָה עִמְּךָ עַד דְּרשׁ אָחִיךָ אֹתוֹ וַהֲשֵׁבֹתוֹ לוֹ.

עד דרש אחיך: וכי תעלה על דעתך שיתנהו לו קודם שידרשהו? אלא דרשהו שלא יהא רמאי.

Until your brother seeks : *Rashi:* And could imagine returning it to him *before* he seeks it? But, rather [it means], inquire after him lest he be a swindler.

Do you see what's bothering Rashi? He asks the question himself.

What is it?

YOUR ANSWER:

WHAT IS BOTHERING RASHI?

An Answer: The verse says, in effect: When you find a lost article, hold on to it until its owner comes looking for it; then return it to him. But of course! Could you possibly return it to him *before* he comes looking for it? Remember, the beginning of the verse says "you don't know him" — you don't know to whom this lost animal belongs, so how could you possibly return it to him, unless he shows up to claim it?

The verse could have simply said: When you find, etc., then return it to your brother.

So Rashi is asking: What could the additional words "Until you brother seeks" possibly mean? How does Rashi's comment deal with this question?

YOUR ANSWER:

UNDERSTANDING RASHI

An Answer: Rashi changes the whole sense of these words. We originally understood the phrase "until your brother seeks it" that the words "your brother" are the subject while "it" is the object of the phrase. Who is doing the seeking? Answer: "Your brother." What is he seeking? Answer: "it" (the lost animal).

Rashi changes all this. Now "your brother" is the object, and "you" is the subject. Who is doing the seeking? "You." What are you seeking (that is: what are you investigating)? "your brother." You have to investigate this man — your brother — who comes to claim the lost animal. Maybe the lost article is not his and he is falsely claiming it. Maybe he's a crook. How can you determine this? By "seeking him out," by investigating him.

How would you do that? By simply asking him to give some evidence that this animal is his. Does it have any distinguishing signs? If he can identify the article in a way that indicates that only an owner would know these signs, then it should be returned to him.

The Hebrew words עד דרש אחיך אתו are translated as if it said עד דרש אחיך – אותו, "Until you investigate him (who?) your brother."

(See *Mizrachi*)

THE *BECHOR SHOR* LEARNS *P'SHAT*

The *Bechor Shor*, always in search of the most straightforward interpretation, offers a *p'shat* understanding of the words עד דרש אחיך which bothered Rashi. He says the meaning is: Until your brother seeks you —

but you are under no obligation to seek him. This means, the finder need not make a special effort to locate the one who lost this article. All he must do is keep it until his brother — the owner — finds it — the lost article.

We see how "a verse never loses it *p'shat* meaning," in spite of the instructive *drash* associated with it. Perhaps Rashi preferred the *drash* because of its practical lesson in living.

THE LESSON

Rashi's comment derives directly from the *midrash* and the Talmud (*Baba Metzia* 28b). It is instructive to see how the Sages have taken an innocent phrase and turned it into an *halachic* stipulation which is to guide us to wisely and responsibly fulfill our obligation when returning a lost article to its owner. This is just one of many examples in the Torah which illustrates how the Oral Law, anchored in the Written Law, expands and elucidates the latter. Rashi's next comment is an even more striking example of this.

Righteous and wise laws are derived from an implied message.

Deut. 22:2 (same verse as above)

וְאִם־לֹא קָרוֹב אָחִיךָ אֵלֶיךָ וְלֹא יְדַעְתּוֹ וַאֲסַפְתּוֹ אֶל תּוֹךְ בֵּיתֶךָ וְהָיָה עִמְּךָ עַד דְּרֹשׁ אָחִיךָ אֹתוֹ וַהֲשֵׁבֹתוֹ לוֹ.

> **וַהֲשֵׁבֹתוֹ לוֹ:** שֶׁתְּהֵא בּוֹ הֲשָׁבָה. שֶׁלֹּא יֹאכַל בְּבֵיתְךָ כְּדֵי דָמָיו וְתִתְבָּעֵם מִמֶּנּוּ. מִכָּאן אָמְרוּ כָּל דָּבָר שֶׁעוֹשֶׂה וְאוֹכֵל יַעֲשֶׂה וְיֹאכַל, וְשֶׁאֵינוֹ עוֹשֶׂה וְאוֹכֵל יִמָּכֵר.
>
> **And you shall return it to him**: *Rashi:* So that there is a [real] returning (restoration). The [animal] should not eat in your house the worth of its own value. And you would then claim this [from the owner]. From here [the Sages] derived the principle: Anything that works and requires food (like an ox) should work and eat. Whatever does not work but requires food (like a sheep) should be sold (and that money returned to the owner).

RASHI SHOWS US THE SPIRIT OF THE LAW

Rashi is telling us to understand the spirit, and not just the words, of the law. When a person loses something and someone finds it and returns it to him, he has done the owner a great service. The man's loss was retrieved. However, if a man finds a sheep and keeps it until its owner seeks it out, this could take weeks, maybe months, before its owner claims it. During all that time the finder must feed the sheep and keep it healthy, otherwise what kind of *chesed* is it to return an emaciated, sickly sheep to its owner? But feeding the animal costs money. Should the finder pay for this out of his own pocket? No, Torah law does not require this of a person. To demand such expenditures from a person would probably discourage most people from "getting involved," and they would pass by a lost article, which they saw on the way. So the Sages gave the following advice. If the animal can do work, like an ox, put it to work, until the owner comes; that would more than cover its eating expenses. But if the animal is one that cannot do work, like a sheep, then in order to "return it" to its owner, you had best sell the sheep (the money received from the sale doesn't cost anything to hold), and give that money to the owner when he comes.

This is brilliant advice. This gets at the spirit of the law, which is to help a person retrieve his loss, without causing him other losses in the process.

An example of how serious the Sages took the mitzvah of returning the value of the lost article and not just the article itself, is the following incident (recorded in the Talmud, *Taanis* 25a).

> "It happened that someone passed the home of Rabbi Chanina the son of Dosa, and left there chickens. His wife found them and Rabbi Chanina said to her 'Don't eat their eggs.' The eggs increased and they sold them and with the money bought sheep. Later the man who had forgotten his chickens passed by Rabbi Chanina's home and said to his friend 'It is here that I forgot my chickens.' Rabbi Chanina overheard this and said to him 'Do you have identification that the chickens are yours?' He gave him a sign and Rabbi Chanina 'returned' to him 'his' sheep!"

We see that the Sages' dedication to living by the spirit of the Torah is no less than their wisdom in interpreting it.

A drash *based on close analysis of the Torah's words.*

Deut. 22:15

וְלָקַח אֲבִי הַנַּעֲרָה וְאִמָּהּ וְהוֹצִיאוּ אֶת־בְּתוּלֵי הַנַּעֲרָה אֶל־זִקְנֵי הָעִיר הַשָּׁעְרָה.

> **אבי הנערה ואמה:** מי שגדלו גדולים הרעים יתבזו עליה.
> **The father of the girl and her mother:** *Rashi:* Those who nurtured this evil plant must suffer the humiliation over her.

Background To the Defamation of a Married Woman

The case described here concerns a young woman who immediately after her wedding night is accused by her husband of not having been a virgin on the wedding night, as had been assumed. The woman's parents protest and deny the accusation. They offer proof that their daughter was, in fact, a virgin. If their evidence is upheld in court their daughter is acquitted. The slanderous husband is fined for spreading malicious rumors about a daughter of Israel and must remain married to this woman, unless she wants out. If, on the other hand, the husband can prove to the court that his accusation is correct, that is, that the woman had relations with a man after their *kiddushin* (betrothal), then the woman is given the death penalty. This is punishment for having had a sexual relationship with a man after she was betrothed, which is equivalent to actual marriage in Jewish law.

Before we investigate any deeper questions, let us understand why Rashi concludes that our verse implies the public embarrassment of the parents. What in our verse led him to that conclusion?

Can you answer?

Hint: Compare our verse with verses 16,19 and 21.

YOUR ANSWER:

What Is Bothering Rashi?

An Answer: The father, not the mother, is the person who gives his daughter over in marriage. The father is the parent who is mentioned in this chapter, not the mother. See verses 16, 19 and 21 where only the father is mentioned. Our verse is the only one where the father *and mother* are both mentioned. It seems inappropriate.

This is what Rashi is reacting to.

How does his interpretation deal with this?

YOUR ANSWER:

UNDERSTANDING RASHI

An Answer: The fact that *both* parents of the young woman are mentioned, that *both* are involved in defending their daughter, alerts our antennas. Why would both be mentioned when only the father is the legal guardian of the young woman? Therefore, Rashi points out that *both* parents, of necessity, suffer embarrassment in their need to publicly defend their daughter against such a shameful accusation.

What would you ask about this matter of parental embarrassment?

YOUR QUESTION:

QUESTIONING RASHI

A Question: The young woman has not yet been proven guilty. She may very well be innocent. Why then does Rashi say that the parents must suffer the embarrassment of a wayward daughter?

YOUR ANSWER:

UNDERSTANDING RASHI

An Answer: She may very well be innocent. But as the saying goes "where there's smoke there's fire." At this point the woman is not guilty in any legal sense, but the fact that she is accused of such a shameful act hints at the possibility that her behavior has been wanting from a moral point of view. Well, you say, there are husbands that are rascals. He may be one of them and he may be totally lying. But we should remember, that he risks being found out as a liar, and if so, would be fined and would be "stuck" with this woman as his wife forever-after (not necessarily "happily ever after"!). See verse 22:19. Considering this, he would think twice before making a false accusation, particularly if the girl had an unblemished reputation to begin with. This in no way means that the woman is, in fact, guilty — no one is ever found guilty in a Jewish court on the basis of circumstantial evidence alone; we must have valid witnesses. But it does open her up to closer scrutiny and exposes her parents to embarrassment.

(See *Silvermann*)

An apparently superfluous comment makes sense in light of a verse in Lamentations

Deut. 23:4

לֹא־יָבֹא עַמּוֹנִי וּמוֹאָבִי בִּקְהַל הי׳ גַּם דּוֹר עֲשִׂירִי לֹא־יָבֹא לָהֶם בִּקְהַל הי׳ עַד עוֹלָם.

> **לֹא יבא עמוני:** לא ישא ישראלית.
>
> **An Ammonite may not enter**: *Rashi:* He may not marry an Israelite woman.

When you look at the Rashi-comment preceding this one, you should have a question.

YOUR QUESTION:

QUESTIONING RASHI

A Question: Rashi made the very same comment on the previous verse. That verse says:

"A *mamzer* shall not enter the congregation of *Hashem*, even their tenth generation shall not enter the congregation of *Hashem*."

On the words "A *mamzer* shall not enter" Rashi comments "He may not marry an Israelite woman." This is identical to his comment on our verse.

Why the need to repeat himself? If the words "He shall not enter" means "Marrying an Israelite woman" in the first verse, we would assume it has the same connotation in our verse. Why did Rashi need to repeat himself?

This is difficult.

Hint: See Lamentations 1:10.

YOUR ANSWER:

WHAT IS BOTHERING RASHI?

An Answer: The Prophet when viewing the destruction of the Temple, says in Lamentations "she saw the gentiles invade her Sanctuary about whom You commanded that *they should not enter the congregation.*" The implication of this verse in Lamentations is that the gentiles (according to the *midrash* "gentiles" refers to Ammon and Maob) should "not enter the congregation" means they should not enter the Temple; I might have thought that this is likewise the meaning of *"they should not enter the congregation"* in our verse as well.

UNDERSTANDING RASHI

Therefore Rashi had to repeat again on our verse that the Simple Meaning of these words is: "He may not marry an Israelite woman."

(See *Amar Nekai*)

Rashi chooses precise wording to joggle our memory.

Deut. 23:8,9

לֹא־תְתַעֵב אֲדֹמִי כִּי אָחִיךָ הוּא לֹא־תְתַעֵב מִצְרִי כִּי־גֵר הָיִיתָ בְאַרְצוֹ.

בָּנִים אֲשֶׁר־יִוָּלְדוּ לָהֶם דּוֹר שְׁלִישִׁי יָבֹא לָהֶם בִּקְהַל ה׳.

לֹא תְתַעֵב אֲדֹמִי: לגמרי, ואף על פי שראוי לך לתעבו שיצא בחרב לקראתך.

לֹא תְתַעֵב מִצְרִי: מכל וכל, אף על פי שזרקו זכוריכם ליאור. מה הטעם? שהיו לכם אכסניא בשעת הדחק. לפיכך **בנים אשר יולדו להם דור שלישי** וגו׳.

Do not despise an Edomite: *Rashi:* Completely, although it would be appropriate for you to despise him as he advanced towards you with the sword.

Do not despise an Egyptian : *Rashi:* Totally, although they hurled your males into the river. What is the reason (for not despising them)? Because they were a home for you in time of need. Therefore **"sons born to them of the third generation"** etc.

Background

Ordinarily, any gentile who wants to convert to become a Jew may do so, providing he converts according to the *halacha*. But there are exceptions. The Ammonite and Moabite can under no circumstances be accepted as a Jew (see verse 23:4). The cases of the Egyptian and the Edomite fall somewhere in between. They may convert, but the convert him/herself and his/her child may not yet join the community of Israel. Only the grandson/daughter of a convert may enter as a Jew into the nation Israel (meaning being allowed to marry another Jew).

With this in mind, let us question Rashi.

Rashi has two similar comments on these two similar phrases.

What would you ask?

Your Question:

Questioning Rashi

A Question: What is the point of Rashi's comment here? The meaning of the verse seems clear enough.

What's bothering Rashi?

Your Answer:

What Is Bothering Rashi?

An Answer: The Torah tells us to despise *neither* the Edomite *nor* the Egyptian. But then it says he may not be admitted to the community of Israel. Only his/her grandson/daughter may be accepted. This contradiction is bothering Rashi.

How does his comment deal with it?

Your Answer:

Understanding Rashi

An Answer: The prohibition "not to despise the Edomite" is a qualified one. He actually deserves to be despised because of his aggressive behavior towards Israel. See Numbers 20:18-20 where the Torah describes

Edom's aggressive stance when Israel requested to peacefully pass through their territory on the way the Land of Canaan. So, Rashi tells us, the Torah is saying "you have reason to despise him (for what he did to you), but don't despise him completely (i.e. forever) because he is nevertheless 'your brother'. His third generation can become a member of Israel."

Likewise, regarding the Egyptian. You have reason to despise him, since he enslaved you in a bitter enslavement for several generations. Nevertheless, we are warned not to despise him completely, because when Jacob was forced to flee Canaan during the famine, Egypt agreed to take him and his family in. So while the Egyptian may not immediately become part of the Nation of Israel, his third generation may. This is the middle ground compromise between either being accepted as a convert immediately or not being accepted at all.

This is the simple meaning of Rashi.

But as you scrutinize and compare Rashi's wording in these two comments, you should have a question.

YOUR QUESTION:

A CLOSER LOOK: QUESTIONING RASHI'S WORDING _____

A Question: Did you notice that in the first comment Rashi uses the word לגמרי to say "completely," but in the second comment he uses the term מכל וכל? This also means "completely." Much speculation has been expended to try to figure out if the switch in Hebrew terms is significant. Most commentators on Rashi conclude that there is no meaningful difference between the two; it is just a stylistic change that Rashi introduces so as not to be repetitive.

A CLOSER LOOK: UNDERSTANDING RASHI'S NUANCES _____

One commentator, the *Devek Tov*, does suggest a reason for Rashi's choice of words. When referring to the Egyptian, Rashi chooses the idiom מכל וכל. This recalls the verse in the beginning of Exodus (Exodus 1:22). There it tells of Pharaoh's evil decree.

וַיְצַו פַּרְעֹה לְכָל־עַמּוֹ לֵאמֹר, כָּל־הַבֵּן הַיִּלּוֹד הַיְאֹרָה תַּשְׁלִיכֻהוּ וְכָל־הַבַּת תְּחַיּוּן.

"And Pharaoh commanded all his people saying, **Every** son that is born shall be thrown in the river; **and every** girl you shall let live."

We have here an exact replication of Rashi's term "מ״כל וכל", as if Rashi is hinting at Pharaoh's exact words. Rashi uses this term in the precise context of Pharaoh throwing the males into the river. He also uses the word יאור (river) as the verse in Exodus does. Rashi could as easily have said מים "water." But he wants us to recall and associate to the verse in Exodus where we also find the words כל...וכל !

A Type II comment clarifies a possible misunderstanding.

Deut. 23:15

כִּי הי אֱלֹקֶיךָ מִתְהַלֵּךְ בְּקֶרֶב מַחֲנֶךָ לְהַצִּילְךָ וְלָתֵת אֹיְבֶיךָ לְפָנֶיךָ וְהָיָה מַחֲנֶיךָ קָדוֹשׁ וְלֹא־יִרְאֶה בְךָ עֶרְוַת דָּבָר וְשָׁב מֵאַחֲרֶיךָ.

> ולא יראה בך: הקב״ה ערות דבר.
>
> **So He shall not see in you** : *Rashi:* The Holy One blessed be He, **a matter of nakedness.**

Questioning Rashi

A Question: Rashi inserts in between the Torah's words, just one term, "the Holy One." Why has he done this?

Hint: See the next Rashi-comment. Who does he rely on?

You can see this is a Type II comment. Its purpose is to avoid a possible misunderstanding. What do you think it is?

Your Answer:

Which Misunderstanding?

An Answer: Rashi in his next comment cites the *Targum Onkelos* as his guide in interpreting the Torah's meaning. He also does so on verse 13 above. He also does so on verse 14 above, albeit without actually mentioning the *Targum* by name. We see that Rashi was closely following the *Targum* on all these verses. Now, if we look at the *Targum* on our verse we find that he translates the words ולא יראה בך as "it shall not be seen in you..." This means "no nakedness shall be seen" by anyone. The *Targum* explicitly does not understand our verse to say that it is G-d, the Holy One, blessed be He, who "shall not see" the nakedness in the camp. Rashi's comment is meant to dispute the *Targum's* understanding. While Rashi agrees with the *Targum's* other interpretations in this section, here, he does not. Here he says, the words refer to G-d and are not to be taken abstractly, as the *Targum* does.

What evidence can you cite to support Rashi?

Hint: Read the whole verse.

YOUR ANSWER:

SUPPORTIVE EVIDENCE FOR RASHI

An Answer: The beginning of this verse mentions "*Hashem*, your G-d" and the end of the verse says clearly "and He will turn away from you." If the words ולא יראה meant "shall not be seen" in the passive sense, then the words "and He will turn away from you" do not follow.

The referent is undoubtedly G-d.

If the meaning is so obvious, why then does the *Targum* translate the words in the passive, avoiding reference to G-d?

Hint: Our introduction to the *Bamidbar* volume of *What's Bothering Rashi?* explains the *Targum's* approach to Biblical translation.

YOUR ANSWER:

UNDERSTANDING THE TARGUM

An Answer: The *Targum,* in principle, avoids any and all references to G-d that imply human qualities. It is his practice to avoid anything that has a human connotation when referring to G-d. Here too he avoids ascribing seeing the nakedness directly to G-d. First of all, seeing is a human behavior. Secondly, seeing nakedness is disrespectful to G-d. For this reason the *Targum* translates the "not seeing" in the passive, "It shall not be seen"; in this way it does not refer to G-d.

Rashi, of course, knew *Targum's* approach to Biblical translation. He also realized that, in the final analysis, the Torah does refer to G-d as having human qualities, but this is only so that we mortals can have some way of grasping His ways in the world and our obligations towards Him. Rashi's comment here brings us back from the *Targum's* sensitivity of being disrespectful to G-d, and places matters in the correct perspective.

Rashi's Style

The *Sefer Zikaron* asks, and leaves unanswered, why Rashi needs to add the words ערות דבר in this comment. They seem unnecessary because the meaning is abundantly clear.

I would say that this is Rashi's style whenever he adds just one word to help us avoid a misunderstanding. See for example Genesis 30:35 where it says:

וַיָּסַר בַּיּוֹם הַהוּא אֶת־הַתְּיָשִׁים וְגוּ׳

Rashi comments on these words:

ויסר לבן ביום ההוא.

See how Rashi adds the one word "Laban" and inserts it between the Torah's words. Here too he adds the words ביום ההוא for no apparent reason.

Also see Deut. 25:18.

אֲשֶׁר קָרְךָ בַּדֶּרֶךְ וַיְזַנֵּב בְּךָ כָּל־הַנֶּחֱשָׁלִים אַחֲרֶיךָ וְאַתָּה עָיֵף וְיָגֵעַ
וְלֹא יָרֵא אֱלֹקִים.

Rashi comments on these words:

ולא ירא: עמלק אלקים

See how Rashi adds the one word "Amalek" and inserts it between the Torah's words.

Here too he adds the word אלקים, for no apparent reason.

It would seem that it is Rashi's method to insert his one word for clarification and then bring us back to the text, to the Torah's own words.

Rashi refers to Targum. We must understand what he means.

Deut. 23:16

לֹא־תַסְגִּיר עֶבֶד אֶל־אֲדֹנָיו אֲשֶׁר־יִנָּצֵל אֵלֶיךָ מֵעִם אֲדֹנָיו.

לֹא תַסְגִּיר עֶבֶד: כתרגומו. דבר אחר אפילו עבד כנעני של ישראל שברח מחוצה לארץ לארץ ישראל.

Do not deliver a slave*: Rashi: As its Targum.* Another interpretation, Even a gentile slave owned by a Jew, who fled from outside the Land to the Land of Israel.

WHAT IS RASHI SAYING?

Rashi refers to *Targum Onkelos*. But there is a controversy as to what the *Targum* says. We highlight his words, which have been interpreted in different ways.

לֹא תמסר **עבד עממין** לות רבוניה די ישתיזיב לותך מן קדם רבוניה.

"Do not deliver an עבד עממין to his master" etc. The word עבד means "slave." The word עממין means "gentile."

The question is: Do these words mean " a gentile slave" or "a (Jewish) slave of a gentile (master)."

The *Mizrachi* translates these words as "a Jewish slave of a gentile master." The Ramban, on the other hand, says this is a gentile slave escaping from his gentile master who wants to join the People of Israel.

In summary: Rashi offers two interpretations, the first from the *Targum* that this is (according to the Ramban) a non-Jewish slave escaping from his gentile master. Rashi's second interpretation is from the Talmud (tractate *Gittin* 45a) which says this is a non-Jewish slave escaping from his Jewish master. In neither case should the slave be returned to his master.

P'SHAT AND DRASH

The first interpretation is *p'shat,* the second, *drash.*

Why do you think the first is *p'shat*?

YOUR ANSWER:

An Answer: The interpretation that this is a slave running from his gentile master fits best with the context of the previous verses. From verse 10 and onwards, the Torah speaks of Israel at war with their gentile enemies. This is the most likely scenario for a slave to escape from his gentile master to the winning side. He may even have heard that Jewish masters must treat their servants with a certain amount of decency.

But whenever Rashi offers two interpretations, we can ask a question:

YOUR QUESTION:

QUESTIONING RASHI

A Question: Once Rashi has given us *p'shat* which is reasonable and fits in well with the context, why does he need to offer a second, *drash*, interpretation?

Can you see why?

YOUR ANSWER:

UNDERSTANDING RASHI

An Answer: The first interpretation is *too* reasonable! Meaning, it is obvious that if a gentile slave escapes from his pagan, idol-worshipping master, that we should not return him to that kind of life, particularly if he begs us not to. This is so self-evident that the Torah doesn't even have to command us regarding this. Therefore, Rashi gives us the second interpretation, which is not at all obvious. This is a case of a gentile running away from his Jewish master. Why shouldn't he be returned? Why is one Jewish master better than another? The answer is that one master lives in the Land of Israel and the other does not.

In the Ramban's words:

"He (the escaping slave) should serve those dwellers of the Land of *Hashem,* and thus be saved from serving those who dwell in the impure lands (outside of the Land of Israel) which have no mitzvos conducted in them."

Spoken as a true lover of Zion! And the Ramban certainly was one.

(See *Amar Nekei; Ramban*)

When positive implies the negative which is the positive!

Deut. 23:20,21

20) לֹא־תַשִּׁיךְ לְאָחִיךָ נֶשֶׁךְ כֶּסֶף נֶשֶׁךְ אֹכֶל נֶשֶׁךְ כָּל־דָּבָר אֲשֶׁר יִשָּׁךְ.

21) לַנָּכְרִי תַשִּׁיךְ וּלְאָחִיךָ לֹא תַשִּׁיךְ לְמַעַן יְבָרֶכְךָ ה' אֱלֹקֶיךָ בְּכֹל מִשְׁלַח יָדֶךָ עַל־הָאָרֶץ אֲשֶׁר־אַתָּה בָא־שָׁמָּה לְרִשְׁתָּהּ.

לַנָּכְרִי תַשִּׁיךְ: ולא לאחיך. לאו הבא מכלל עשה, עשה. לעבור עליו בשני לאוין ועשה.

To a stranger you may pay interest: *Rashi:* But not to your brother. A negative commandment that derives from a positive commandment is considered a positive commandment. So that (in paying interest to a Jew) he transgresses two negative commandments and one positive commandment.

WHAT IS RASHI SAYING?

Rashi mentions a rule of the Talmudic Sages regarding calculating the commandments. When the Torah states an obligation in a positive phrase, then the negative inference of this command is considered to be an additional *positive commandment*. Our verse says "You may pay interest to a gentile" — the inference is, but you may not pay interest to a Jew. Notice that the previous verse and the very next words of our verse state this prohibition explicitly. Nevertheless, the positive phrasing has the effect of creating an additional prohibition, albeit in positive phrasing. This then is considered to be a positive commandment. So we have, as Rashi says, two negative and one positive commandments that are transgressed if a person pays interest to a Jew.

QUESTIONING RASHI

A Question: Why would the statement "To a stranger you may pay interest," which says nothing about paying interest to a Jew, imply that if one does pay interest to a Jew he is guilty of another, positive, transgression?

Why so?

YOUR ANSWER:

Understanding Rashi

An Answer: It seems quite unnecessary and perhaps even out of place for the Torah to tell us we should or even, that we may, pay interest to a gentile. Why should we pay him interest? Is the Torah *commanding us* to pay interest to a gentile? Unlikely. Why then does the Torah tell us this? The only reasonable interpretation is that the significance of this phrase is in its opposite — to a gentile, you may pay interest, but to a Jew you may not.

With this background knowledge we can understand a puzzling Rashi-comment that appeared earlier in *Devarim*.

In *parashas Re'eh* the Torah teaches us the laws of the Seventh year, the year of *Shemita*, and the mitzvah to release (relinquish) unpaid loans. Just as the land is to lie fallow and not be worked on the Seventh year, so, too, no unpaid loans can be claimed by the creditor.

Deut. 15:2,3

2) וְזֶה דְּבַר הַשְּׁמִטָּה שָׁמוֹט כָּל־בַּעַל מַשֵּׁה יָדוֹ אֲשֶׁר יַשֶּׁה בְּרֵעֵהוּ לֹא־יִגֹּשׂ אֶת־רֵעֵהוּ וְאֶת־אָחִיו כִּי־קָרָא שְׁמִטָּה לַה'.

3) אֶת־הַנָּכְרִי תִּגֹּשׂ וַאֲשֶׁר יִהְיֶה לְךָ אֶת־אָחִיךָ תַּשְׁמֵט יָדֶךָ.

את הנכרי תגש: זו מצות עשה.

From gentile you shall exact payment: *Rashi:* This is a positive mitzvah.

A Question

This comment, which stems from the *midrash Sifrei*, has caused much discussion among the commentators. They ask: Is it a *bona fide* mitzvah, one of the 613 mitzvahs, to claim your debt from a gentile? There is no need for a mitzvah to allow him to claim his debt from a gentile. The gentile doesn't observe the laws of the *Shemita* year, and he would claim his debt from you, if you borrowed money from him. So why can't you claim your money from him? Why is this a mitzvah?

A Misunderstanding

But all these questions stem from a misunderstanding of this comment. If we look at the verse we discussed above, we see that this is not what Rashi had in mind. Just as Rashi explains the words "You may pay interest to a gentile," in our verse, as a positive command, so, likewise, the meaning here is *not* that it is a mitzvah to "exact payment" from the gentile, it is rather a mitzvah for a Jew *not* to exact payment from his brother Jew in the Year of Release. The Torah just phrases this mitzvah in its opposite form — you may exact payment from the gentile — but not from a Jew

The Lesson: "Words Poor in One Place and Rich in Another"

We were better able to understand one Rashi-comment by seeing another one of his comments. This is as it says about the Torah Itself — "The words of the Torah are 'poor' in one place and 'rich' in another" (*Tos. Krisus* 14a), meaning that in places where the meaning of the Torah's words are unclear ("poor"), its meaning can be understood by looking at other relevant places in the Torah which are clearer ("rich").

A brief comment clarifies matters.

Deut. 25:18

אֲשֶׁר קָרְךָ בַּדֶּרֶךְ וַיְזַנֵּב בְּךָ כָּל־הַנֶּחֱשָׁלִים אַחֲרֶיךָ וְאַתָּה עָיֵף וְיָגֵעַ וְלֹא יָרֵא אֱלֹקִים.

> **וְלֹא יָרֵא אֱלֹקִים:** עמלק מלהרע לך.
> **And he had no fear**: *Rashi*: Amalek **of G-d**: from harming you.

This is a typical Type II comment. See how Rashi weaves his short comment in between the Torah's words.

What question would you ask?

Your Question:

Questioning Rashi

Remember that Type II comments, as we have explained, are usually intended to help us avoid a misunderstanding. The question here is: Which misunderstanding is Rashi helping us avoid? In other words: Who else, beside Amalek, might we have thought was not G-d fearing?

Your Answer:

What Misunderstanding Are We to Avoid?

An Answer: Verse 17 begins "Remember what Amalek did to you …when you were going out of Egypt." Two subjects are included in this verse, "Amalek" and "you" meaning Israel. The ambiguity in the verse is, was it Amalek or was it Israel who did not fear G-d?

Rashi's one word comment, "Amalek," answers the question.

What evidence can you find in the Torah's words which supports Rashi's comment? What evidence is there in the text that Amalek is referred to as not fearing G-d, and not Israel?

Your Answer:

Supportive Evidence for Rashi

An Answer: Did you notice that this whole section (verses 17-19) speaks to Israel in the second person. "Amalek did to *you...your* going out...met *you* on the way...and *you* were tired.." etc. Amalek is referred to in the third person, "*he* did to you... *he* met you...*he* smote your hindmost." In light of this we can assume that if the reference were to Israel it should have said "and *you* did not fear G-d." But the Torah says "He did not fear G-d." Clearly referring to Amalek.

This is a subtle but indisputable grammatical support. The words יָרֵא אֱלֹקִים are written with a *kametz* under the י, which means "he did not fear G-d." Had it been written slightly differently, with a *shevah* under the י its meaning would be "and was not G-d-fearing." Phrased in this way, it would refer to Israel. Rashi's brief comment makes its meaning clear.

Probing Deeper

But we might ask: Why should we expect Amalek to be G-d fearing? This complimentary appellation was used in reference to Abraham after he was willing to sacrifice his son Isaac. This is a level of righteousness that we would not expect from any nation; certainly not from Amalek. Why is it used here?

Hint: Look at the continuation of Rashi's comment.

YOUR ANSWER:

A DEEPER UNDERSTANDING

An Answer: In Rashi's next comment (actually the connecting half of the first comment) he says: "**of G-d:** from harming you." This comment, I believe, is related to our question. Amalek attacked a weak and tired ragtag group of escapees. And he made a point of attacking just those that straggled at the end of the group. The tail-end, the weakest end of a weak group. Certainly Amalek had no fear of losing this battle. Their attack clearly indicated that they had no qualms, no second thoughts about such a cowardly act. Nor did they fear, the Torah informs us, the wrath of the gods. The Torah uses the term אלקים to convey the idea of a G-d of retribution, as well as a God that even the gentiles believe in. The next verse, on the other hand, uses the unique name of יה-ו-ה, the G-d of the Jews. But our verse which refers to Amalek, uses the name אלקים.

In short, Rashi tells us the significance of Amalek's lack of fear of G-d — He saw a weak potential victim and attacked with no qualms. He attacked because he didn't fear any higher power. His might made right. This is the significance of his not fearing G-d.

פרשת כי תבוא

Rashi shows us how behavior speaks louder than words.

Deut. 26:3

וּבָאתָ אֶל־הַכֹּהֵן אֲשֶׁר יִהְיֶה בַּיָּמִים הָהֵם וְאָמַרְתָּ אֵלָיו הִגַּדְתִּי הַיּוֹם
לַה' אֱלֹקֶיךָ כִּי־בָאתִי אֶל־הָאָרֶץ אֲשֶׁר נִשְׁבַּע ה' לַאֲבֹתֵינוּ לָתֶת לָנוּ.

> **וְאָמַרְתָּ אֵלָיו:** שאינך כפוי טובה.
>
> **And you will say to him**: *Rashi*: That you are not un-grateful.

The comment should lead you to ask …

YOUR QUESTION:

QUESTIONING RASHI

A Question: How does Rashi derive this comment from these words?

Rashi has lifted this comment straight out of the *midrash Sifrei*. But he wouldn't have included it in his commentary if it weren't connected with the words of the Torah.

What is his reason for including it?

Hint: Read the whole verse and see what the man who brings his first fruits goes on to say.

YOUR ANSWER:

WHAT IS BOTHERING RASHI?

An Answer: If you read the verse you certainly saw that before he gives the new fruits to the Priest, he has said nothing of significance, at least no words of gratefulness. He says only that he has come to the Land that G-d promised, but that is quite apparent. Only later (verses 5-10) does he thank G-d for the Land of milk and honey. So why, in these verses, does he say the obvious and only the obvious?

That is what Rashi is bothered by.

Can you now see the connection between these words and Rashi's comment?

Hint: See the very next words, הגדתי היום.

YOUR ANSWER:

UNDERSTANDING RASHI

An Answer: Notice that the very next words which the man says are: "I have declared today…" in *the past tense*! But he has yet to declare anything. This is a clue.

The Hebrew word להגיד, "to declare" does not necessarily mean to declare verbally. See, for example, these verses:

In Psalms 19:2:

$$\text{וּמַעֲשֵׂה יָדָיו מַגִּיד הָרָקִיעַ.}$$

"The works of His hands, the heavens **declare**."

This definitely is a non-verbal declaration, for the heavens don't speak.

See also II Samuel 19:7 where we are told that after David's rebellious son, Abshalom, dies, David publicly mourns his death. Then David's general, Yoav (who fought Abshalom in order to save David's kingdom), rebukes him saying:

$$\text{"הִגַּדְתָּ הַיּוֹם כִּי אֵין לְךָ שָׂרִים וַעֲבָדִים..."}$$

"You have **declared** today that you have no officers or servants…"

Nowhere did David make such a declaration. What Yoav meant was that David's mourning behavior was, in effect, such a declaration.

We see from these examples that behavior also "speaks" and can make declarations. We know that 'action speaks louder than words.' That is what is meant in our verse. The man has already brought his fruits to Jerusalem (therefore the past tense of הגדתי). Bringing the fruits is the man's behavioral declaration that he has not only come to the Land, but that he has clearly benefited from living in the Land.

Rashi related to the words ואמרת אליו because what the man is about to say is evidence that he is not ungrateful. He says "I have declared already," meaning that his act of bringing the fruits all the way to Jerusalem (and not just by thanking G-d at home) is in and of itself, even without any other verbal declaration, an indication of his gratefulness to G-d.

(See *Mizrachi, Tosephes Berachah*).

Seeing the forest and the trees when serving G-d.

Deut. 26:13

וְאָמַרְתָּ לִפְנֵי הי אֱלֹקֶיךָ בִּעַרְתִּי הַקֹּדֶשׁ מִן־הַבַּיִת וְגַם נְתַתִּיו לַלֵּוִי וְלַגֵּר לַיָּתוֹם וְלָאַלְמָנָה כְּכָל־מִצְוָתְךָ אֲשֶׁר צִוִּיתָנִי לֹא־עָבַרְתִּי מִמִּצְוֹתֶיךָ וְלֹא שָׁכָחְתִּי.

> **וְלֹא שָׁכָחְתִּי:** מלברכך על הפרשת מעשרות.
> **Neither have I forgotten**: *Rashi:* To bless You on the occasion of giving the tithes.

The source of Rashi's comment is a *mishneh* in *Masser Sheni* (5:11).

QUESTIONING RASHI

A Question: Why does Rashi comment here and on what basis does he draw the particular conclusion that one has to make a blessing on separating tithes?

Can you see what's bothering him?

Hint: Read the whole verse.

YOUR ANSWER:

WHAT IS BOTHERING RASHI?

An Answer: The words "I have not forgotten" are both unclear (what hasn't he forgotten?) and also seem to be redundant. The latter part of our verse says "[I have done] according to all Your commandments which You have commanded me. I have not transgressed Your commandments, *neither have I forgotten.*

After the person proclaims that he has done *all* that G-d commanded him without transgressing His commands, what need is there to say any more? What could the words "neither have I forgotten" possibly add?

This is what is bothering Rashi.

How does his comment deal with this?

YOUR ANSWER:

UNDERSTANDING RASHI

An Answer: One may do all the mitzvos precisely according to the *halacha*, yet miss the essence of things. We must not lose sight of the ultimate goal of mitzvos. The commandments are *from G-d* and their spiritual goal is to direct us *back to G-d*. At times, being preoccupied with the details of a mitzvah, one may *forget* its essence. In our verse Rashi tells us that this person makes clear that he has *not forgotten* the essence – he has remembered Him, Who has given him his plentiful harvest and has remembered to thank Him for it.

We have explained Rashi's interpretation above, but it cannot be considered *p'shat*.

Can you think of a *p'shat* interpretation of the words "and I have not forgotten"?

YOUR ANSWER:

A *P'SHAT* INTERPRETATION

An Answer: The *Nachlas Yaakov*, a commentary on Rashi, suggests a very simple explanation for the inclusion of the words "and I have not forgotten." He says that the words "I have not transgressed Your commandments" mean I have not *intentionally* transgressed any mitzvah while "and I have not forgotten" means that I have not even *unintentionally* transgressed. This makes perfect sense, for "forgetting" means an unintentional sin of omission, an unintentional transgression of G-d's commandments. With this quite reasonable interpretation we are reminded once again of the rule that no Torah verse ever losses it's *p'shat* sense — אין מקרא יוצא מידי פשוטו.

A Deeper Look

We find a rarely noticed consistency in the Torah. When the Torah describes the blessings of the Land that are to redound to Israel's benefit, we almost invariably find immediately afterwards warnings of forgetting *Hashem*. See the following examples of this connection:

> *Deut. 8:10:*
> "And you will eat and you will be satisfied, then you shall bless *Hashem* your G-d for the good Land which He has given you."

The very next verse says:
> "Take heed lest you forget *Hashem,* your G-d" etc.

> *Deut. 8:12–14:*
> "Lest you will eat and be full and build good houses….and silver and gold will multiply for you…and your pride increases and you forget *Hashem,* your G-d…"

> *Deut. 11:14–16*
> "And I will provide rains of your Land…and you will harvest your grain…and you will eat and be satisfied. Be careful for yourselves lest your heart mislead you and you turn away and serve other gods."

> *And in Deut. 28:47*
> "Since you did not serve *Hashem,* your G-d, with joy and good heartedness, when you had all the good."

> *And again in Deut. 32:15*
> "And Yeshurun grew fat (i.e. blessed with plentitude) and kicked (i.e. rebelled against G-d.)" etc.

Clearly, the blessings of plentitude are a two-edged sword. In addition to their blessing they also carry within them a potential risk of forgetting the source of all blessings. Forgetting G-d, it would seem, is an occupational hazard of receiving His bounty. Therefore the Torah constantly stresses that once we have received His blessings we should be mindful not to forget the source of this goodness; not to forget *Hashem,* Himself, Who has "given us the strength to make our wealth".

We can now understand, as Rashi did, that the words in our verse "neither have I forgotten" refer to remembering *Hashem* and thanking Him with a blessing.

Understanding Rashi leads us to a realization about the Torah's subtle style.

Deut. 26:16

הַיּוֹם הַזֶּה ה' אֱלֹקֶיךָ מְצַוְּךָ לַעֲשׂוֹת אֶת־הַחֻקִּים הָאֵלֶּה וְאֶת־הַמִּשְׁפָּטִים וְשָׁמַרְתָּ וְעָשִׂיתָ אוֹתָם בְּכָל־לְבָבְךָ וּבְכָל־נַפְשֶׁךָ.

> **וְשָׁמַרְתָּ וְעָשִׂיתָ אוֹתָם:** בַּת קוֹל מְבָרַכְתּוֹ, הֲבֵאתָ בִּכּוּרִים הַיּוֹם תִּשְׁנֶה לְשָׁנָה הַבָּאָה.
>
> **And you shall observe and do them**: *Rashi:* A heavenly voice blesses him "You have brought the first fruits on this day, may you repeat [to do so] next year."

What would you ask on this comment?

YOUR QUESTION:

QUESTIONING RASHI

A Question: The simple meaning of these words would seem to be an admonishment to keep the mitzvah in the future. Why doesn't Rashi accept the simple meaning? Why the need for this "*Bas Kol*"?

Can you think of a reason for this *drash*?

YOUR ANSWER:

WHAT IS BOTHERING RASHI?

An Answer: Various explanations have been suggested to make sense of this comment. Following is one of them.

These words seem completely out of place, since the whole section tells us that the man has already performed the mitzvah, has come to the

Priest and has just made his declaration. Why, then, the necessity to tell him "you shall observe and do" ? He has just observed and done!

How does this comment deal with this difficulty?

YOUR ANSWER:

UNDERSTANDING RASHI

An Answer: Rashi's *drash* reinterprets these words from a command ("you shall do") to a blessing ("you will be enabled to do") — next year you will also be blessed with produce and again will come to acknowledge your thanks by offering your first fruits.

Can you see on what basis Rashi derived this *drash*?

YOUR ANSWER:

UNDERSTANDING THE *DRASH*

An Answer: The late Lubavitcher Rebbe, Menachem Mendel Schneerson, offered an interesting insight. He points out that the *sedra Ki Savo* is built on a reciprocal relationship between the Israelite and *Hashem*. A measure for measure relationship. This is expressed here in the poetic chiastic form, that is, of the form of ABBA.

> First *Hashem* gives of His bounty, (A)
> then man acknowledges it.   (B)
> Man expresses his gratefulness,   (B)
> and then G-d gives His bounty.   (A)

Regarding the first fruits we read:

Hashem gives: "And He brought you...and He gave you this Land of milk and honey." (26:9) (A)

Man acknowledges : "And now I have brought the first fruits of the soil (note: this is the produce of the Land of Milk and Honey) which You have given me, *Hashem*." (26:12) (B)

Regarding the tithes we find the same idea in reversed order:

First, man fulfills his obligation and expresses his gratefulness: "[I have done] all that You commanded me ..I have not forgotten.." (26:13) (B)

Then *Hashem* is asked to give of His bounty: "View from Your sacred residence in the heavens and bless Your people…"(26:15) (A)

But, (and now we come to the point), we have yet to see G-d's blessing, only the request for it.

Then comes our verse.

"This day *Hashem*, your G-d, commands you to do the statues and the laws and you *will be enabled to observe and do them.*"

This is the blessing! The poetic couplet is complete now. G-d makes a promise by means of His heavenly voice, that this man will be blessed again next year and will also be able to bring his first fruits once again.

(See *Mizrachi; Biurim l'Pirush Rashi*)

Rashi and Bechor Shor view the verse differently.

Deut. 27:18

אָרוּר מַשְׁגֶּה עִוֵּר בַּדָּרֶךְ וְאָמַר כָּל הָעָם אָמֵן.

> **מַשְׁגֶּה עִוֵּר:** הסומא בדבר ומשיאו עצה רעה.
> **Whoever misleads the blind:** *Rashi*: One who is blind regarding a particular matter and he offers him bad advice.

Rashi takes this verse in a metaphorical sense, that is, not one who is physically blind, but one who is ignorant regarding a particular issue. The prohibition is against intentionally giving bad advice to someone ("lead him astray"), since he cannot adequately evaluate the advice, as he is "blind" in this particular area of expertise. This is similar to Rashi's comment on Leviticus 19:14.

QUESTIONING RASHI

A Question: The simple meaning of this verse is not to lead a blind man in the wrong direction while he is walking on the road. Why does Rashi prefer the allegorical interpretation to the simple meaning?

Hint: See this verse in its context.

YOUR ANSWER:

WHAT IS BOTHERING RASHI?

An Answer: All the curses in this section (27:16–26) refer to transgressions done in secret, out of sight of potential witnesses. See verse 16 where it speaks of making idols and placing them "in a hidden place." And verse 24, which speaks of one who hits another "in a hidden place." All the other curses refer to transgressions which are either done at home or can be done in a surreptitious way. But our verse does not seem to fit with that theme. It speaks of misleading a blind man "on the way." If we take the verse at face value, meaning misguiding a blind man as he walks on the road, that is an act done in full public view and would deviate from the list of hidden transgressions recorded in this section of accursed behaviors. Therefore Rashi looks for an interpretation that will fit the context.

How does his comment accomplish that?

YOUR ANSWER:

UNDERSTANDING RASHI

An Answer: Rashi transforms our verse into a "hidden transgression." No one can see another man's intentions. So that when he gives his misleading advice he can always claim that he did so innocently, with no devious intent. In this sense it is a "hidden transgression."

BECHOR SHOR OFFERS P'SHAT

The *Bechor Shor,* always in pursuit of the simple *p'shat,* has suggested something quite straight forward. He takes Rashi's idea a step further and thus brings it nearer to a *p'shat* interpretation. He says we should take the verse at face value. The man actually misled a blind man on the way. Nevertheless, this can rightfully be considered a "hidden transgression" since the perpetrator can always defend himself by saying he did so innocently; he didn't realize he was guiding him wrongly. Nobody can know another person's intention, it remains hidden.

Again we see how *p'shat* is available, if we only open ours eyes to see it.

Rashi's close reading and clear thinking help us understand the verse.

Deut. 28:6

בָּרוּךְ אַתָּה בְּבֹאֶךָ וּבָרוּךְ אַתָּה בְּצֵאתֶךָ.

בָּרוּךְ אַתָּה בְּבֹאַךְ וּבָרוּךְ אַתָּה בְּצֵאתֶךָ: שֶׁתְּהֵא יְצִיאָתְךָ מִן הָעוֹלָם
בְּלִי חֵטְא כְּבִיאָתְךָ לָעוֹלָם.

**Blessed are you in your coming in, and blessed are
you in your going out** *Rashi:* Your leaving this world
should be without sin as was your entry into this world.

Rashi abandons the Simple Meaning of the verse — that a person will
be blessed when he enters his home as when he leaves it — and ex-
changes it for a more spiritual concept. As Rashi sees it, "coming in and
going out" refers to being born and to dying.

YOUR QUESTION:

QUESTIONING RASHI

A Question: Why does Rashi take the verse out of its Simple Meaning? Remember, when Rashi cites a *midrash* as interpretation of a verse,
we can safely assume that some anomaly in the verse lead him to
it.

Do you see what is bothering him?

Hint: Notice the order of the words here.

YOUR ANSWER:

WHAT IS BOTHERING RASHI?

An Answer: The verse starts with coming in and ends with going out. Ordinarily a person begins by going out (of his home) and only later
"comes in"(some examples: Numbers 27:16, and Deut. 31:2) This
reversed order is what caught Rashi's eye.

How does Rashi's comment rectify matters?

YOUR ANSWER:

UNDERSTANDING RASHI

An Answer: True that most "goings out" precede most "comings in" in this world. The one glaring exception is being born and dying. A person first "comes into" this world, when he is born, and then, after 120 years, he leaves ("goes out of") this world. So Rashi chose this case to fit the order of the words in our verse. Once this was established, he sought to turn it into a blessing. The meaning then became: that his leaving(when he dies), should be without sin as was his entry (when born) into this world.

A DEEPER QUESTION

A Question: The *Mizrachi,* who suggested the above answer, then poses a question: What can we say about verse 19 where it says:

אָרוּר אַתָּה בְּבֹאֶךָ וְאָרוּר אַתָּה בְּצֵאתֶךָ.

"Cursed are you in your coming in and cursed are you in your going out."

Here, too, we have "coming in" before "going out" but here it is a curse. If the person came into the world without sin, how can we explain this verse, which is a curse?

Can you think of an answer?

YOUR ANSWER:

A DEEPER UNDERSTANDING

An Answer: It can be explained as follows. Granted the person came into this world without sin, as we said above, but he also came in without merit. So the curse would be, that just as a person came into the world without merit, so too he will leave the world without merit. Having lived here a lifetime and not having acquired any merits, could certainly be considered a curse.

Another explanation given is that when an evil person dies, people curse the day he was born. So just as he will be cursed "in his going out" so too will he be cursed "in his coming in."

(See *Mizrachi; Zichron Moshe*)

Without saying so, Rashi teaches us a rule of Biblical Hebrew.

Deut. 28:47

תַּחַת אֲשֶׁר לֹא־עָבַדְתָּ אֶת הֹ' אֱלֹקֶיךָ בְּשִׂמְחָה וּבְטוּב לֵבָב מֵרֹב כֹּל.

> **מֵרֹב כֹּל:** בְּעוֹד שֶׁהָיָה לְךָ כָל טוּב.
> **When everything was abundant:** *Rashi:* While you had all good things.

QUESTIONING RASHI

A Question: Why has Rashi said this? What is he adding to our understanding of this verse?

Hint: Think. How else could we have understood these words? It is a short comment of the Type II style. Is he guiding us around a possible misunderstanding?

YOUR ANSWER:

WHICH MISUNDERSTANDING?

An Answer: The Hebrew letter מ in the words מֵרֹב כֹּל is generally understood to mean as "due to" or "because of." That would give our verse the meaning: "Since you did not serve *Hashem* with joy and a good heart *because of* your having all good things." This is because the מ sometimes carries the sense of "because of."

As in Exodus 6:9

...וְלֹא שָׁמְעוּ אֶל־מֹשֶׁה מִקֹּצֶר רוּחַ וּמֵעֲבֹדָה קָשָׁה.

"...And they didn't listen to Moses **because of** shortness of breath and **because of** hard work."

Rashi rejects this interpretation and says that the מ is to be understood as "while" or "at the time of." But for the מ to mean "at the time of" is unusual.

How can he do that? How can we understand this unusual use of מ here? This is difficult.

YOUR ANSWER:

Understanding Rashi

Mizrachi explains that Rashi has given the מ the meaning of a ב, "with" or "at the time when," as if it said כל ברב.

A close reading of the Torah shows that the מ and ב are sometimes interchanged.

Some examples are:

Leviticus 6:13

זֶה קָרְבַּן אַהֲרֹן וּבָנָיו אֲשֶׁר־יַקְרִיבוּ לַחי בְּיוֹם הִמָּשַׁח אֹתוֹ וְגוֹ׳

"This is the offering of Aaron and his sons that they shall offer to *Hashem* **on** the day that he is anointed etc."

The meaning here is really "from the day he is anointed" as if it said מיום המשח (See Ibn Ezra).

Leviticus 8:32

וְהַנּוֹתָר בַּבָּשָׂר וּבַלָּחֶם בָּאֵשׁ תִּשְׂרֹפוּ.

"And the remnant **of the** meat and **of the** bread shall be burnt in fire."

This is as if it were written מהבשר ומהלחם.

And in Genesis 19:34

וַיְהִי מִמָּחֳרָת וַתֹּאמֶר הַבְּכִירָה אֶל־הַצְּעִירָה הֵן־שָׁכַבְתִּי אֶמֶשׁ אֶת־אָבִי וְגוֹ׳

"And it was **on the** morrow that the older girl said to the younger, 'Last night I slept with my father etc."

The word ממחרת here does not mean "from the morrow" for the daughter slept with her father only once — on the morrow. It is if it says במחרת "on the morrow".

See also Proverbs 5:18.

Why Does Rashi Prefer the Less Likely Interpretation?

Rashi is particularly difficult to understand because he not only stretches for an unusual interpretation, he also rejects the most obvious and meaningful interpretation of this verse. The version we offered above, "Since you did not serve *Hashem* with joy and a good heart *because of* your having all good things" sounds right and makes sense. This means that they strayed from the way because of their luxurious and G-d-given blessings.

As it says in Deut. 32:15:

וַיִּשְׁמַן יְשֻׁרוּן וַיִּבְעָט

"And Yeshurun grew fat (i.e. blessed with plentitude) and kicked (i.e. rebelled against G-d.)" etc.

Why didn't Rashi accept this interpretation?

Any ideas?

Hint: Look at the next verse.

YOUR ANSWER:

A Deeper Understanding

An Answer: There may be two reasons that Rashi opts for this interpretation.

One is that our verse is parallel (but opposite) to the next verse.

Verse 47	Verse 48
Because you did not serve	So you will serve
Hashem, your G-d	your enemies….
in gladness and goodness of heart,	in hunger, in thirst and in nakedness
מרב כל *when everything was abundant.*	ובחסר כל *and without anything.*

Our phrase above, with the מ, is parallel to the phrase in verse 48 with the ב. So it is reasonable to assume that our phrase has a similar meaning.

Another reason for Rashi rejecting the more obvious interpretation may be that Moses is here reprimanding the People (this is the "Rebuke/ Curse"). If he is reproving them, why should he give them even the slightest excuse for their evil deeds? Psychologists know of what has been called the "Abuse-excuse," and this could be called the "Profuse-excuse" — because they had a profusion of every material wealth. But the problem is that by saying "you did this because of your wealth" he is, in a way, "understanding" this all-too-human frailty for their back-sliding. Such "understanding" takes the moral sting out of Moses' rebuke. Rashi prefers a straight objective statement about their sins, which doesn't even hint at an excuse.

(See *Mizrachi, Lifshuto shel Rashi*)

Rashi clues us in to grammatical nuances.

Deut. 28:63

וְהָיָה כַּאֲשֶׁר־שָׂשׂ הי עֲלֵיכֶם לְהֵיטִיב אֶתְכֶם וּלְהַרְבּוֹת אֶתְכֶם כֵּן יָשִׂישׂ הי עֲלֵיכֶם לְהַאֲבִיד אֶתְכֶם וּלְהַשְׁמִיד אֶתְכֶם וְנִסַּחְתֶּם מֵעַל הָאֲדָמָה אֲשֶׁר־אַתָּה בָא־שָׁמָּה לְרִשְׁתָּהּ.

> כן ישיש הי: את אויביכם **עליכם להאביד** וגו'.
>
> **So will *Hashem* (be) make happy:** *Rashi:* Your enemies **over you to obliterate** etc.

In this comment, Rashi adds just two words — "Your enemies" — to the Torah's words. This a typical Type II comment. Rashi is helping us avoid a possible misunderstanding.

What is it?

YOUR ANSWER:

WHICH MISUNDERSTANDING?

An Answer: The verse begins with "And it will be that as *Hashem* rejoiced over you to benefit you" and verse continues with our words "*so He will rejoice* over you to destroy you" etc. This translation is the most reasonable culmination of the thought of this verse. But Rashi says this is incorrect. Not "*He* will rejoice over you" but "*your enemies* will rejoice over you."

Certainly it is somewhat more comforting to know that not G-d, Himself, will rejoice at Israel's destruction. Only our enemies will rejoice! In Yiddish that is called "a *halba tzarah*," in Talmudic language, a נחמה פורתא, and in English "small consolation." (It seems all languages are familiar with such depressing optimism!)

But Rashi is not in the business of giving consolation, large or small. He is a Torah commentator and we must understand on what basis he can change the meaning of these words.

Hint: Knowledge of grammar is helpful here.

YOUR ANSWER:

UNDERSTANDING RASHI

An Answer: In fact Rashi changes nothing. The word יָשִׂישׂ (its root = to rejoice) is in the causative form. That means literally "to make (others) joyous." Who could these "others" possibly be? Of course, Israel's enemies, who are G-d's rod to punish His People Israel. These mortal enemies of Israel would rejoice at their downfall. (Anyone familiar with the State of Israel's neighbors/enemies today, knows very well how true this is.)

A CLOSER LOOK

In light of the above grammatical understanding, we can point out an important nuance in our verse. Notice that when the Torah speaks of Israel being punished, it is their enemies who rejoice; not G-d. The verb "rejoice" — יָשִׂישׂ — is in the causative construction. But at the beginning of the verse when it speaks of Israel having been blessed, it is G-d Himself who rejoices. There it says:

כַּאֲשֶׁר שָׂשׂ ה׳ עֲלֵיכֶם לְהֵטִיב אֶתְכֶם
"As *Hashem* had rejoiced over you to do you good..."

Here the verb "rejoice" — שָׂשׂ — is in the simple, intransitive, construction, meaning G-d, Himself, will rejoice. G-d is always happy when Israel prospers and is never happy when they fall, even if this is due to their own doing.

(See *Mizrachi*)

What is p'shat? Rashi & Rashbam differ.

Deut. 28:67

בַּבֹּקֶר תֹּאמַר מִי־יִתֵּן עֶרֶב וּבָעֶרֶב תֹּאמַר מִי־יִתֵּן בֹּקֶר מִפַּחַד לְבָבְךָ
אֲשֶׁר תִּפְחָד וּמִמַּרְאֵה עֵינֶיךָ אֲשֶׁר תִּרְאֶה.

> **בבקר תאמר מי יתן ערב:** וְיִהְיֶה הָעֶרֶב שֶׁל אֶמֶשׁ.
>
> **ובערב תאמר מי יתן בקר:** שֶׁל שַׁחֲרִית. שֶׁהַצָּרוֹת מִתְחַזְּקוֹת תָּמִיד
> וְכָל שָׁעָה מְרוּבָּה קִלְלָתָהּ מִשֶּׁלְּפָנֶיהָ.
>
> **In the morning you will say 'Would that it be evening'**:
> *Rashi:* That it would be yesterday evening.
> **And in the evening you will say 'Would that it be morn-
> ing'**: *Rashi:* This morning. Because the tribulations in-
> crease constantly, and every moment it (the curse) is worse
> than the previous one.

WHAT IS RASHI SAYING?

The verse tells of the people's distress who are suffering all the horrors
of the Rebuke/Curse. They are so distraught that whenever they think of
their situation they wish that the clock could be turned and they would
be freed of their travail.

Rashi adds that their desire in the morning is that it should be evening,
means that the clock should be turned *back* to last night. It does not
mean, as we might have expected, that the clock should be turned *forward* so that their trouble would already be behind them.

Why does Rashi reject the more obvious interpretation which is, in fact,
the Rashbam's interpretation?

THE RASHBAM'S P'SHAT INTERPRETATION

'Would that it be morning': *Rashbam*: According to the
p'shat, [it means] the evening that will come, for such is
the way of the sick.

The Rashbam points out that a person in distress always looks forward
to the day he will be finished with his troubles. Just as a sick man looks
forward toward his recovery.

But Rashi chose another way. Why?

Can you explain Rashi's view?

Your Answer:

Understanding Rashi

An Answer: The Rashbam is right in that this is the way a person usually reacts to ordinary troubles — he looks forward to the day that they will all be behind him. But Rashi's view reflects a deeper psychological despair, that of a person suffering from *unrelenting and ever-increasing* distress. There comes a point when a person loses all hope. If he has been subject to ongoing terror, terror with no reprieve, terror with no "light at the end of the tunnel," he realizes that his salvation hasn't come, in spite of all his prayers and hopes — then he can only look backward to "the good old times," because he no longer has any faith in the future. He is truly depressed.

Rashi has grasped the true hopelessness of the Rebuke/Curse that Moses is describing.

Rashbam: "According to the *P'shat*"

The Rashbam will often begin an interpretation with the words "according to the *p'shat*…" Often this in contradistinction to what other commentators have written, including Rashi. Rasbam feels that Rashi has not always chosen the path of *p'shat* even though he had declared (Genesis 3:8) "I have only come for *p'shuto shel mikra*."

Many times when we probe Rashi's meaning further, we find that his interpretation is, in fact, a better fit with *p'shat* than is that of the Rashbam. Our verse above is, I believe, a good example of this.

Rashi points out the significance of "today."

Deut. 29:14

כִּי אֶת־אֲשֶׁר יֶשְׁנוֹ פֹּה עִמָּנוּ עֹמֵד הַיּוֹם לִפְנֵי הִי אֱלֹקֵינוּ וְאֵת אֲשֶׁר אֵינֶנּוּ פֹּה עִמָּנוּ הַיּוֹם.

> **וְאֵת אֲשֶׁר אֵינֶנּוּ פֹּה:** וְאַף עִם דּוֹרוֹת הָעֲתִידִים לִהְיוֹת.
>
> **And those who are not here**: *Rashi*: Even generations destined to be [born].

Questioning Rashi

A Question: Rashi's comment seems somewhat far out. Why the need for the it? Why can't he understand these words simply, i.e. all those not present at this assembly? And how does someone make a covenant with someone not yet alive?

Hint: See the previous verses.

What's bothering Rashi?

Your Answer:

What Is Bothering Rashi?

An Answer: The first verse in the *sedra* (29:9) says explicitly who were present at this assembly. They included "the heads of the tribes, your elders, your law officers, *every man of Israel*."

If every man of Israel was present, who could be meant by "those not present here today"?

This is what's bothering Rashi.

How does Rashi's comment deal with this?

Nitzavim

Your Answer:

Understanding Rashi

An Answer: "Those not here today" means "those not here *today!*" The emphasis is on "today," which implies those here at some other time — in the future.

But the question has been asked: How can an agreement be made with someone not yet born?

Can you answer this?

Your Answer:

A Fuller Understanding

An Answer: From a legal point of view this may be difficult to justify. But from a historical or sociological perspective this is quite normal. Of all the possible legacies that parents could hand over to their children, religion is the most universal and most long-lasting. Parents can pass on to their offspring any one of a number of allegiances — political, national, intellectual, social philosophical and others. But none is as common as transmitting one's religious affiliation to the next generation. Nor is any as binding as the religious commitment. Why this is so may be a mystery, but it remains a fact of human society. Rashi's comment reflects this phenomenon. The nation that stood at Sinai and the next generation who heard Moses' final oration in the land of Moav, accepted G-d's covenant, thereby obligating themselves and all their future generations to its fulfillment.

"Today" — The Seven Code

I have shown elsewhere (*"Studying the Torah: A Guide to In-depth Interpretation"*) how the Torah emphasizes a theme by repeating a key word seven times within one *parashah*. The word "today" היום is repeated seven times in chapter 29, which delineates a *parashah* (from 29:9-28). (Interestingly enough, also chapter 30 has "today" repeated seven times.)What is the message? Obviously "today" was an important day for those present. It was the last day of Moses' life; it was a day that the covenant was made (renewed), the people were warned "today," and they were sustained "today" as G-d's nation. But in spite of the emphasis on today, even "those *not here* today" were also included in the ceremony and the commitment. And that may be because only if "today" has the seeds of future "today"s within it, does it have any lasting significance.

There is more to knowing than meets the eye.

Deut. 29:25

וַיֵּלְכוּ וַיַּעַבְדוּ אֱלֹהִים אֲחֵרִים וַיִּשְׁתַּחֲווּ לָהֶם אֱלֹהִים אֲשֶׁר לֹא־יְדָעוּם
וְלֹא חָלַק לָהֶם.

לֹא יְדָעוּם: לא ידעו בהם גבורת אלהות.
Whom they knew not: *Rashi:* Whom they had never experienced any divine power.

What would you ask on this comment?

YOUR QUESTION:

QUESTIONING RASHI

A Question: Why does Rashi not accept the more obvious meaning of these words — gods whom they did not know, foreign gods ?

What is wrong with such an interpretation?

YOUR ANSWER:

WHAT IS BOTHERING RASHI?

An Answer: The verse condemns worshipping "gods they had not known." But if they worshipped them, in what sense can we say they didn't know them? They knew them enough to worship them! So these words cannot be taken at face value.

How does Rashi's comment deal with this?

Your Answer:

Understanding Rashi

An Answer: According to Rashi, "known" does not mean "being aware of" as we might say "I know who he is." Here it means "knowing these gods to be gods," that is, to be powers that have manifested their might to the benefit of their worshippers. But these gods do not have such power and the people could not have "known" them in such a god-like capacity.

Great is the day of the Ingathering of the Exiles...even the exiles of the nations.

Deut. 30:3

וְשָׁב הִי אֱלֹקֶיךָ אֶת־שְׁבוּתְךָ וְרִחֲמֶךָ וְשָׁב וְקִבֶּצְךָ מִכָּל־הָעַמִים אֲשֶׁר הֱפִיצְךָ הִי אֱלֹקֶיךָ שָׁמָּה.

וְשָׁב הִי אֱלֹקֶיךָ אֶת שְׁבוּתְךָ: הֵיה לוֹ לכתוב יוהשיב את שבותְךָ'
רבותינו למדו מכאן כביכול שהשכינה שרויה עם ישראל בצרת
גלותם וכשנגאלין הכתיב גאלה לעצמו - שהוא ישוב עמהם.
ועוד יש לומר שגדול יום קבוץ גליות בקושי כאלו הוא עצמו
צריך להיות אוחז בידיו ממש איש איש ממקומו, כעניין שנאמר
[ישי' כז:יב]'ואתם תלקטו לאחד אחד בני ישראל' ואף בגליות
שאר האמות מצינו [יחזקאל כט:יד] 'ושבתי את שבות מצרים'.

And *Hashem*, your G-d, will return (with) your captives: *Rashi:* It should have written והשיב את שבותְךָ 'And He will cause the captives to return.' Our Rabbis derive from here that the *Shechina* (Divine Presence), so to speak, resides with Israel in the suffering of their exile. And when they are redeemed, He ascribes redemption to Himself; that is, that He will return (together) with them. And additionally one may interpret (this verse), that the day of the ingathering of the Exiles is so momentous and difficult, it is as if He, Himself, would need to grasp with His hands literally each Jew from his place (in Exile) as it

> says (Isaiah 27:12) 'You, the Children of Israel, shall be plucked one by one.' And also with regard to the other nations we find this (Ezekial 29:14), 'I shall return the captivity of Egypt.'

QUESTIONING RASHI

Since Rashi himself states his difficulty, we will go straight to his problem.

WHAT IS BOTHERING RASHI?

An Answer: Rashi states the problem clearly. It appears that the grammar is amiss in this verse. The Hebrew word ושב is intransitive; it literally means "and He (G-d) will (Himself) return." But since the Torah is speaking of G-d gathering in the Jews from the exile, it should have said והשיב which is transitive; meaning "He will cause the captives to return." Rashi offers two approaches to explain why the Torah used the apparently inappropriate word.

How do his answers deal with this question?

YOUR ANSWER:

UNDERSTANDING RASHI

An Answer: Let us take Rashi's two interpretations one at a time.

His first explanation is that the verse says what it intends to say. That is, that G-d, in fact, is in Exile. He went into Exile together with His people Israel. So, when G-d will return Israel from its Exile, He, Himself, will also return from Exile. The thought is an uplifting one; one that offers the exiled nation inspiration during their difficult years away from home. It recalls an earlier Rashi in Exodus (3:2) when Moses saw the Burning Bush, which symbolized "I am with them in their distress."

Rashi's second *drash* is that G-d will be in Exile because He will have to go there personally, take a hold of each Jew individually and pull him out of Exile. Apparently the Jew's attachment to life in the Exile would be so strong that G-d, Himself, and no mere angel, would be needed to accomplish this feat.

The first explanation highlights G-d's love of His People. The second highlights the People's love of the good life in Exile. Both interpretations explain why the word ושב is used. The reason: Because G-d Himself is in Exile.

But Rashi's last comment, regarding the nations of the world ("also with regard to the other nations, we find this"), is strange. Can you see a question here?

YOUR QUESTION:

QUESTIONING RASHI

A Question: The point of this comment is unclear. Is Rashi telling us, that G-d also loves the nations so much that He will also go into exile to be with them in their distress? That is a bit strange. In fact, the prophets do speak of G-d returning the gentile nations to their homeland. See Jeremiah (48:47) where it says "I will bring back the captivity of Moab, in the end of days." And later on he says (49:6) "And afterwards I will bring back the captivity of the children of Ammon." And we also have the verse quoted in Rashi about G-d returning the captivities of Egypt. So we see that G-d does intend to return all these nations to their original homeland, in the end of days. But returning them to their national homeland is one thing and going into Exile with them is quite another matter. Does Rashi mean to say that G-d will go into exile with these gentile nations as He does with Israel?

How do you understand his last comment?

YOUR ANSWER:

UNDERSTANDING RASHI

An Answer: Rashi's latter comment is connected to his second *drash* and not to the first one. The second interpretation stresses the difficulty of bringing the Jewish captivity back to its homeland. This was based on the use of the intransitive ושב — He, Himself, will return. Rashi wants to show us that the intransitive word שב is used as well with other nations, because they, too, will be reluctant to return to their homeland. So it as if G-d would have to go after them into their exile in order to bring them back to their homeland. But Rashi does not mean that G-d *resides* with them in their exile (Rashi's first explanation), suffering their suffering, as He does with Israel.

THE RETURN OF NATIONS TO THEIR HOMELAND _____

We could ask why is it so important for the nations to be returned to their own lands. But the question reflects a narrow view of G-d's sovereignty in this world. *Hashem* is the Lord of the earth and the fullness thereof. He is the G-d of all nations. He gave each their parcel of land, as He gave Israel theirs. Each nation is entitled to live in its G-d-given territory. Reading the chapters of Jeremiah, we learn that just as Israel was exiled for its sins, so too other nations were exiled for their sins. Their sins always included idol worship and their affliction of Israel. In the end of days, after all nations recognize *Hashem* as the one G-d, then Israel and all other nations will be returned to their rightful places. And that is as it should be, for that was G-d's original plan.

The Talmudic Sage, Samuel, said something similar. He said "there is no difference between our times (before the Messiah) and the days of Messiah, except for [Israel's] subjugation to the nations." That means that the most outstanding change that will take place when the Messiah arrives will be that Israel will no longer be subjugated to other nations. Because Israel has always been the weakest of nations, this means that in the End of Days, no longer will Might be Right. Weak Israel will be treated with the same respect as any strong country because G-d will have manifested His dominion over all the nations. Then Right will be Might. And all nations will live in their land in peace, according to G-d's will.

A CLOSER LOOK_____

Rashi's two interpretations can be seen as two complementary interpretations.

Our verse has the word ושב twice.

1) **וְשָׁב** ה' אלקיך את שבותך ורחמך

2) **וְשָׁב** וקבצך מכל העמים

The *Meshech Chachmah* offers an enlightening explanation for the repetition.

The first phrase, he says, refers to the Jewish exiles who long to return to their homeland. They are referred to as שבותך "your captives" because they are in Exile against their will, they are aware that they are in exile. The second phrase refers to those Jews who are scattered among the nations of the world but have no real desire to return to Eretz Yisrael. They are not called "captives" in this phrase because they don't see themselves as captives. They have integrated and assimilated themselves into their homes in exile. Yet, they too will be returned by G-d to their home-land.

With this in mind, we can better understand Rashi's two interpretations. The first comment, which tells us that G-d goes into Exile with His People, refers to the first group. The group of "captives" who feel that they are in captivity because they have not forgotten their G-d. They long for Him. He is with them; He has even gone into captivity with them.

The second group of exiles do not see themselves as "captives" nor are they referred to as such. This group, who have found a comfortable home in Exile, Rashi tells us, will require *Hashem* to go after them into Exile and pull them back one by one ("kicking and screaming"?) to their heri-tage and their homeland.

Rashi alerts us to a subtle implication that we might have missed.

Deut. 30:12

לֹא בַשָּׁמַיִם הִוא לֵאמֹר מִי יַעֲלֶה־לָּנוּ הַשָּׁמַיְמָה וְיִקָּחֶהָ לָּנוּ וְיַשְׁמִעֵנוּ אֹתָהּ וְנַעֲשֶׂנָּה.

> **לֹא בשמים הוא:** שאלו היתה בשמים היית צריך לעלות אחריה ללמדה.
>
> **It is not in the heavens**: *Rashi:* For if it were in the heav-ens, you would be obligated to go up after it to learn it.

QUESTIONING RASHI

A Question: Why does Rashi add these words? What is bothering him?

Hint: As you look at the verse, how would you have interpreted its mean-ing?

YOUR ANSWER:

WHAT IS BOTHERING RASHI?

An Answer: One might have thought that Moses is comforting Israel, by telling them that the Torah is easily attainable ("in your mouth and in your heart to do it"). Fortunately it is not in the heavens, for if it were, then we certainly wouldn't be expected to "go up to the heavens" to get it.

Rashi rejects this reading. He says that were the Torah in the heavens, that would not exempt us from learning it; we would have "to go up" there to get it and learn it.

Why does Rashi choose this interpretation instead of the one he rejected?

Can you see what about this verse makes Rashi's reading more reasonable?

Hint: What is the general message of Moses' words here?

YOUR ANSWER:

UNDERSTANDING RASHI

An Answer: Moses is encouraging the people. He tells them how fortunate they are that the Torah is not distant from them, rather it is "very near to you" (verse 14). He is stressing that it is near and thus easy to fulfill. He is not saying, how fortunate you are that it is near, for if it were far from you (in the heavens or over the sea) then you wouldn't be obligated to go that far to fulfill it. This is no way to encourage them. They might have said, "too bad it isn't in the heavens, because then we would be free of it and would not have the burden of fulfilling it."

Do you see what in the verse supports this interpretation?

YOUR ANSWER:

A CLOSER LOOK

An Answer: The last words of the verse are ויקחה לנו וישמענו אתה ונעשנה "and he will take it for us and make us hear it so that we will do it."

We see that the emphasis is on "doing it." This implies that we must, under any circumstances, fulfill it, even if it were in the heavens. We would have to find someone to retrieve it for us. This is exactly what Rashi has said.

(See *Sefer Zikaron*)

Rashi clarifies a point easily overlooked.

Deut. 30:15

רְאֵה נָתַתִּי לְפָנֶיךָ הַיּוֹם אֶת־הַחַיִּים וְאֶת־הַטּוֹב וְאֶת־הַמָּוֶת וְאֶת־הָרָע.

> **את החיים ואת הטוב:** זה תלוי בזה אם תעשה טוב הרי לך
> חיים ואם תעשה רע הרי לך המות. והכתוב מפרש והולך.
> **Life and Good:** *Rashi:* This one is dependent on the other.
> If you do the good then, behold, you have life; and if you
> do evil; behold, you have death. And the verse goes on to
> explain.

QUESTIONING RASHI

A Question: Why does Rashi say "one is dependent on the other"? Isn't that obvious. What else could the verse mean?

YOUR ANSWER:

WHAT IS BOTHERING RASHI?

An Answer: The verse could be interpreted to mean: G-d is placing before us two rewards, "Life" and the "Good." If we follow His way then we will be rewarded with *both* life and goodness.

But Rashi says this is not its meaning.

How does he interpret the verse? And, why?

YOUR ANSWER:

UNDERSTANDING RASHI

An Answer: Rashi rejects the interpretation that G-d is offering two rewards, life *and* goodness. Instead, he says, G-d is offering one reward and one obligation. The reward is life and the obligation or condition for receiving life, is doing the good, i.e, doing His mitzvos. Thus receiving life is dependent on our doing the good.

How does Rashi know that this is the correct interpretation?

Hint: See the continuation of Rashi's comment.

YOUR ANSWER:

SUPPORT FOR RASHI'S INTERPRETATION

The Answer: Rashi ends his comment by saying that the following verses confirm this interpretation. On the following verse (30:16) Rashi says:

אֲשֶׁר אָנֹכִי מְצַוְּךָ הַיּוֹם לְאַהֲבָה: הרי הטוב ובו תלוי **וְחָיִיתָ וְרָבִיתָ:**
הרי החיים.

Which I command you today to love: *Rashi:* This is 'the good', and on it is dependent **And you will live and flourish**: *Rashi:* This is 'the life.'

WHAT IS RASHI SAYING?

See how Rashi interprets "the good" as what we are to do. This is obviously the meaning because the verse says that we are *commanded* to "love *Hashem*...to go in His ways" etc. Then we will receive the promise of a reward "you will live and you will flourish." This is the "life" mentioned in verse 15.

Rashi's interpretation of verse 16 validates his understanding of verse 15.

A CLOSE LOOK AT THE TORAH'S WORDS

There is another indication that the correct interpretation is that we have here both obligation and reward and not two rewards. It comes from the Torah's words themselves.

The Torah says "I have *placed before you* today life and good and death and bad." G-d is offering a choice, He is *placing before us a choice* — לְפָנֶיךָ, He is not giving us an outright gift. Now as you think about it, what kind of choice is there between life and death? Who would choose death over life? And if "good" meant a reward (and not an obligation to do the good) who would choose bad over good? There would be here no real choice, no real struggle.

If, on the other hand, the choice was between doing the good, heeding G-d's mitzvos or doing the bad, i.e. not heeding His mitzvos, that is a real choice, one that demands an exercise in free will.

Thus Rashi wisely points out that Life is dependent on our doing the good and Death would be dependent on our doing the bad. That is a true choice, the ultimate existential choice.

A non-comment sparks thoughts.

Deut. 31:1

וַיֵּלֶךְ מֹשֶׁה וַיְדַבֵּר אֶת־הַדְּבָרִים הָאֵלֶּה אֶל־כָּל־יִשְׂרָאֵל.

וילך משה וגו':

And Moses went etc.: [no comment]

This "Rashi-comment" is a bit strange, for there is no comment here.

The question is: Why does Rashi give us a *dibbur hamaschil* when he has no comment to offer on these words.

Many have wondered about this strange phenomenon.

UNDERSTANDING RASHI'S *DIBBUR HAMASCHIL*

The answer is quite simple. We have already explained (see *What's Bothering Rashi? Bamidbar* Verse 1:1) that Rashi begins his commentary to every sedra in the Chumash by quoting the first words of the sedra which form the name of that sedra, *whether or not he has a comment to make.* Our sedra is named *Vayelech,* so Rashi quotes the words וילך משה, even though he has no comment to make on these words.

There are similar instances of this in the book of *Devarim.* See the first comment in *parashas Re'eh* (Deut.11:26) and *parashas Ki Savo* (Deut. 26:1). Many other such cases can be found throughout Rashi's Torah commentary. Rashi's lack of commentary is more obvious in our verse, because here Rashi has no other comment on this verse, whereas in the two cases cited above Rashi does have a comment on other words in the first verse, although his comment has nothing to do with his first *dibbur hamaschil.* That *dibbur,* as we said, is placed there because it is the first words of the sedra.

This custom of quoting the first words of each sedra probably was done to show the student where a new *sedra* began. Remember, originally, Rashi's commentary was hand written on a separate scroll, without the words of the Chumash accompanying it. Only after the printing press was invented (several hundred years after Rashi's death) was the Torah printed together with commentaries. Then Rashi's commentary was on the same page as the Torah's words themselves. Since we mention the printing press, it is interesting to note that the first Hebrew book printed (*circa* 1470) was Rashi's Torah commentary. At this first publication it was printed without the Chumash. In other words, Rashi was printed even before the Torah itself was printed! This is some indication of the high regard his commentary had already gained among the people by the 15th century.

Although Rashi does not comment on the words "And Moses went" other commentators do. As you look at the verse, can you think of the question they deal with?

YOUR QUESTION:

OTHER COMMENTATORS' QUESTION

A Question: The Ramban, Ibn Ezra, Abarbanel and others ask: Where did Moses go to? The Torah only says "And Moses went," but doesn't say where he went or why he needed to go anywhere. In the previous *sedra, Nitzavim*, it says that Moses addressed the whole nation (Deut. 29:9). What need then was there for him to go anywhere since, in our *sedra,* he continued to speak to the people and the whole nation was present?

Can you suggest an answer?

YOUR ANSWER:

SOME COMMENTATORS' ANSWERS

Some Answers: The Ramban explains that after Moses finished his address to the people (in *Nitzavim*) the people returned to their tents. Now Moses wanted to bid them farewell before his death. This was a personal message and he wanted to deliver it personally. And so "He went" from the Camp of the Levites, where he resided, to the Camp of Israel, where the people resided and personally bid them farewell.

The Ibn Ezra gives an interesting explanation of the reason for Moses' going to each tribe. He says that Moses wanted to console them on his imminent death. He told them they should not fear, for *Hashem* would guide Joshua who would take care of them after his death. The Ibn Ezra speculates that it was at this time, on these individual visits with each tribe, that Moses gave them his final blessings, as is recorded later in *parashas V'Zos haBrachah*.

THE LESSON: MOSES' MODESTY

Moses could just as easily (actually, more easily for him) have called the people to assemble before him, as he had done whenever he had a message for them. But his humility prevented him from exploiting his lofty position as leader and the respect the people had for him. Instead, he personally went from tribe to tribe to pay his last farewells. Moses' modesty is thus as evident on the last day of service to his people as it was on his first day, forty years earlier, when he was chosen to lead them. At that time he said, in his self-effacing manner, "Who am I that I should go to Pharaoh?" (Exodus 3:12). The circle is now closed when Moses, at the end of his public service, humbly makes his way to each tribe to speak with them personally and convey his blessings to them.

Rashi teaches us the versatility of the letter ו

Deut. 31:1-2

וַיֵּלֶךְ מֹשֶׁה וַיְדַבֵּר אֶת־הַדְּבָרִים הָאֵלֶּה אֶל־כָּל־יִשְׂרָאֵל. וַיֹּאמֶר אֲלֵיהֶם־ בֶּן־מֵאָה וְעֶשְׂרִים שָׁנָה אָנֹכִי הַיּוֹם לֹא־אוּכַל עוֹד לָצֵאת וְלָבוֹא וַה' אָמַר אֵלַי לֹא תַעֲבֹר אֶת־הַיַּרְדֵּן הַזֶּה.

> **וה' אמר אלי:** זהו פירוש ילא אוכל עוד לצאת ולבאי לפי שה' אמר אלי.
>
> **And *Hashem* said to me:** *Rashi:* That is the meaning of "I can no longer go out and come in" *because* "Hashem, said to me."

WHAT IS RASHI SAYING?

Rashi has given the letter ו the meaning of "because" and not its usual meaning of "and." Instead of "I can no longer go out and come in *and* Hashem has said to me."

The verse now reads: "I can no longer go out and come in *because Hashem* has said to me."

It is our job to understand why Rashi has made this change. It should be said that having the ו mean "because" is quite unusual, and if Rashi makes this change, then he should have cogent justification for doing so.

Why do you think he made the change?

YOUR ANSWER:

WHAT IS BOTHERING RASHI?

An Answer: The previous words "I can no longer go out and come in" can mean either "I am not able" or "I am not allowed." Rashi had explained these words to mean "I am *not allowed* to go out and come in." This is because the Torah testifies to Moses' healthy physical state at the time of his death, when it says "his eyes had not dimmed and his freshness did not fade" (Deut. 34:7). So it couldn't be that he was physically unable.

In addition to this, were the meaning "I am not *able*" then the next words make no sense "And G-d said 'You shall not pass over this Jordan.'" If Moses was physically unable "to go out and come in" then there was no need for G-d to tell him 'You will not pass over this Jordan.' If he was unable, he could not pass over, in any event.

Do you see how Rashi's comment makes sense out of the verse?

YOUR ANSWER:

UNDERSTANDING RASHI

An Answer: It is for these reasons that Rashi understood the words לא אוכל to mean "I am not allowed." Once these words are interpreted in this way, the next words והי אמר לי take on the meaning "*because Hashem* said to me."

QUESTIONING THE ו AS "BECAUSE"

But we are left with the question: How can Rashi interpret the ו as "because"?

Actually the *Mizrachi* asks this question but has no answer to offer.

Can you think of another place in the Torah where the ו has this meaning?

A difficult question.

YOUR ANSWER:

A BETTER UNDERSTANDING

An Answer: In Genesis 2:5 on the words ואדם אין לעבוד את האדמה – "*and* there was not yet a man to work the soil." Rashi says this means **לפי** שאדם אין לעבוד את האדמה —"*because* there was not yet a man to work the soil." Here we have ו meaning "because." This additional instance affords Rashi's present interpretation some legitimacy.

There are also instances in the Torah where the ו has the meaning of "so that" or "in order that." See, for example, Leviticus 21:14,15; Numbers 17:5; and Deut. 17:17.

We see from our verse and from other examples, that in the Tanach the letter ו has meanings other than its usual "and."

(See *Tzaidah laDerech*)

Grammatical differences make a difference.

Deut. 31:7

וַיִּקְרָא מֹשֶׁה לִיהוֹשֻׁעַ וַיֹּאמֶר אֵלָיו לְעֵינֵי כָל־יִשְׂרָאֵל חֲזַק וֶאֱמָץ כִּי אַתָּה תָּבוֹא אֶת־הָעָם הַזֶּה אֶל־הָאָרֶץ אֲשֶׁר נִשְׁבַּע הי לַאֲבֹתָם לָתֵת לָהֶם וְאַתָּה תַּנְחִילֶנָּה אוֹתָם.

כי אתה תבוא את העם הזה: ארי את תעול עם עמא הדין. משה אמר ליהושע, זקנים שבדור יהיו עמך, הכל לפי דעתן ועצתן אבל הקב"ה אמר ליהושע כי אתה תביא את בני ישראל אל הארץ אשר נשבעתי להם ־ תביא על כרחם, הכל תלוי בך, טול מקל והך על קדקדן. דבר אחד לדור ולא שני דברים לדור.

Because you will come with this people: Rashi: (As *Targum Onkelos* translates) Because you will come with this people. Moses said to Joshua "The elders of the generation will be with you. Everything [should be decided] according to their opinion and their advice." But the Holy One, blessed be He, said to Joshua (verse 31:23) "Because you will bring the Children of Israel to the Land which I swore to them" — "Bring them" even against their will, everything is dependent on you. Take a stick and hit them over their head! One leader in a generation, not two leaders in a generation.

Rashi is relating to an apparent contradiction between two verses. Can you see what it is?

YOUR ANSWER:

WHAT IS BOTHERING RASHI?

An Answer: In our verse and in verse 23 Joshua is told that he will be the one who will lead the nation as it enters the Holy Land. But while the phrasing is similar, there are some differences. Rashi centers in on one of them. Our verse has כי אתה **תבוא את** העם הזה while verse 23 has כי אתה **תביא את** בני ישראל אל הארץ. The first means "you **will come (or enter) with** this nation," the second means "you **will bring** the Children of Israel..." Rashi is asking: What is the meaning of this different phrasing?

Do you see how he answers this question?

YOUR ANSWER:

UNDERSTANDING RASHI

An Answer: Rashi explains that the difference between these two verses — one saying that Joshua *will come with* the people, the other saying he *will bring* the people — is due to who is the one speaking to Joshua. In our verse, it is Moses speaking to Joshua; in verse 23 it is *Hashem* speaking to him. When Moses speaks, he tells Joshua to treat the people's representatives (the Elders) as equals. He should not make decisions unilaterally; he must consult with them before doing anything. On the other hand, when *Hashem* speaks to Joshua, He gives him a free hand, even encourages him to take the lead. The rule: There can be only one leader in the generation, not two, otherwise the people will be confused and there will likely be only qualified loyalty to the leader, which means he will have questionable authority. Such a leader cannot lead.

(See *Mizrachi*)

QUESTIONING THE RATIONAL FOR THIS DIFFERENCE _____

A Question: Why do you think Moses told Joshua "you will come with the people" while *Hashem* told him "you will bring the people"? Can you explain the different approaches?

YOUR ANSWER:

THE *BECHOR SHOR* AND *CHIZKUNI* EXPLAIN _____

The *Bechor Shor* suggests that since Moses himself conducted his leadership with modesty and humility, so when he passed on the mantle of leadership to his student and successor, he instructed him to act likewise. But when G-d spoke to Joshua, He told him that he would have to exert his authority. G-d realized that some people *command* the privilege of authority by their mere presence, as Moses did, while others must *demand* that privilege, as Joshua would have to.

The *Chizkuni* makes another distinction. He points out that our verse says that when Moses spoke to Joshua he did so before all Israel. In their presence he didn't want to alienate the people against their new leader. So he showed them that Joshua would lead them with their consent, he would come "together with them." When *Hashem* spoke to Joshua regarding his role as leader (verse 23), the people were not privy to that command. Thus their sensitivities did not have to be taken into account.

Rashi clarifies an apparent contradiction.

Deut. 31:9

וַיִּכְתֹּב מֹשֶׁה אֶת־הַתּוֹרָה הַזֹּאת וַיִּתְּנָהּ אֶל־הַכֹּהֲנִים בְּנֵי לֵוִי הַנֹּשְׂאִים אֶת־אֲרוֹן בְּרִית ה' וְאֶל־כָּל־זִקְנֵי יִשְׂרָאֵל.

> **ויכתב משה, ויתנה:** כשנגמרה כלה נתנה לבני שבטו.
> **And Moses wrote, and he gave it**: *Rashi:* When it was completely finished he gave it to the sons of his tribe (Levi).

It is noteworthy to pay attention to the *dibbur hamaschil*. See how Rashi selects the words he wants to comment on and leaves out those that he is not focusing on, i.e. only those that are the direct subject of his commentary.

What would you ask on his comment?

YOUR QUESTION:

QUESTIONING RASHI

A Question: What has Rashi told us here? He seems to say more or less what the Torah itself says. He does replace the Torah's words "to the Priests, the sons of Levi" with "to the sons of his tribe (Levi)." That needs to be understood.

What is bothering him?

Hint: Look at the *dibbur hamaschil.*

YOUR ANSWER:

WHAT IS BOTHERING RASHI?

An Answer: Rashi is mainly troubled by the word ויתנה "and he gave it" in the past tense. How can the Torah say "and he *gave* it"? This would mean that Moses gave the Torah to the sons of Levi when it was not yet complete. Significant sections were yet to be written — the Song of *Ha'azinu* and Moses' blessings in *V'Zos haBrachah*. This can't be the correct meaning, for he wouldn't have handed over an incomplete Torah.

Furthermore, we are told that only later did Moses hand over the complete Torah (Deut. 31:24):

"And it was when Moses finished writing the words of this Torah in a book till they were complete. And Moses commanded the Levites, the bearers of the Ark of the covenant of *Hashem,* saying. Take this book of the Torah and place it on the side of the Ark of the covenant of *Hashem,* your G-d, and it will be there as a witness against you."

We see that only later was the complete Torah handed over. Notice also that this verse says it was handed over to the Levites, this is different from our verse which says Moses gave it to the Priests, the sons of Levi, and to the Elders.

Do you see what Rashi's comment does and why?

YOUR ANSWER:

UNDERSTANDING RASHI

An Answer: First of all, Rashi says that the words ויכתב ויתנה must not be translated "And he wrote and he gave over"; rather their meaning is "And *when* he wrote the *complete* Torah, then he gave it over to his tribe."

Secondly, Rashi corrects the possible misconception that only the Priests received the Torah. In fact, the whole Tribe of Levi received it, which includes the Priests.

That explains matters. But the question now is, how can Rashi change what the verse in fact says? How can he say that Moses gave over the Torah when it was completed when the verse says that he now gave over the Torah, before it was completed?

YOUR ANSWER:

A DEEPER UNDERSTANDING

An Answer: The simplest answer is that Rashi realized that verse 31:24 contradicted our verse, and of the two verses, verse 24 most likely reflected what actually happened. Because it makes more sense to say that Moses gave the *complete* Torah to the Levites, than it does to think that he gave them an incomplete Torah.

The problem is not with Rashi; it is with the Torah itself! Why does our verse say something that is not so? Why does our verse say Moses gave over the Torah to the Levites, when, in fact, he had not yet done so?

YOUR ANSWER:

THE TORAH'S COMPOSITIONAL STYLE

An Answer: The Torah has its own stylistic compositional characteristics in addition to the important content it conveys. One of those characteristics is that the Torah will complete recounting an episode before another event is recorded, even if that event took place earlier. An example of this can be found in Genesis (11:32). Terach's death is recorded before Abram sets out on his journey to the land of Canaan. In actuality Abram left Haran *before* Terach died. This non-chronological order was chosen by the Torah in order to first have closure on the story of Terach, before going on to the significant and sweeping story of Abram's travels.

Our verse, which tells of Moses giving over the Torah, is immediately followed by the laws of *Hakhail*, which are unrelated to our verse. It is understandable that the Torah would "tie up" the previous section, which speaks of Moses' last words to Joshua and his last act of handing over the Torah, before beginning the laws of *Hakhail.* So our verse is a midway summary statement about Moses giving over the book of the Torah. Later, in verse 24, we have the Torah's recording of the actual event.

(See *Mesiach Ilmim*)

A lesson in child rearing.

Deut. 31:12

הַקְהֵל אֶת־הָעָם הָאֲנָשִׁים וְהַנָּשִׁים וְהַטַּף וְגֵרְךָ אֲשֶׁר בִּשְׁעָרֶיךָ לְמַעַן יִשְׁמְעוּ וּלְמַעַן יִלְמְדוּ וְיָרְאוּ אֶת הי אֱלֹקֵיכֶם וְשָׁמְרוּ לַעֲשׂוֹת אֶת־כָּל־דִּבְרֵי הַתּוֹרָה הַזֹּאת.

> **הָאֲנָשִׁים:** לִלְמוֹד. **וְהַנָּשִׁים:** לִשְׁמוֹעַ. **וְהַטַּף:** לָמָּה בָּא? לָתֵת שְׂכַר לִמְבִיאֵיהֶם.
>
> **The men:** *Rashi:* To learn. **And the women:** *Rashi:* To listen. **And the infants:** *Rashi:* Why did they come? To give merit to those who brought them.

RASHI'S TALMUDIC SOURCE

Rashi's comment is a direct quote from the Talmud (*Chagigah* 3a).

"There was an incident with Rabbi Yochnana son of Beroka, and Rabbi Eliezer Chasma who were going to greet Rabbi Yehoshua in P'kein. He (Rabbi Yehoshua) said to them 'What new insight (*chidush*) did you learn in the Bais Midrash today?' They replied: 'We are your students and from your waters (Torah) we drink' (meaning, you are our teacher and you can teach us, we cannot teach you). He replied: 'Nevertheless, it is impossible that there is a Bais Midrash without a *chidush*.' (They then proceeded to tell him the drash about *Hakhail,* which we have in our Rashi-comment.) Rabbi Yehoshua then replied: 'You had a beautiful pearl in your possession and you intended to keep it from me!'"

Background

On this Talmudic passage the *Mar'shah* explains the following point. The טף in this verse must be referring to children under Bar/Bas Mitzvah age, for if they were already Bar/Bas Mitzvah they would themselves be commanded to come to the *Hakhail,* for they too are bound by all the mitzvos. And if these under-Bar/Bas Mitzvah-age children were old enough to benefit from education, גיל חינוך, which is above the age of six years, then their parents would be obligated to bring them as part of their mitzvah of *Chinuch* (one's obligation to educate one's child.) Such children are actually referred to in the very next verse "And their children who did not know etc." So, our verse must be referring to mere toddlers and infants, even below the age of education.

In light of this, what question begs to be asked on this comment?

YOUR QUESTION:

Questioning Rashi

A Question: It is understandable that men come to learn and that woman come to listen, (and today, we might add, listen *and* learn) but if the infants have no educational benefit from being at this Assembly, why should their parents receive merit for bringing them?

This question has stumped many a Torah commentator. Can you think of an answer?

YOUR ANSWER:

Understanding Rashi

Several answers have been suggested. I prefer the following ones.

One Answer: Note that it was Rabbi Yehoshua who learned this *chidush* from his students and praised them highly for the idea. We should also note that Rabbi Yochanan ben Zakai praised his student, Rabbi Yehoshua (*Pirkei Avos* Ch. 2:8) with the words "Happy is the one who gave birth to him." This is explained by reference to another story in the

Talmud (Jerusalem Talmud, *Yevamos* Ch. 9), where we are told that Yehoshua's mother would bring him as an infant, while still in his carriage, to the entrance of the Bais Midrash, so his tender ears could hear the sounds of the Torah discourse taking place there.

How fitting, therefore, that this very same Rabbi Yehoshua, should appreciate the significance of the *drash* which tells us that parents receive reward for bringing their infants to hear the words of Torah at the *Hakhail* Convocation. His mother had done this and she was praised through her son's praise — "Happy is the one who gave birth to him."

(See Meshech Chochmah)

The Lesson

There is a message here. When children of school age apply themselves to learning or, on conversely, when they find ways to avoid learning, they, themselves, deserve the credit for their efforts. This is not to deny the influence that parents have on the development of motivation of their children, yet even the most dedicated and caring parents are limited in their influence. On the other hand, when mere infants are exposed to learning, they are but passive participants in the experience. In such cases, these influences on the child are much more due to their parents' efforts. Such influences, which take root below the level of the child's awareness, exist primarily because of the parents' dedication to creating an all-inclusive educational environment to help their child develop according to their expectations. The results, evident only years later, are best summed up by Rabbi Yochanon's words about Rabbi Yehoshua's mother "Happy is the one who gave birth to him."

Another Suggested Answer:

If we remember that the טף referred to here were mere infants, we realize that if all family members above the age of six went to *Hakhail,* we wonder who would stay home with these infants. In such a case the parents were forced to make the choice between staying home, babysitting with their infants and missing the *Hakhail* ceremony, or taking them along so that they, the parents, could hear *Hakhail.* Rashi's words can now be understood: "Why did the infants come? To give merit ("merit" = being present and hearing the Torah lessons of *Hakhail*) to those that brought them (the parents)."

Rashi alerts us to a subtle change in a word's meaning.

Deut. 31:14

וַיֹּאמֶר הִי אֶל־מֹשֶׁה הֵן קָרְבוּ יָמֶיךָ לָמוּת קְרָא אֶת־יְהוֹשֻׁעַ וְהִתְיַצְּבוּ בְּאֹהֶל מוֹעֵד וַאֲצַוֶּנּוּ וַיֵּלֶךְ מֹשֶׁה וִיהוֹשֻׁעַ וַיִּתְיַצְּבוּ בְּאֹהֶל מוֹעֵד.

וַאֲצַוֶּנּוּ: ואזרזנו.

And I will command him: *Rashi:* I will exhort him.

WHAT IS RASHI SAYING?

Rashi alters the meaning of the word ואצונו, which ordinarily means "to command." In this case, Rashi says, it means "to exhort," to urge him. The word does have this meaning elsewhere in the Torah, as Rashi points out in the beginning of *parashas Tzav*. (Leviticus 6:2).

Granted that ואצונו could mean "to exhort" or "to urge," we can still question Rashi's comment.

Hint: See verses 31:10, 31:23 and 31:25.

YOUR QUESTION:

QUESTIONING RASHI

A Question: In all the verses referred to above, the word צו means to command. Why doesn't Rashi interpret this word in our verse as it is interpreted in most cases in the Torah?

Hint: Look at those verses and their context.

YOUR ANSWER:

UNDERSTANDING RASHI

An Answer: In each of the verses cited above the word ויצו is followed by a mitzvah (the laws of *Hakhail*; telling the Levites to take the Torah), while our verse has no mitzvah following this "command." In fact, what Moses does say is recorded in verse 23. There it tells us that his צו to Joshua was "be strong and courageous." Those are words of exhortation and encouragement, not words commanding a mitzvah.

(See *Mizrachi*)

A clarification and evidence to support it.

Deut. 31: 23

וַיְצַו אֶת־יְהוֹשֻׁעַ בִּן־נוּן וַיֹּאמֶר חֲזַק וֶאֱמָץ כִּי אַתָּה תָּבִיא אֶת בְּנֵי
יִשְׂרָאֵל אֶל־הָאָרֶץ אֲשֶׁר־נִשְׁבַּעְתִּי לָהֶם וְאָנֹכִי אֶהְיֶה עִמָּךְ.

ויצו את יהושע בן נון: מוסב למעלה כלפי שכינה כמו שמפורש
יאל הארץ אשר נשבעתי להם׳.

And He commanded Joshua, the son of Nun: *Rashi:*
This is to be connected [to verse 14] above referring to
the *Shechinah*, as it states explicitly "to the Land which *I
have sworn* to them."

WHAT IS RASHI SAYING?

Rashi tells us that our verse is to be connected with the section beginning with verse 14 above. There *Hashem* is speaking, as it says "And
Hashem said to Moses…" Rashi is clarifying an ambiguity in this verse.

What is unclear? What could be misunderstood here?

YOUR ANSWER:

WHAT IS UNCLEAR IN THIS VERSE?

An Answer: The verse says "And *he* commanded Joshua…" Who commanded
Joshua? It would seem to be referring to Moses, because he was
the subject of the previous verse. As it says "And *Moses* wrote…"
So, I would be inclined to think that it is Moses also who is commanding Joshua.

Rashi tells us this is incorrect. It is *Hashem* who is commanding Joshua.

How does Rashi know this?

Hint: Rashi tells us himself!

YOUR ANSWER:

UNDERSTANDING RASHI

An Answer: Our verse continues to state "to the Land which *I* swore to them."
This could only refer to *Hashem,* for it was *Hashem*, not Moses,
who swore to give the Land to Israel.

But while this is what Rashi says, it is not unequivocal evidence that this was *Hashem* talking. For as the Ramban makes clear (in his commentary on Deut. 4:4), throughout the book of *Devarim* Moses speaks in G-d's name. The chapters of the *Shema*, for example, say "And I will give the rains in their time" but this is Moses speaking. He certainly isn't the power that gives rains in their time. It is G-d, but Moses speaks in His name.

But we have better evidence in verse 14, that our verse is speaking of G-d addressing Joshua. Here it says explicitly "And *Hashem* said to Moses, Behold the days of your death are approaching, call Joshua and place yourselves in the Appointed Tent *and I will command him...*" Our verse continues where that statement left off. It tells us what G-d's command to Joshua was. It was the exhortation "to be strong and firm."

פרשת האזינו

Introduction to the Song _Ha'azinu_

The major portion of this sedra is devoted to the poem _Ha'azinu_. It is instructive to note that this poem or song is different in significant ways from other Songs in the Tanach. There are four other famous Songs, two in the Torah — the Song of the Sea (Exodus 15:1ff) and the Song of the Well (Numbers 21:17ff). There is also the Song of Deborah in the Book of Judges (Ch. 5) and, of course, the Song of Songs of King Solomon. All these Songs are attributed to specific people. The Song of the Sea begins, "Then sang Moses and the Children of Israel." The Song of the Well begins, "Then sang Israel." The Song of Deborah begins, "And Deborah and Barak sang." The Song off Songs begins, "The Song of Songs that were Solomon's." But _Ha'azinu_ begins without any appellation. It is as if the Song itself sings, as it says (Deut. 31:21) "And it will be when these many evils and vicissitudes befall him then this Song will testify before him as a witness..."

Another difference between _Ha'azinu_ and other Biblical songs is that the other songs are praises of G-d for miracles that He wrought for Israel, (or a paean of G-d's love of His people, as in Solomon's Song). In contrast, _Ha'azinu_ is a look into the future and a pessimistic look at that. It is a not a Song of praise, nor a Song of jubilation, it is rather a Song of warning and chastisement.

In spite of these differences, _Ha'azinu_ is a poem like the other Songs and it has the characteristics of a poem, it speaks in allusions, alliterations and parallelisms. This leaves much room for commentary.

The Ramban on _Ha'azinu_

The Ramban has these significant words to say about the _Ha'azinu_ Song:

> "This Song is an assured guarantee of the future redemption, in spite of the nonbelievers. And so is stated in the _Sifrei_. 'This Song

is great in that it contains the present, the past and the future; it contains issues of this world and of the World to Come. And this is what is alluded to when the Scriptures say 'And Moses came and he spoke all the words of this Song in the ears of the people.' It says "all" to intimate that it contains [a prophecy for] all matters regarding their future. And while it (the Song) is small in size, nevertheless it explains many things. And were this Song one of the writings of the astrologers which predicted future events, it would justifiably command our belief, because all of its predictions have been fulfilled up until the present. Nothing has gone unfulfilled. We therefore should also believe and anticipate (the future fulfillment of this Song) with all our heart, for these are the words of G-d, as conveyed by His prophet (Moses) 'the faithful one of His house."

Rashi imposes clarity on a verse with confusing syntax.

Deut. 32:5

שִׁחֵת לוֹ לֹא בָּנָיו מוּמָם דּוֹר עִקֵּשׁ וּפְתַלְתֹּל.

שחת לו וגו': כתרגומו, חבילו להון לא ליה.

בניו מומם: בניו היו, והשחתה שהשחיתו היא מומם.

בניו מומם: מומם של בניו היה ולא מומו.

Corruption is His, etc.: *Rashi:* As the Targum renders: "Corruption is theirs, not His.

It is His children's blemish: *Rashi:* They were His children, and the corruption which they wrought is their blemish.

It is His children's blemish : *Rashi:* It was the blemish of His children, not His blemish.

An Introductory Thought

Before we look at Rashi's comment, let us mention something about the verse itself. The word שחת is central in our verse. We should note that the word שחת appears previously in the Torah. When G-d informs Moses that the Israelites had made themselves a Golden Calf, He says (Exodus 32:7):

לֵךְ רֵד כִּי שִׁחֵת עַמְּךָ...

"Go down (from the mountain) because your people have
acted *corruptibly*...."

Likewise, in the previous sedra (Deut. 31:29), the people are accused of
acting corruptibly in their straying after foreign gods.

כִּי יָדַעְתִּי אַחֲרֵי מוֹתִי כִּי־הַשְׁחֵת תַּשְׁחִתוּן וְסַרְתֶּם מִן־הַדֶּרֶךְ וְגוֹ׳

"For I know that after my death you will surely act
corruptibly and stray from the way..."

So when our verse says שחת לו לא בניו מומם, that word is chosen so as to
ignite an association in our mind which would carry with it all the weight
this word bears. It refers to the people of Israel when they turn away
from G-d. Now let us look at Rashi.

Questioning Rashi

A Question: Rashi seems to be struggling with something here. His last two
comments are on the same words. Can you see what's bothering
him with this verse?

Hint: Read the verse over in Hebrew. Do you see different possible ren-
ditions?

Your Answer:

What Is Bothering Rashi?

An Answer: If we read (and translate) this verse literally we have:

"Corruption is His; not to His sons is the blemish; a stubborn and convo-
luted generation." The sentence is constructed in an odd way and easily
leads to misunderstanding. Did you notice that the words לו לא ("to Him,
not") seem to be reversed? If the Torah had meant that G-d is not the
corrupt one, it would be more appropriate to say:

שִׁחֵת לֹא לוֹ

"Corruption is not His."

But our verse has it just reversed — שחת לו לא — and that does not
sound right. This reading seems to ascribe corruption to G-d and perfec-
tion to His people. That is certainly not the Torah's message. (As we
pointed out above, the word שחת is associated with Israel's backsliding.)
Rashi searches for a more appropriate interpretation.

How do his comments give the verse a new sense?

YOUR ANSWER:

UNDERSTANDING RASHI

An Answer: Rashi turns to *Targum Onkelos* for guidance. The *Targum* separates the word שחת from the word לו. It now means "Corruption [is
theirs]. Not His." The latter is a reversal of a literal reading of the
Hebrew words. It is as if the *Targum* read לו? לא! as "To Him? No!"
Rashi adopts this as the correct interpretation of these words.

Now we come to Rashi's next comment.
It is His children's blemish: *Rashi:* They were His
children and the corruption which they wrought is their
blemish.

Do you see what Rashi is doing with this comment? Why does he add
"They were His children"?

YOUR ANSWER:

WHAT IS BOTHERING RASHI?

An Answer: This verse, as we have pointed out, can be read in various ways.
One is to connect the word לא with the next word בניו. That would
be read as follows:

שִׁחֵת לוֹ----לֹא בָּנָיו

The (mistaken) meaning would be: They are not His children. Rashi
first clarifies that this is not the correct reading. "They were His children"

But then we might wonder why the past tense is used "they *were* His
children."

This leads us to consider another reason for Rashi's comment.

Israel is referred to in various ways in this Song. As "His people" or as
"Jacob" (32:9), or as "nation" (32:6), or as "Yeshurun" (32:15) and most
often, in the anonymous, third person ("He found *him* in the desert"
32:10). Our verse has the more intimate term "children." Rashi is reacting to this deviance.

How does his comment relate to this?

Your Answer:

Understanding Rashi

An Answer: Rashi's comment "They were His children" is meant to emphasize this relationship and the shameful ingratitude of His children towards their Father in Heaven. The emphasis is that they were His children when they acted sinfully. That this is the point of emphasizing the word בנים, can be seen when we look at the very next verse.

...הֲלוֹא־הוּא **אָבִיךָ** קָּנֶךָ הוּא עָשְׂךָ וַיְכֹנְנֶךָ

"... is He not **your Father**, who has obtained you? He has made you and established you."

Here too, the father/child relationship is stressed, because the recalcitrance of a child towards a loving father reveals an ungrateful, inconsiderate, attitude toward one who loves him.

The second part of this comment "and the corruption which they wrought is their blemish" makes a different point. Can you see what is bothering him?

Hint: Read the words בניו מומם carefully. Could they be misinterpreted?

Your Answer:

What Is Bothering Rashi?

An Answer: The words בניו מומם could possibly be read "Being His children, that is their blemish!" This means that being G-d's children is itself a blemish. But certainly this must be rejected outright, because being G-d's children is an honor not a blemish. This you will say is obvious. But it is Rashi's way to make clear the implicit, even if it is obvious. Not the fact that they are G-d's children is the blemish, rather their corrupt behavior is their blemish. So these words mean: "the corruption which they wrought is their blemish." This comment tells us what the word מומם refers to.

(See *Knizel*)

בניו מומם: מומם של בניו היה ולא מומו.

The last Rashi comment, which is on these same words, deals with the suffix ם in the word מומם "their blemish."

This comes to strengthen the beginning comment, that the people's evil ways are the reference of the word מומם. Their evil ways is *their* blemish, not His.

Rashi and Ramban: differing approaches, different interpretations.

Deut. 32:6

הֲלַיהוָה תִּגְמְלוּ־זֹאת עַם נָבָל וְלֹא חָכָם הֲלוֹא־הוּא אָבִיךָ קָּנֶךָ הוּא עָשְׂךָ וַיְכֹנְנֶךָ.

> **עם נבל:** ששכחו את העשוי להם.
>
> **ולא חכם:** להבין את הנולדות ,שיש בידו להיטיב ולהרע.
> **A debased people:** *Rashi:* Who have forgotten [the good] that was done for them.
> **And not wise:** *Rashi:* To understand future events, that He has the power to cause benefit or harm.

QUESTIONING RASHI

A Question: The meaning seems quite clear, why does Rashi see the need to comment here? We would also ask why Rashi brings up such issues as forgetting the [good] that *Hashem* did for them or their not having foresight to realize what may happen to them in the future.

What's bothering him in this verse?

Hint: What is the relationship between the two words נבל and לא חכם?

YOUR ANSWER:

WHAT IS BOTHERING RASHI?

An Answer: The words נבל and לא חכם as used here, would seem to be synonymous terms. But in fact they are not. The term נבל means a base or debased person. See the following verse from Samuel I 25:25:

אַל־נָא יָשִׂים אֲדֹנִי אֶת־לִבּוֹ אֶל־אִישׁ הַבְּלִיַּעַל הַזֶּה עַל־נָבָל כִּי כִשְׁמוֹ
כֶּן־הוּא נָבָל שְׁמוֹ וּנְבָלָה עִמּוֹ וגו'

"Let my lord not set his heart against this base man, against
Naval, for he is as his name implies — Naval is his name
and degradation is his trait etc."

This verse indicates that the word נבל has the connotation of a degraded
or base person. Degraded, in the sense of being ungrateful, as Naval was
(see the Ramban below). This is not the same as "not wise." More appropriate as a synonym to "not wise" would be a word such as כסיל, "a
fool" as we find in Ecclesiastes 10:2:

לֵב חָכָם לִימִינוֹ וְלֵב כְּסִיל לִשְׂמֹאלוֹ

The heart of the wise is to his right; the heart of the fool is
to his left.

In short, the rhythm of our verse leads us to feel that these two words are
intended to be similar, yet, in fact, they are not similar.

It is for this reason that Rashi sees the need to comment on each word
individually, in order to show the specific meaning of each one and their
similarity.

How do his comments clarify matters?

YOUR ANSWER:

UNDERSTANDING RASHI

An Answer: The people act as an עם נבל. The people have been ungrateful, the
essential element of the "Naval." Rashi tells us that this ungratefulness is the result of "forgetting" all the good they have received
from G-d. "Forgetting" is a mental state; it is a sign of intellectual
weakness as opposed to wisdom. This is why Rashi chooses particularly "forgetting" for it is parallel to "not wise."

It is for this reason that Israel is called an עם נבל. For they were un*mind*-
ful of the many benefits that G-d had bestowed upon them. They *forgot*
and did not apply themselves wisely to understand all they had received
from G-d.

When Rashi comes to the words לא חכם, he shows us in what way the
people lacked wisdom. They did not understand that their future is in
G-d's hands, as their past had been until now.

Rashi's wording is reminiscent of a well-known Talmudic saying (*Tamid* 32b) which equates wisdom with the ability to anticipate future events.

איזהו חכם? הרואה את הנולד.

"Who is a wise man? He who foresees future events."

The same idea is expressed further on in the Song (verse 29), which says:

לו חכמו ישכילו זאת, יבינו לאחריתם.

"Would that they were wise they would comprehend this,
they would discern it from their end."

We see that wisdom is equated with seeing what will happen to them in the future.

Rashi accordingly interprets the words לא חכם in our verse in that sense.

The people were not wise in that they didn't give thought to the future and to the reality that their fate is dependent on the quality of their relationship with G-d.

We now realize that the two terms (נבל and לא חכם) have a similar dimension — both refer to the lacunae in their thinking. The people have forgotten all the good G-d had given them and they did not understand what awaited them in the future as a consequence of their irresponsible actions and ungrateful attitude.

THE RAMBAN'S INTERPRETATION

The Ramban explains the meaning of the word נבל and the meaning of the verse:

> "In my opinion one who repays evil to one who did him favors is called a נבל. That is why it says about Naval, the Carmelite 'as his name is, so is he' because David had done him a great favor by watching all his possessions and he [Naval] did not want to repay him a favor, instead he insulted him…And it is possible that he was called [נבל] because he has fallen [נפלה] from the status of being a person. Likewise a dead animal is called a נבלה because it has fallen to the ground and died.
>
> Therefore the meaning of our verse is 'Is this the way you repay *Hashem* for all the good He did for you? You Naval-nation who repays evil for the good received. And not wise enough to know that to yourself you have done this evil, not to G-d…'"

We see how the Ramban deals with the two terms נבל and לא חכם. He does attempt to equate them, as Rashi did. He adds his own flare for searching for the etymology of Hebrew terms, by comparing the word נבל to the word נפל.

A Deeper Look

The *Mesiach Illmim*, one of the early commentaries on Rashi, offers a cogent insight here. He points out that the *Ha'azinu* Song is divided into four sections.

- G-d's kindness to Israel (verses 3-14)

- Israel's rebellion (verse 15-20)

- G-d's vengeance against Israel (verses 21-35)

- G-d's vengeance against Israel's enemies (verses 36-43)

Our verse, with its mention of Israel's ungrateful behavior and foolish disregard for their own fate, summarizes the first three sections of the Song. The verse stands at the entrance of the Song and, in a sense, foretells its major message.

The Lesson

Rashi's comment gives us the moral meaning of this message as he relates Israel's ungratefulness to G-d with their later sufferings.

"Will you requite this to *Hashem*,"	meaning: after all the good He has done to you
"you degraded"	will you act in an ungrateful manner?
"and unwise people?"	Don't you realize that just as He did you good, He can also do you evil?

Rashi's super-sensitivity to nuances leads to precise definition of a common word.

Deut. 32:31

כִּי לֹא כְצוּרֵנוּ צוּרָם וְאֹיְבֵינוּ פְּלִילִים.

> **כי לא כצורנו צורם:** כל זה היה להם לאויבים להבין שהשם
> הסגירם ולא להם ולאלהיהם הנצחון שהרי עד הנה לא יכלו
> כלום אלהיהם כנגד צורינו כי לא כסלענו סלעם. **כל צור**
> **שבמקרא לשון סלע.**
>
> **For not as our Rock is their rock**: *Rashi:* All of this the
> enemies should have understood, that it is *Hashem* who
> has delivered them (Israel) to their hands, and not to them
> nor to their gods is the victory, for until now their gods
> could achieve nothing against our Rock, for "not as our
> Rock is their rock." **Any time the word צור occurs in
> Scriptures it means rock**.

WHAT IS RASHI SAYING?

Rashi is explaining the thrust of these verses (20-31). Israel receives a
terrible setback as their punishment. Yet the gentile nations, who have
inflicted this punishment, should not think it was their power and their
deity who effectuated their victories. *Hashem* has delivered Israel into
their hands. They should have understood this.

This much is clear. It is the last phrase in Rashi's comment (the words in
bold letters), that should awaken our curiosity. What would you ask here?

YOUR QUESTION:

QUESTIONING RASHI

A Question: Why would Rashi need to explain such a familiar word as צור?
When it occurred in the Torah previously Rashi saw no need to
explain it then. Most striking is the fact that this word appears in
our sedra, *Ha'azinu*, already five times (count them: 32:4; 13; 15;
18; 30). So we have two questions: Why does Rashi explain such a
common word? And if there is need to explain it, why didn't Rashi
do so when the word first appeared in the Torah, or at least when it
first appeared in this sedra?

Note: Rashi would not explain a word that is familiar to us, unless he saw a particular need to do so.

What is bothering him here?

Hint: This is not easy. Compare our verse with the others in our sedra where the word צור appears.

YOUR ANSWER:

WHAT IS BOTHERING RASHI?

An Answer: The word צור has two possible meanings. One is rock, meaning strength, and one is creator as in יוצר אור "He who creates light." As we also have in the songs for Shabbos eve — כי ביה ה׳ צור עולמים "For with [the name] יה *Hashem* created worlds" (see Rashi Genesis 2:4). Now, when we look at the previous verses where the word צור is used in our *sedra* we see that it always refers to *Hashem*. Our verse, for the first time, uses it in reference both to *Hashem* and to the god of the gentiles. Can you see why that could make a difference? How could that possibly explain Rashi's need here to explain the meaning of the word.

YOUR ANSWER:

UNDERSTANDING RASHI

An Answer: Rashi is first and foremost a teacher. So when צור occurred previously, it referred exclusively to *Hashem* and it made little difference to our understanding if the word צור was translated as "rock" or as "creator," because *Hashem* is both a Rock (in the sense of strength) and a Creator. Therefore, on the those verses Rashi saw no urgency to give the precise definition of the word. Whether the student understood the word to mean "rock" or whether he thought it meant "creator" made no difference since in either case it referred to *Hashem*. But once he came to our verse where צור refers both to *Hashem* and to a gentile deity, then Rashi had to make matters clear. He had to clarify that צור in the Scriptures never means creator and it certainly does not mean that here, since "their rock" is not a creator. On the other hand, the foreign god may be considered a "rock" because he gives strength to those that believe in him.

(As heard from Nechama Leibowitz)

THE LESSON

It is important to note that while Rashi often translates difficult words in the Torah, he will never translate a familiar word, unless there is some difficulty in understanding the verse and a precise translation is essential to a correct understanding. The difficulty that Rashi relates to is not always readily apparent. But in these cases we must think deeply and ask "What's bothering Rashi?"

A drash *that must be understood to be fully appreciated.*

Deut. 32: 48

וַיְדַבֵּר ה' אֶל מֹשֶׁה בְּעֶצֶם הַיּוֹם הַזֶּה לֵאמֹר.

וַיְדַבֵּר ה' אֶל מֹשֶׁה בעצם היום הזה: בשלשה מקומות נאמר 'בעצם היום הזה' נאמר בנח 'בעצם היום הזה בא נח' וגו' (בראשית ז:יב) במראית אורו של היום, לפי שהיו בני דורו אומרים בכך וכך אם אנו מרגישין בו אין אנו מניחין אותו לכנס בתיבה ולא עוד אלא אנו נוטלין כשילין וקרדומות ומבקעין את התיבה. אמר הקב"ה הריני מכניסו בחצי היום וכל מי שיש בידו כח למחות יבא וימחה. במצרים נאמר 'בעצם היום הזה הוציא ה'' (שמות יב:יא) לפי שהיו מצריים אומרים בכך וכך אם אנו מרגישין בהם אין אנו מניחין אותם לצאת ולא עוד אלא אנו נוטלין סייפות וכלי זין והורגין בהם. אמר הקב"ה הריני מוציאן בחצי היום וכל מי שיש בו כח למחות יבא וימחה. אף כאן במיתתו של משה נאמר בעצם היום הזה לפי שהיו ישראל אומרים בכך וכך אם אנו מרגישין בו אין אנו מניחין אותו. אדם שהוציאנו ממצרים וקרע לנו את הים והוריד לנו את המן והגיז לנו את השליו והעלה לנו את הבאר ונתן לנו את התורה אין אנו מניחין אותו. אמר הקב"ה הריני מכניסו בחצי היום וכו'.

And *Hashem* spoke to Moses on that self-same day: *Rashi:* In three places it says 'on the self-same day.' It is said about Noah 'on the self-same day Noah entered, etc.' when the light of day was in full view. Because his contemporaries said, 'By this and by that (an oath) if we sense him [entering the ark] we won't let him enter the ark and not only that, we will get sledgehammers and axes and smash the ark!' The Holy One, blessed be He, said, 'I will bring him [into the ark] in mid-day. Let anyone who has the power to protest, do so. Concerning Egypt, it is said, 'on the self-same day *Hashem* took out, etc.' Because the Egyptians had said 'By this and by that, if we sense [them leaving] we won't let them go. And not only that, we will get swords and other weapons and kill them. The Holy One, blessed be He, said 'I will take them out [of Egypt] in mid-day. Let anyone powerful enough to protest, do so.' Here as well, concerning Moses' death, it is said 'on the self-same day.' Because the Israelites said 'By this and by that, if we sense him [leaving] we won't let him [go]. The man who took us out of Egypt, split the Sea for us, and brought down the Manna for us, brought us the quail and raised up the well and gave us the Torah – we won't let him! The Holy One, blessed be He, said 'Behold I will take him in mid-day etc.'

This is a beautiful *midrash* which emphasizes the people's love and appreciation of Moses. It is important to stress this, considering all the trouble the people had made for him during the forty years of his leadership.

UNDERSTANDING THE *DRASH*

The *drash* is based on the fact that the word עצם translated here as "self same" and in the *drash* as "mid-day" is superfluous. The verse would have the same meaning were it omitted. The *drash* takes the word to mean "in the strength of the day." This is because the word עצם can also mean "strength." As in Deut. 8:17

כֹּחִי וְעֹצֶם יָדִי עָשָׂה לִי אֶת־הַחַיִל הַזֶּה.

"My power and the strength of my hand made for me this wealth."

Thus the "strength of the day" becomes "in mid-day," when the sun is strongest.

Now let us question Rashi.

YOUR QUESTION:

QUESTIONING RASHI

Some Rashi commentaries have questioned Rashi's statement "in three places it says 'on the self same day.'" They point out that there is another place, which Rashi doesn't mention here, where the words בעצם היום הזה appear. This in *parashas Lech Lecha*. (Genesis 17:23):

וַיִּקַּח אַבְרָהָם אֶת־יִשְׁמָעֵאל בְּנוֹ וְאֵת כָּל־יְלִידֵי בֵיתוֹ וְאֵת כָּל־מִקְנַת כַּסְפּוֹ כָּל־זָכָר בְּאַנְשֵׁי בֵּית אַבְרָהָם וַיָּמָל אֶת־בְּשַׂר עָרְלָתָם בְּעֶצֶם הַיּוֹם הַזֶּה כַּאֲשֶׁר דִּבֶּר אִתּוֹ אֱלֹקִים.

Rashi even comments on this verse in Genesis and says:
"By day and not by night. He was not afraid of the scoffers so that his enemies should not say 'Had we seen him we would not have let him do the circumcision and fulfill G-d's commandment.'"

Since Rashi commented on the verse, he was aware of it when he wrote his commentary on our verse. The question is: Why didn't he include it in his list of verses that had the words בעצם היום הזה?

Can you see why? Can you see a difference between this verse and the three that Rashi does cite?

YOUR ANSWER:

UNDERSTANDING RASHI

An Answer: The verse in *Lech Lecha,* while it has the same phrase, doesn't use it in the same way as in the other three. The three verses that Rashi cites all tell us that G-d made certain that no one would interfere with His plan. Noah was allowed to enter the Ark; the Israelites were allowed to leave Egypt. But in Abraham's case the point of the verse was different. It was Abraham's courage, not G-d's intervention, that was the issue. And since Rashi's whole point on our verse is to show how *Hashem* made sure that His plan was executed, he cites only those verses that are relevant to this point.

(See *Nachlas Ya'akov*)

A DEEPER LOOK

But as we look at the last part of Rashi's comment, which refers to Moses' death, we could ask a question. Rashi says:

"Here as well, concerning Moses' death, it is said 'on the self-same day.' Because the Israelites said 'By this and by that, if we sense him [leaving] we won't let him [go]. The man who took us out of Egypt, split the Sea for us, and brought down the Manna for us, brought us the quail and raised up the Well and gave us the Torah — we won't let him!'"

YOUR QUESTION:

QUESTIONING RASHI

A Question: How is our verse about Moses' death similar to the case of Noah entering the Ark or to that of Israel leaving Egypt? A jealous mob could conceivably stop Noah from entering the Ark; incensed hooligans could possibly stop Israel from escaping their country, but how can any human stop another person from dying? How could the anxious Israelites prevent Moses' death?

What does Rashi mean?

YOUR ANSWER:

A DEEPER UNDERSTANDING

An Answer: The next verses (32:49,50) tells us what G-d said to Moses on that "self-same day."
"Go up to this Mount Ha'avarim, Mount Nevo, which is
in the land of Moab, that faces Jericho....and die on the
mountain, upon which you are going up there…"

We see that a precondition for Moses' death was that he go up the mountain. He was to die on the mountain and had first to ascend the mountain. It was this ascension that the people thought they could prevent. If they stopped Moses from going up Mount Nevo, they would prevent his imminent death. Or so they thought. That is exactly what Rashi means when he says: "Because the Israelites said 'By this and by that, if we sense him [leaving] we won't let him [go].'

A familiar Rashi-comment, but what's behind it?

Deut. 33:2

וַיֹּאמַר הי מִסִּינַי בָּא וְזָרַח מִשֵּׂעִיר לָמוֹ הוֹפִיעַ מֵהַר פָּארָן וְאָתָה
מֵרִבְבֹת קֹדֶשׁ מִימִינוֹ אשׁדת (קרי אֵשׁ דָּת) לָמוֹ.

> וזרח משעיר **למו**: שפתח לבני עשו שיקבלו את התורה ולא
> רצו.
>
> הופיע מהר **פארן**: שהלך שם ופתח לבני ישמעאל שיקבלוה
> ולא רצו.
>
> **ואתה**: לישראל.
>
> **He shone forth from Seir to them**: *Rashi:* He addressed
> the sons of Esau that they should accept the Torah, but
> they did not want to.
>
> **He appeared from Mount Paran**: *Rashi:* He went there
> and addressed the sons of Ishmael that they should accept
> it, but they did not want to.
>
> **And He came**: *Rashi:* To Israel.

WHAT IS RASHI SAYING?

The verse describes G-d's appearance at Mount Sinai when He gave the
Torah to Israel. Rashi's comment is meant to explain the relevance of
places like Seir and Mount Paran which are mentioned in the verse. He
identifies Esau as the nation that dwells in Seir (see Genesis 36:8) and
Ishmael as the people who dwell in Paran (see Genesis 21:21).
Furthermore, he concludes that G-d first went to these nations to offer
them the Torah. Only after they refused, did He offer it to Israel.

What would you ask on this comment?

YOUR QUESTION:

QUESTIONING RASHI

A Question: The whole thrust of this comment seems strange. Did G-d go first to other nations to offer them the Torah and only later turned to Israel, as a last choice?! Rashi's *midrashic* source (the *Sifrei*) actually says that G-d went to *all* the nations first before Israel. Where do we find even a hint of this in the Torah?

Can you explain it?

YOUR ANSWER:

UNDERSTANDING RASHI

An Answer: In fact, the Torah says this quite explicitly. The first chapters of Genesis detail G-d's search for loyal followers. G-d first gave his commandments to Adam, the father of mankind. But Adam slipped early on, transgressing G-d's first commandment by eating from the Tree of Knowledge. Then Adam's son, Cain, perpetrated the ultimate crime against humanity by committing the first homicide when he killed his own brother. Mankind continued on this downward spiral until the generation of the Flood, when all mankind had descended to depths of moral depravity. As a result they were destroyed by the Flood. Only Noah and his family were saved in order to make a new covenant with G-d and became the chosen family. But once again Noah's offspring failed to remain at an acceptable moral and spiritual level. Then Abram was chosen. But this choice was not absolute; and even within Abraham's family further selection was invoked. Isaac and not Ishmael, and of Isaac's sons, Jacob/Israel and not Esau was chosen.

So we see that, in fact, Israel (Abraham's grandson) was chosen *only* *after* the rest of mankind had failed to live up to Divine expectations. Rashi's comment is in accordance with this and should be seen in this light.

A FURTHER QUESTION

A Question: Why does Rashi refer only to Ishmael and Esau when the *midrash* mentions *all* the nations?

YOUR ANSWER:

UNDERSTANDING RASHI

An Answer: Since the verse mentions Seir and Paran this seems to refer just to Esau and Ishmael. But there may be another reason for Rashi's choice.

Let us compare Rashi's interpretation with those of the *Rashbam* and the *Bechor Shor*.

RASHBAM'S AND BECHOR SHOR'S INTERPRETATION

The *Rashbam* interprets these words as following:

"From the four sides of Mount Sinai the light and the angels came by way of Seir and Paran until they reached Mount Sinai."

The *Bechor Shor* has a similar approach:

"From the side of Seir the lightening was first seen….and the appearance of lightening also came by way of Paran…"

These commentaries offer a simpler, less *aggadic*, interpretation. The unnatural, divine light that accompanied the Revelation at Sinai came from all directions towards the focal point of Sinai.

Why did Rashi choose the *aggada* here instead of the simpler interpretation that the *Ba'alei haTosafos* followed?

RASHI'S ANTI-CHRISTIAN AGENDA

A Possible Answer: Here we come to an interesting, lesser known aspect of Rashi's commentary. Some modern students have noticed in Rashi's commentary (particularly on Psalms and Isaiah) that Rashi will prefer an interpretation which refutes a Christian interpretation. Towards the end of Rashi's life the Christians began their death-wielding crusades and anti-Jewish battles. These battles took place both on the battlefields and in the world of scholarly discourse. The Christian clerics vigorously strove to reinterpret the Torah and the Tanach's verses in a way that would seem as if they were prophesying the coming of their god, Yeishu.

Rashi and other Torah commentators showed how these interpretations were incorrect and usually farfetched.

As an example of this see Rashi's commentary to Psalms 2:1:

לָמָּה רָגְשׁוּ גוֹיִם וּלְאֻמִּים יֶהְגּוּ־רִיק.

"Why are the nations in an uproar and the peoples mutter in vain?"

Rashi understands this verse as the battle between the nations of the world and G-d's anointed king. He comments on these words:

> "Our Rabbis learned this matter in reference to the anointed King (the Messiah), but according to its meaning (and as an answer to the nonbelievers)* it is correct to interpret it in reference to David himself."

> *These words have been censored in most printed editions.

In this commentary to Psalms, Rashi makes a point of disabusing the "nonbelievers" of their incorrect understanding of this verse. It does not refer to the Messiah, who would come in the End of Days, which the nonbelievers could interpret as a reference and prophecy of their god, Yeishu. This is definitely not a correct reading; rather, Rashi says, the correct interpretation is that it refers to King David, the first Messiah. Seen in this way, the nonbelievers have no Scriptural "proof" for their dogma.

So perhaps we can theorize that in our verse, Rashi had the same goal. He intentionally made a point of showing a Scriptural basis for rejecting the claims of the Muslims (Ishmael) and of the Christians (Esau) to be the followers of the true Messiah. Our verse says that they had been offered G-d's Torah, but had rejected it.

This would explain why Rashi preferred this interpretation over the simpler *p'shat,* as interpreted by the *Rashbam* and *Bechor Shor.* It would also explain why Rashi emphasized just Ishmael and Esau, while the *midrash* mentioned all the nations. Ishmael and Esau were the forefathers of the two major religions that vied with Judaism. Rashi's comment was intended to defend his faith. It should be mentioned that Rashi's Torah commentary was diligently studied and highly respected by Christian clerics in the Middle Ages.

One of Rashi's one-word clarifications.

Deut. 33:5

וַיְהִי בִישֻׁרוּן מֶלֶךְ בְּהִתְאַסֵּף רָאשֵׁי עָם יַחַד שִׁבְטֵי יִשְׂרָאֵל.

> **וַיְהִי:** הקב״ה. **בִישֻׁרוּן מֶלֶךְ:** תמיד עול מלכותו עליהם.
> **And He was:** *Rashi:* The Holy One blessed be He. **King in Yeshurun**: *Rashi:* The yoke of His sovereignty is always upon them.

QUESTIONING RASHI

Rashi says the king referred to here is G-d. One-word comments like these are usually intended to help us avoid a misunderstanding.

A Question: What other king could be intended?

YOUR ANSWER:

An Answer: It is interesting to note that the three giants of Torah interpretation of the Golden Age in Spain (10th-13th centuries) — Ibn Ezra (1092-1167), Rabbi Yehuda haLevy (1086-1145) and the Ramban (1194-1270) — each have suggested different interpretations to this verse. The Ibn Ezra believes the 'king' is Moses. This is a reasonable possibility because the previous verse also has Moses as the subject. "Moses commanded us the Torah" etc. The Ramban agrees with Rashi that the 'king' refers to G-d. Rabbi Yehuda haLevy suggests an original idea that the 'king' is the Torah. He bases this on the fact that in the previous verse the Torah was the object. "Moses commanded us the Torah" etc.

We must try to understand the basis for Rashi's (and the Ramban's) thinking that the 'king' is *Hashem* and not Moses.

Can you defend this interpretation?

YOUR ANSWER:

UNDERSTANDING RASHI

An Answer: There are several pieces of evidence which support Rashi's opinion here. The Ramban, who agrees that the 'king' is G-d, sees our verse in its context as it is connected with the previous verse. The two verses:

"The Torah that Moses commanded us is the heritage of the congregations of Jacob. He was King over Yeshurun when the heads of the nation gathered — the tribes of Israel — as one."

This, the Ramban says, refers to the Divine revelation of the Torah at Sinai. All of Israel was present, "as one man" and at that moment, more than at any other in history, G-d was manifest as King of the universe.

Another reason for not thinking this refers to Moses is that Moses himself is speaking. It would be a bit strange for the most modest man on the face of the earth (Numbers 12:3) to refer to himself as King of Israel.

The Sages also understood this 'king' to be G-d. The Ramban points out that our *Shemoneh Esrei* prayer on Rosh Hashanah incorporates this idea. In the *Musaf* prayer we recite ten Scriptural verses, which illustrate G-d's kingly status, three from the Torah, three from the Prophets and three from the Writings. It closes with the tenth verse from the Torah. The three from the Torah are:

הי יִמְלֹךְ לְעֹלָם וָעֶד. (שמות טו:יח)

"*Hashem* will reign forever (Exodus 15:18);

הי אֱלֹקָיו עִמּוֹ וּתְרוּעַת מֶלֶךְ בּוֹ (במדבר כג:כא)

"*Hashem*, his G-d is with him, the trumpet blast of the King is with him (Numbers 23:21)

וַיְהִי בִישֻׁרוּן מֶלֶךְ...

"And He was King in Yeshurun."

This is indisputable evidence that the Sage's understood "king" in our verse as referring to G-d.

ANOTHER QUESTION

We can ask another question, this one about Rashi's last words in this comment. Why does he add the words: "The yoke of His sovereignty *is always upon them.*"

Can you think of a reason for the necessity of this comment?

YOUR ANSWER:

UNDERSTANDING RASHI

An Answer: It is possible that Rashi was focusing on the word ויהי which is in the past tense: "and He *was.*" This implies that G-d *was* King in Israel — but is no longer! This is certainly not its meaning. By saying that "His sovereignty *is always* upon them" Rashi is correcting this misinterpretation. The word ויהי here may have the same meaning it has in Genesis 1:3:

וַיֹּאמֶר אֱלֹקִים יְהִי־אוֹר וַיְהִי אוֹר.

"And G-d said 'Let there be light' and **there was** light."

The meaning here is that there was and that there *continued to be* light. Likewise, Rashi tells us here that the meaning of ויהי is, G-d was King (at Sinai) and He continues to be King.

Rashi shows the future and past allusions of Moses' blessing.

Deut. 33:7

וְזֹאת לִיהוּדָה וַיֹּאמַר שְׁמַע ה' קוֹל יְהוּדָה וְאֶל־עַמּוֹ תְּבִיאֶנּוּ יָדָיו רָב לוֹ וְעֵזֶר מִצָּרָיו תִּהְיֶה.

וְעֵזֶר מִצָּרָיו תִּהְיֶה: על יהושפט התפלל על מלחמת רמות גלעד ויזעק יהושפט וה' עזרו (ד"ה ב' יח:לא). דבר אחר, שמע ה' קול יהודה, כאן רמז ברכה לשמעון מתוך ברכותיו של יהודה, ואף כשחלקו ארץ ישראל נטל שמעון מתוך גורלו של יהודה, שנאמר' מחבל בני יהודה נחלת בני שמעון' (יהושע יט:ט) ומפני מה לא ייחד לו ברכה בפני עצמו? שהיה בלבו עליו על מה שעשה בשיטים (במדבר כה:יד). (כן כתוב באגדת תהילים.)

And You shall be a help to him from his adversaries: *Rashi:* Here he (Moses) prayed for [King] Yehoshaphat in his battle at Ramos Gilad. (Chronicles II 18:31) "And Yehoshaphat cried out and *Hashem* helped him."

Another interpretation,

Hear, O *Hashem*, the voice of Judah. Here he alluded to a blessing for Simeon in the midst of Judah's blessings. So too when they divided the Land of Israel, Simeon took his portion in the midst of Judah's as it says "Within the portion of the Children of Judah was the heritage of the Children of Simeon." (Joshua 19:9). And why did he not assign to him a separate blessing? Because he had something in his heart against him on account of what he had done in *Shittim* (Numbers 25:14). (So it is written in Aggada of Psalms.)

There are two Rashi-comments here. Let us take one at a time.

WHAT IS RASHI SAYING? _____

The first comment associates Moses' prayer "And You (G-d) shall be a help to him etc." with King Yehoshaphat. Yehoshaphat was the third king of Judah after King Solomon. (The unified Davidic kingdom split into two states after Solomon's death. The Southern state, known as Judah had kings who were offspring of David and Solomon. The Northern state, known as Israel, had a series of kings who were not of the Davidic line.) Being that Yehoshaphat was a king of Judah, this verse, which is part of Judah's blessing, could very well apply to him.

UNDERSTANDING RASHI _____

The association is based on two textual elements, which connect our verse with the one in the Book of Chronicles.

Do you see them?

YOUR ANSWER:

An Answer: The word עזרו in Chronicles is associated with the words ועזר מצריו in our verse. Also Yehoshaphat, the Judaic king, "cried out" and G-d heeded his prayer, which is what our verse says שמע ה' קול יהודה.

A CLOSER LOOK _____

These associative elements in the verse in Chronicles which connect that verse with our verse in Deuteronomy, explain another point. The original Biblical documentation of Yehoshaphat's war, when he was saved by *Hashem,* is recorded in I Kings 22. Why did Rashi need to find a verse in Chronicles, which is much more distant from our verse (in the order of the Scriptures), than the Book of Kings? As a rule, when Rashi quotes a supporting verse he will usually choose a verse as close as possible to the verse he is commenting on.

The answer is that Rashi chose the verse in Chronicles, because it had the two similarities with our verse which we noted above. There was no verse in I Kings 22 which had these similarities with our verse.

Let us now examine the second Rashi-comment.

Questioning Rashi

Rashi says there is a hint in Judah's blessing to a blessing for Simeon.

Can you think what might be the basis for Rashi drawing this conclusion?

Hint: Where elsewhere in the Torah do these words appear?

Your Answer:

Understanding Rashi

An Answer: The words שמע הי are reminiscent of the verse in Genesis 29:33 where Leah gives Simeon his name:

וַתֹּאמֶר כִּי־**שָׁמַע** הי כִּי־שְׂנוּאָה אָנֹכִי וַיִּתֶּן־לִי גַּם־אֶת־זֶה וַתִּקְרָא שְׁמוֹ שִׁמְעוֹן.

This is the allusion that Rashi has in mind. The verse in Genesis has the same words as we have in this verse. Thus, the verse hints at Simeon while speaking of Judah.

Another Question and Answer

In light of all of the above, we are led to another question, which Rashi himself deals with.

At the end of the above comment, Rashi asks:

"And why did he (Moses) not assign to him a separate blessing?

"[Rashi answers] Because he had something in his heart against him on account of what he had done in *Shittim* (Numbers 25:14)."

Simeon was not given his own blessing by Moses because of the sin of Simeon's tribal prince, *Zimri son of Salu.*

The Twelve-Tribe Constant

We see that even without Simeon included among those blessed openly, there are, nevertheless, twelve tribes accounted for. How does this happen? There were twelve sons to Jacob, if one is missing we should have only eleven remaining. Who filled in for Simeon here?

Your Answer:

An Answer: The two sons of Joseph, Ephraim and Menasseh, are each counted. Taking Joseph out and putting in two in his place makes up for the missing Simeon.

The Ramban has an enlightening comment on this verse regarding the consistency of having only twelve tribes, never more and never less.

THE RAMBAN ON THE NUMBER OF TWELVE TRIBES

Within the Ramban's lengthy comment to Deut. 33:6 he has this to say:

"The correct understanding, in my opinion, is that the Scriptures will always enumerate only twelve tribes. And thus it says in Jacob's blessing (Genesis 49:25) "all these are the tribes of Israel, *twelve*." Now Jacob mentioned his twelve sons and he mentioned Joseph as (only) one tribe [not including Joseph's sons Ephraim and Menasseh]. Moses saw fit to reckon Joseph as two tribes, as it says 'and they are the ten thousands of Ephraim and they are the thousands of Menasseh.' And this was because of two reasons. One is because the Holy One blessed be He commanded Moses to include them as two tribes at the dedication of the Altar and the banners (the tribes' encampment in the wilderness) and by the inheritance of the Land, he perforce had to count them as two for (these) blessings. And another reason is that he mentioned Joshua who caused them to possess the Land and he was from Ephraim the younger son and therefore he needed to mention his older brother [Menasseh]. (Thus he included the two sons of Joseph but not Joseph.) Now he also wanted to mention the [tribe of] Levi for through his blessing all Israel would be blessed. Hence it was necessary to omit one of the tribes, *for nowhere [in Scripture] are they enumerated except as twelve,* corresponding to the twelve constellations in the heavens, the twelve months of the year ... Accordingly Simeon was left out [of Moses' blessings] since his tribe was not large and it was not the intention of the blessing of Jacob, their father, that they become numerous. Instead he 'divided them in Jacob and scattered them in Israel' and to that extent they too were blessed through the blessing of the rest of the tribes."

The Ramban makes an important point. Never do we find more than twelve tribes mentioned in the Torah. Sometimes we find Joseph, other times, Ephraim and Menasseh, but then some other tribe must be omitted, either Levi or, as in our verse, Simeon, so as to summate to twelve.

A Closer Look

Let us look at the various circumstances when the tribes are enumerated and see if we can see any method in it.

Levi & Joseph included	**Ephraim & Menasseh included**
Shoham Stones (Exodus 28:9)	Dedication of Tabernacle (Numbers 7:2)
Princes bring Jewels for Breastplate (Exodus 28:21)	Banners and encampment in Wilderness (Numbers 2:18)
	The Spies (Numbers 13:2)
The Staves (in *parashas Korah*) (Numbers 17:17)	
	Inheritance of the Land (Numbers 34:23)
Blessings at Mt. Gerezim (Deut. 27:12)	

We see that there are times when Joseph is counted as but one tribe and other times when his sons, Ephraim and Menasseh are counted individually, replacing the one tribe of Joseph with two tribes. Of course, in such cases one of the other tribes must be omitted, so as to preserve the twelve total.

Can you see any method in the above division? What would determine when Ephraim and Menasseh are counted and, alternatively, when Joseph is counted?

Your Answer:

Deciphering the Twelve Tribe Code

An Answer: Did you notice that whenever the tribes participated in a real event, as opposed to a symbolic one, Ephraim and Menasseh were included? Ephraim and Menasseh were real tribes. This was based on Jacob's blessing to Joseph. "Ephraim and Menasseh are like Reuben and Simeon to me" (Genesis 48:5). So the two families existed as real tribal units and were on an equal status with the other tribes ("as Reuben and Simeon"). Therefore, when the Temple was dedicated, real-life representatives of each tribe had to bring their sacrifices. When the tribes encamped in the wilderness, real people encamped, including the tribes of Ephraim and Menasseh. Likewise when they inherited geographic portions in the Land of Israel. Also, when the Spies were sent to the Land of Canaan, the purpose was to prepare for the conquest, whose goal was to secure the Land for the tribes who were to dwell there, including Ephraim and Menasseh.

On the other hand, all the instances where Joseph is counted and not his two sons, are instances that have symbolic, though not real-life, significance. This includes the precious stones in the High Priest's breastplate; the sticks that Aaron placed in front of the Ark, after the rebellion of Korah, to see which family of Levi would be chosen; and the stationing of tribal representatives for the Blessing and Curse ceremony on the mountains Gerezim and Aval, after entrance into the Land. These were all symbolic ceremonies, and the tribe of Joseph (which was no longer a real individual tribe) was included together with the rest of Jacob's sons.

❖❖❖

Rashi questions the meaning of the verse.

Deut. 33:24

וּלְאָשֵׁר אָמַר בָּרוּךְ מִבָּנִים אָשֵׁר יְהִי רְצוּי אֶחָיו וְטֹבֵל בַּשֶּׁמֶן רַגְלוֹ.

בָּרוּךְ מִבָּנִים אָשֵׁר: רָאִיתִי בְּסִפְרֵי אֵין לְךָ בְּכָל הַשְּׁבָטִים שֶׁנִּתְבָּרֵךְ בְּבָנִים כְּאָשֵׁר וְאֵינִי יוֹדֵעַ כֵּיצַד.

The most blessed of sons is Asher: *Rashi:* I have seen in the *Sifrei* that you will not find among all the tribes one who was as blessed with sons as was Asher. But I don't know how this is so.

WHAT IS RASHI'S DIFFICULTY?

In attempting to understand in what way Asher was blessed more than his brothers, Rashi cites the *midrash Sifrei*. This *midrash* explains that Asher's blessing was that he would have more sons than the other tribes. Rashi adds that he doesn't understand this. His difficulty is that of the twelve tribes, Asher was not the largest. When we check the first census of the people (Numbers 1:40) we find that Asher had only 41,500 fighting age sons. This is, by far, not the largest tribe. Many tribes had larger populations and Judah, the largest, had 74,600. A second census was taken after the forty years of wandering in the wilderness. At that time

Asher's population had increased to 53,400 (Numbers 26:47), but it still was not the largest of the tribes. So in what way was Asher's blessing manifested?

Can you think of an answer?

YOUR ANSWER:

The Ba'alei haTosafos' Explanation

An Answer: Rabbi Judah son of Eliezer (the *Riva*, lived in the early 1300's) is one of the *Ba'alei haTosafos*. In his book *Minchas Yehuda*, he explains that Asher's growth from 41,500 at the first census, to 53,400 at the second (an increase of 11,900) was the largest *increase* of the tribes. And "blessing" in the Torah usually means "increase."

The *Riva* questioned this explanation. He points out that the tribe of Menasseh increased from 32,200 to 52,700. This is an increase of 20,500, even greater than Asher's. This raises the question: In what way was Asher more blessed than Menasseh? His answer is that Moses' blessing stated "The most blessed *of sons* is Asher" and Menasseh was not a son of Jacob (he was Joseph's son, a grandson of Jacob). So, in comparison to his own brothers, Asher did have the largest increase.

This may be an answer to Rashi's question. Yet we can also understand why Rashi did not accept this answer and remained with his question. The *Sifrei* says "among all *the tribes*" and Menasseh was a tribe like any other, even if he was not a direct son of Jacob.

Let us see how other commentaries interpret this verse.

Bechor Shor

Following is the *Bechor Shor's* interpretation of this verse:

> "[Asher is] blessed by the other sons, for all the sons bless him, as the continuation of this verse testifies 'he will be acceptable to his brothers...'"

The *Bechor Shor* understands the מ in the word מבנים to mean "*from* (or by) the sons." He is blessed from his brothers (Jacob's sons). Rashi, on the other hand, had understood the מ as a ב meaning "with" as he said שנתברך בבנים "blessed *with* sons."

The *Ramban* surveys different interpretations, emphasizing the different meanings of the letter מ.

THE RAMBAN'S INTERPRETATION

Following is a paraphrase of part of the Ramban's comment on this verse.

"The מ means "more than" as in

הַנֶּחֱמָדִים מִזָּהָב וּמִפַּז רָב

They are desirable **more than** gold, **more than** much fine gold.(Psalms 19:11).

But this is surprising that Moses would bless them more than the other sons of Jacob and furthermore this was never fulfilled. The Rabbis (in the *Sifrei* Rashi quoted) intended ברוך מבנים אשר to be read as ברוך בבנים by having many sons born to him. Similar to the מ in (Deut. 33:13)

מְבֹרֶכֶת הי אַרְצוֹ מִמֶּגֶד שָׁמַיִם מִטָּל...

"*Hashem* blesses his Land, **with** the bounty of the heavens from the dew…"

[Asher's blessing of sons] can be understood, because Moses blessed the other tribes with strength or with inheritance while Asher was blessed with sons. But to understand this according to the *p'shat* we would say that Asher was blessed *by* the other sons as it says 'he shall be pleasing to his brothers.' (Note: this is the same as *Bechor Shor*.) Here the מ means "from" as in the verse (Genesis 24:50):

מֵהי יָצָא הַדָּבָר

"The matter came **from** *Hashem*"

The Ramban has shown us how the versatile letter מ can be translated in three different ways; he supports each interpretation by citing similar uses of מ in other places in Tanach.

A comment built on a grammatical rule.

Deut. 33:26

אֵין כָּאֵ-ל יְשֻׁרוּן רֹכֵב שָׁמַיִם בְּעֶזְרֶךָ וּבְגַאֲוָתוֹ שְׁחָקִים.

> אֵין כָּאֵ-ל יְשֻׁרוּן: דע לך ישורון שאין כא-ל בכל אלהי העמים ולא כצורך צורם.
> **There is none like G-d, Jeshurun:** *Rashi:* Know, Jeshurun, that there is none like G-d among all the gods of the peoples and that your Rock is not like their rock.

QUESTIONING RASHI _____

As we compare the verse in Hebrew with Rashi's comment on it, it is hard to see what he has added.

What is Rashi clarifying?

Hint: First translate the verse yourself from the Hebrew and see how you understand it. Does this coincide with what Rashi says?

YOUR ANSWER:

WHAT IS RASHI CLARIFYING? _____

An Answer: The words אין כאל ישורון look like they mean: "There is none like the G-d of Yeshurun." But Rashi says this is incorrect. The correct reading, Rashi says, is "There is none like G-d — Yeshurun." That is, Moses is speaking directly to Israel (Yeshurun), he addresses the people 'Yeshurun' and says to them "Yeshurun, be aware, that there is none like G-d ."

How does Rashi know that this is the correct meaning? Maybe these words do mean "The G-d of Yeshurun"?

A "PAINLESS" EXPLANATION OF THREE GRAMMATICAL RULES _____

To understand this we must understand some Biblical grammar. We will discuss three grammar rules; hopefully the discussion will be (relatively) painless!

1) The rule of linking two nouns together, called סמיכות "*smichus*."

2) The rule that the *smichus* construction never begins with a ה הידיעה.

3) The rule for combining the definite article with a preposition.

The three relevant rules, briefly stated, are:

1) THE GRAMMATICAL RULE OF סמיכות (*SMICHUS*) _____

Two nouns can be linked together to create a combined term. This is called *smichus*. Some common examples:

בית **שֶׁל** מדרש = בית המדרש = "the house-**of**-learning."

בית **שֶׁל** התכנסות = בית הכנסת which means literally "the house-**of**-gathering" which we call a synagogue.

משפחות **שֶׁל** בנים **שֶׁל** ישראל = משפחות בני ישראל = "the families **of** the sons **of** Israel."

See that the connecting word **שֶׁל**, "of", is dropped and the vowels are slightly changed. The word בַּיִת is changed to בֵּית. The word בָּנִים becomes בְּנֵי and the word מִשְׁפָּחוֹת becomes מִשְׁפְּחוֹת.

2) THE ABSENCE OF THE INITIAL ה הידיעה IN THE *SMICHUS* CASE _____

In Hebrew the definite article — "***the*** book" הספר as opposed to ספר "*a* book" — is expresed with the letter ה, punctuated usually as הַ. It is called ה הידיעה. **But the *smichus* construction does not take a ה הידיעה, because it doesn't need the ה הידיעה to be "definite".** This means we do not say הבני ישראל, nor do we say הבית מדרש. The correct way is בית המדרש.

3) THE RULE OF COMBINING ה הידיעה WITH A PREPOSITION _____

When ה הידיעה occurs together with the preposition letters לְ ("to"), כ ("as"), and בְ ("in").

An example of a preposition letter is: לְ plus בית = לְבֵית "to a house."

When the preposition words "in," "with," "as," or "to" are used together with the ה הידיעה, the ה is dropped and the vowel from under the ה is applied to the preposition letter. Thus בית -הַ- לְ "to *the* house" becomes לַבֵּית which also means "to *the* house." If it were "to *a* house" it would be punctuated as לְבֵית.

With this background let us look at our verse.

The phrase כאל ישורון can either be in the possessive *smichus* format — without the definite article — or begin with a definite article (combined in this case with a preposition) and *not* be in the possessive form.

The words כאל ישורון look like they mean "like the G-d *of* Yeshurun" with the words אל ישורון being connected in a *smichus* link.

However, the *kametz* under the כ in the word כאל is our clue that there is a hidden ה הידיעה.

Thus Rashi knew this could not be a *smichus* construction, because there is no ה הידיעה the *smichus* construction. Thus it could not mean "like *the* G-d *of* Yeshurun." It could only mean ישורון — כ אל "like G-d — Yeshurun."

We went through this grammatical labyrinth in order to show how sensitive Rashi is to the subtle nuances in the text. The *kametz* under the כ made all the difference.

(See *Lashon Chaim*)

Death sweet as a kiss.

Deut. 34:5

וַיָּמָת שָׁם מֹשֶׁה עֶבֶד־הי בְּאֶרֶץ מוֹאָב עַל־פִּי הי.

עַל פִּי הי: בנשיקה.

By the word of *Hashem*: *Rashi:* With a kiss.

Do you see why Rashi chose this unusual interpretation?

What is bothering him?

YOUR ANSWER:

WHAT IS BOTHERING RASHI?

An Answer: The verse says that Moses died "by the word of *Hashem*." This means by G-d's will or command. But then, doesn't everyone die by G-d's will? What is so unusual about Moses' death that the Torah has to tell us that he died according to G-d's will?

This may have been what was bothering Rashi.

How does his unusual interpretation help matters?

YOUR ANSWER:

UNDERSTANDING RASHI

An Answer: The verse says על פי הי which is an idiom which means "by the order of *Hashem*" (see Numbers 9:18). Translated literally it means "by the *mouth* of *Hashem*." So when taken literally, the verse tells us that "Moses died by the mouth of *Hashem*." In other words "with a kiss of *Hashem*."

What does it mean to die with a kiss from G-d? It means that the dreaded experience of death is, for the righteous, as sweet and as soothing as a kiss. So it was for Moses.

While this interpretation likely reflects Moses' unusually peaceful death experience. Nevertheless, as an interpretation of the Torah's words, it is a *drash*.

Can you think of a *p'shat* interpretation of these words?

YOUR ANSWER:

A P'SHAT INTERPRETATION

It is possible to understand this verse otherwise, according to a *p'shat* interpretation. The verse says "And Moses, the servant of *Hashem*, died there, in the land of Moab, by the word of *Hashem*." We should recall two previous verses where G-d told Moses to ascend Mount Nevo (Deut. 32:49,50):

> "Go up this Mount Ha'avarim, Mount Nevo, which is in the land of Moab, which faces Jericho and see the Land of Canaan which I give to the Children of Israel as a possession. And die on the mountain which you ascend..."

A precondition for Moses' death was that, in accordance with G-d's command, he ascend the mountain in the land of Moab Moses did as he was told, he went up the mountain to his certain death. We know he had a burning yearning to enter the Land of Israel and he could have rebelled the word of G-d and attempted to enter Canaan on his own. But he didn't do that. Being a "servant of G-d" he did as he was told. As our verse points out and even emphasizes, "he died *there*, in the land of Moab, by the word of *Hashem*." It was not that he died by the word of G-d, for everyone does; it was that he died in the land of Moab, by the word of *Hashem*, as G-d had commanded him. He did not try to circumvent this eventuality. He died there on the mountain "by the word of *Hashem*," because to the end, he remained the faithful servant of G-d and did, without questioning, as he had been instructed.

תם ונשלם. שבח לבורא עולם